THE HISTORY OF FREEMASONRY

ITS LEGENDS AND TRADITIONS

ITS CHRONOLOGICAL HISTORY

BY ALBERT GALLATIN MACKEY, M.D., 33°

VOLUME SEVEN

PART 4. - SYMBOLISM OF FREEMASONRY

CHAPTER III

SYMBOLISM OF NUMBERS

THE best way, says Lawrie in his preface, "of refuting the calumnies which have been brought against the fraternity of Freemasons is to lay before the public a correct and rational account of the nature, origin, and progress of the institution, that they may be enabled to determine whether or not its principles are, in any shape, connected with the principles of revolutionary anarchy, and whether or not the conduct of its members has ever been similar to the conduct of traitors." And from the publication of such sentiments it must be evident to every Brother's experience that the feeling against Freemasonry, which displayed itself so openly only a few years ago, has assumed a much milder form, if it be not entirely removed.

It will not, however, be difficult to account for the dearth of Masonic writers in a preceding age.

Before the 18th century symbolical masonry, being limited to the simple ceremonial, needed few illustrations; because, as the science was chiefly operative, the most valuable secrets would be those which had a reference to building, to the scientific ornaments and decorations of each particular style of architecture as it flourished in its own exclusive period; and these mysteries were communicated gradually, as the candidate rose through the different stages of his order or profession.

There appears to have been one general principle, which extended itself over every style from the early English to the florid, decorated, and perpendicular, and constituted one of the most ineffable secrets of the Masonic lodges.

It is now known to have been the hieroglyphical device styled Vesica Piscis; "which may be traced from the Church of St. John Lateran, and the old St. Peter's at Rome, to the Abbey Church at Bath, which is one of the latest Gothic buildings of any consequence in England.

It was formed 1733 by two equal circles cutting each other in the centers, and was held in high veneration, having been invariably adopted by Master Masons in all countries.

In bas-reliefs, which are seen in the most ancient churches, over doorways, it usually circumscribes the figure of our Saviour.

It was indeed a principle which pervaded every building dedicated to the Christi6an religion, and has been exclusively attributed to the scientific acquirements of Euclid."[1]

Oliver, in Pythagorean Triangle, says: "The secret meetings of master masons, within any particular district, were confined to consultations with each other, which mainly tended to the communication of science, and of improvement in their art.

An evident result was seen in the general uniformity of their designs in architecture, with respect both to plan and ornament, yet not without deviations.

We may conclude that the craft or mystery of architects and operative masons was involved in secrecy, by which a knowledge of their practice was carefully excluded from the acquirement of all who were not enrolled in their fraternity.

Still, it was absolutely necessary, that when they engaged in contracts with bishops or patrons of ecclesiastical buildings, a specification should be made of the component parts, and of the terms by which either contracting party should be rendered conversant with them.

A certain nomenclature was then divulged by the master masons for such a purpose, and became in general acceptation in the middle ages."[2]

The abstruse calculations which accompanied the sciences of geometry and arithmetic are no longer necessary to Freemasonry as an institution purely speculative; and they were accordingly omitted in the revised system, as it was recommended to the notice of the Fraternity by the Grand Lodge in 1717, and we retain only the beautiful theory of these sciences, with their application to the practice of morality, founded on the power and goodness of T.G.A.O.T.U.

---

[1] Kerrich in "Archaeol.," vol. vxi., P. 292.
[2] Dallaway, "Archit.," p. 410

It would be an injustice to our Brethren of the last century to believe that they did not entertain a profound veneration for the principles of the Masonic order.

But the customs and habits of the people of England, living in that day, differed materially from our own.

There were times when conviviality and a love of social harmony prevailed over the more sedate pursuits and investigations of science, in which such an astonishing progress distinguishes the present times.

In the seventeenth and eighteenth centuries London was an atmosphere of clubs, and a society of this kind existed in every street for the peculiar use of its inhabitants, besides those which were exclusively frequented by persons possessing similar tastes or habits of amusement.

And it will be no disparagement to masonry if we believe that its private Lodges did not sustain a much higher rank than some of these celebrated meetings, for the Kit-Cat, the Beefsteak, and other clubs were frequented by the nobility and most celebrated characters of that polished era.

It was the organization of Freemasonry that gave it the distinctive character which elevated its pretensions above the common routine of club-life, and although it is admitted that the members of the latter entertained a strong attachment to their several institutions, yet none were so enthusiastic as those who had enlisted in the pause cause of masonry as we may learn from the few testimonies which remain.

A mason of high standing, more than a century ago, thus expresses his feelings respecting the order: "Masonry is the daughter of heaven, and happy are those who embrace her.

By it youth is passed over without agitation, the middle age without anxiety, and old age without remorse. Masonry teaches the way to content, a thing almost unknown to the greater part of mankind.

In short, its ultimate resort is to enjoy in security the things that are, to reject all meddlers in state affairs or religion, or of a trifling nature; to embrace those of real moment and worthy tendency with fervency and zeal unfeigned, as sure of being unchangeable as ending in happiness.

They are rich without riches, intrinsically possessing all desirable good, and have the less to wish for by enjoyment of what they have.

Liberty, peace, and tranquillity are the only objects worthy of their diligence and trouble.'"[3]

"But this, as well as almost all the testimonies of that period to its superior excellence, is confined exclusively to the practice and rewards of Christian morality.

"Modern revision has, however, extended the limits of scientific investigation in the order of Freemasonry beyond what was intended by those who decreed that 'the privileges of masonry should no longer be restricted to operative masons, but extend to men of various professions, provided they were regularly approved and initiated into the order.' And Dr. Hemming and his associates, in the year 1814, thought it expedient to introduce some peculiar disquisitions from the system of Pythagoras on the combinations of the point, the line, the superfice, and the solid, to form rectangular, trilateral, quadrilateral, multilateral figures and the regular bodies, the latter of which, on account of their singularity and the mysterious nature usually ascribed to them, were formerly known by the name of the five Platonic bodies; and they were so highly regarded by the ancient Geometricians that Euclid is said to have composed his celebrated work on the Elements, chiefly for the purpose of displaying some of their most remarkable properties.

These disquisitions usually conclude with an explanation of the forty-seventh problem of Euclid, which is called the Eureka of Pythagoras.

"That great philosopher, Pythagoras, who, by the superiority of his mind, infused a new spirit into the science and learning of Greece, and founded the Italic sect, taught his disciples Geometry that they might be able to deduce a reason for all their thoughts and action, and to ascertain correctly the truth or falsehood of any proposition by the unerring process of mathematical demonstration.

Thus being enabled to contemplate the reality of things and to detect imposture and deceit, they were pronounced to be on the road to perfect happiness.

Such was the discipline and teaching of the Pythagorean Lodges.

It is related that when Justin Martyr applied to a learned Pythagorean to be admitted as a candidate for the mysterious dogmata of his philosophy, he was asked whether, as a preliminary step, he had already studied the sciences of Arithmetic, Music, Astronomy, and Geometry, which were esteemed the four divisions of the mathematics;

---

[3] "Pocket Companion," P. 296

and he was told that it was impossible to understand the perfection of beatitude without them, because they alone are able to abstract the soul from sensibles, and to prepare it for intelligibles.

He was further told that in the absence of these sciences no man is able to contemplate what is good.

And because the candidate acknowledged his ignorance of them he was refused admission into the society.

"Above all other sciences or parts of the mathematics, however, the followers of Pythagoras esteemed the doctrine of Numbers, which they believe to have been revealed to man by the celestial deities.

And they pronounced Arithmetic to be the most ancient of all the sciences, because, being naturally first generated, it takes away the rest with itself, but it is not taken away with them.

For instance, animal is first in nature before man; for by taking away animal we take away man; but by taking away man we do not take away animal.

They considered numbers extending to the decad, to be the cause of the essence of all other things; and therefore esteemed the creation of the world as nothing more than the harmonious enect of a pure arrangement of number.

This idea was adopted by Dryden:

'From harmony, from heavenly harmony, This universal frame began; From harmony to harmony, Through all the compass of the notes it ran, The diapason closing full in man.'

Pythagoras had another idea, as we are informed by Censorinus, respecting the creation of the world, and taught that it was fashioned according to the principles of musical proportion; that the seven planets which govern the nativity of mortals have a harmonious motion, and intervals corresponding to musical diastemes, and render various sounds, according to their several distances, so perfectly consonant that they make the sweetest melody, but inaudible to us by reason of the greatness of the noise, which the narrow pasage of our ears is incapable of receiving.'

"And further, he esteemed the monad to represent the great and good Creator, under the name of Dis, or Zeus, or Zau; and the duad he referred to as the evil and counteracting principle or daemon, 'surrounded,' as Plutarch expresses it, 'with a mass of matter.' And Porphyry adds, that the monad and duad of Pythagoras seem to have been the same with Plato's peras and apeiron, his finite and infinite in his Philebus; the former of which two only is substantial, that first most simple Being, the cause of unity and the measure of all things.

"According to the above doctrine, the monad was esteemed the father of Number, and the duad its mother; whence the universal prejudice in favour of odd numbers, the father being had in greater honour than the mother.

Odd numbers being masculine, were conduced perfect, and applicable to the celestial gods, while even numbers, being female, were considered imperfect, and given to the terrestrial and infernal deities.

Virgil has recorded several instances of this predilection in favour of odd numbers. In his eighth Eclogue, he says (thus translated by Dryden):

'Around his waxen image first I wind Three woollen fillets of three colours join'd; Thrice bind about his thrice devoted head, Which round the sacred altar thrice is led.

Unequal numbers please the gods.'

"The Eastern nations of the present day appear to reverse this principle.

When two young persons are betrothed, the number of letters in each of their names is subtracted the one from the other, and if the remainder be an even number, it is considered a favourable omen, but if it be odd, the inference is that the marriage will be unfortunate.

"Every tyro knows that odd numbers are masonic; and if he be ignorant of the reason why 3, 5, 7, and 11, have been adopted as landmarks, let him apply to the Master of his Lodge for information, and he will then be satisfied of the wisdom of the appropriation, because number forms one of the pillars which contribute to the support of scientific masonry, and constitutes an elementary principle of Geometry.

Thus, in the celebrated Pythagorean triangle, consisting of ten points, the upper single dot or jod is monad or unity, and represents a point, for Pythagoras considered a point to correspond in proportion to unity; a line to 2; a superfice to 3; a solid to 4, and he deemed a point as a monad having position, and the beginning, of all things; a line was thought to correspond with duality, because it was produced by the first motion from indivisible nature, and formed the junction of two points.

A superfice was compared to the number three, because it is the first of all causes that are found in figures; for a circle, which is the principal of all round figures, comprises a triad, in centre, space, circumference.

But a triangle, which is the first of all rectilineal figures, is included in a ternary, and receives its form according to that number; and was considered by the Pythagoreans to be the author of all sublunary things.

The four points at the base of the Pythagorean triangle correspond with a solid or cube, which combines the principles of length, breadth, and thickness, for no solid can have less than four extreme boundary points.

"Thus it appears that in applying number to physical things, the system of Pythagoras terminated in a tetrad, while that of Aristotle, by omitting the point, limited the doctrine of magnitude to a triad, viz., line - surface - body.

In divine things, however the former philosopher profusely used the number three, because it represented the three principal attributes of the Deity.

The first whereof, as we are informed by Cudworth, is infinite with fecundity; the second infinite knowledge and wisdom; and the last active and perceptive power.

From which divine attributes the Pythagoreans and Platonists seem to have framed their trinity of archical hypostases, such as have the nature of principles in the universe, and which, though they be apprehended as several distinct substances gradually subordinate to one another yet they many times extend the to Theion so far as to comprehend them all within it.

While employed in investigating the curious and unique properties which distinguish many of the digits, we no longer wonder that the inhabitants of the ancient world, in their ignorance of the mysterious secrets of science, and the abstruse doctrine of causes and effects, should have ascribed to the immediate interposition of the Deity those miraculous results which may be produced by an artful combination of particular numbers.

Even philosophy was staggered; and the most refined theorists entertained singular fancies, which they were unable to solve without having recourse to supernatural agency.

Hence the pseudo-science of Arithomancy, or divination by numbers, became very prevalent in the ancient world; and was used by Pythagoras as an actual emanation of the Deity.

By this means, according to Tzetzes, he not only was able to foretell future events, but reduced the doctrine to a science, governed by specific rules, which he transmitted to posterity in his Book of Prognostics.

"The ancients had a kind of onomantic arithmetic, the invention of which was in like manner ascribed to Pythagoras, whether truly or not is of no importance here, in which the letters of the alphabet, the planets, the day of the week, and the twelve zodiacal signs, were assimilated with certain numbers; and thus, by the use of prescribed tables, constructed astrologically according to the aspects, qualities, dignities, and debilities of the planets relatively towards the twelve signs, etc., the adept would authoritatively pronounce an opinion on questions affecting life and death, good and evil fortune, journeys, detection of theft, or the success of an enterprise.

It must be confessed, however, that these predictions were not always correct; for the rules laid down in different systems varied so essentially that the wisest magician was frequently puzzled to select an appropiate interpretation.

The numeral system has been introduced into the modern practice of astrology, and very important results appear to depend on the trine, quartile, and sextile aspect of the planets in the horoscope.

"Something of this sort was used by the Jewish cabalists; and hence one of the rules of their cabala was called gemetria, or numeration, which was chiefly confined to the interpretation of their sacred writings.

The letters of the Hebrew language being numerals, and the whole Bible being composed of different combinations of those letters, it was supposed that the correct meaning of difficult passages could only be ascertained by resorting to their numerical value.

The Talmudists entertained an opinion that the mystery of numbers was actually taught in their scriptures; because after the idolatrous priests of Baal had accepted the challenge of Elijah, that prophet constructed his altar of twelve stones, corresponding with the twelve tribes of Israel; but they say that when he took this number for the special purpose of conciliating the favor of Jehovah, it was not merely because the sons of Jacob were twelve in number, but because that particular number was supposed to contain a profound and unfathomable mystery.

"Divination by numbers was not confined to Jewish or heathen nations, but occupied much attention at different periods of Christianity; and superstitious properties, I am afraid, are still attached to particular numbers, as forming climacterics, or grand climacterics; for the days of a man's life are usually considered to be affected by the septenary year, which, as it is frequently believed, produces considerable changes in both body and mind.

But the most remarkable change in a person's life is at the climacteric, or 7 x 7, 49 years; or the grand climacteric, 7 x 9, 63 years; or 9 x 9, 81 years; each of which is conceived to be fraught with a peculiar fatality.

And there are numbers of persons, even in the nineteenth century, who contemplate these periods with some degree of terror, and esteem it a relief when they have passed away.

"The exalted ideas which were entertained by the ancient poets and philosophers respecting the mysterious properties of numbers, may be estimated from the superstitious uses to which they were made subservient in all countries, whether inhabitants were savages or refined. The former saw that the number of his fingers ended at ten; and this constituted the amount of his knowledge. It formed the standard of all his computations.

When a savage, on his warpath, was asked the number of his enemies, if few, he would hold one or more of his fingers; if many, them all.

And in whatever manner his ideas of units might be designated, the calculation would always end in ten.

Thus, in Homer, Proteus counts his sea-calves by fives, or in other words by the number of fingers on his hand. Several nations in the wilds of America have to this day no other instruments of calculation. It is another strong presumption of the truth of what I now advance, that all civilized nations count by tens; tens of tens, or hundreds; tens of hundeds, or thousands; and so on, but always from ten to ten.

We can discover no reason why this number should be chosen rather than any other for the term of numeration, except the primitive practice of counting by the fingers."[4]

"Arithmetical operations," says the Abbe Pluche, "were facilitated and shortened first by the use of counters, and afterwards by figures or chalked letters.

Thus the Romans, when they had a mind to express unity, either held up, one finger or chalked the figure I.

To express the succeeding numbers they drew II, III, IIII. For the number five they depressed the three middle fingers, and extended the thumb and little finger only, which formed the V. They signified ten by putting two V's, one upon the other, thus X, or by joining them together, which formed X. Then they combined the X, the V, and the I, till they came up to fifty, or five tens, which they expressed by laying the five upon its side. The figure in this posture assumed the form of an L. A hundred was marked with two L's put one upon the other which was subsequently rounded into a C. Five hundred was expressed by LC, and a thousand by CLO.

---

[4] Goguet, "Origin of Laws," vol. iv., P. 216

These figures were afterwards changed, the one into D, and the other into CLO, or M. The Greeks and Hebrews employed the letters of the alphabet ranged in order, to express all imaginable numbers.

Amongst these sages, the Monad represented the throne of the Omnipotent Deity, placed in the centre of the empyrean, to indicate T.G.A.O.T.U., by whom all things were made and preserved.

This disposition was symbolised by the hierogram of a point within a circle or equilateral triangle, to exemplify equally the unity of the divine essence, and His eternity, having neither beginning of years nor end of days.

And this deduction appears perfectly reasonable, because the Monad or Point is the original and cause of the entire numeral system, as God is the cause of all things, being the only and great Creator on whom everything depends: for, if there were more all-powerful Beings than one, none would be independent, nor would all perfection be centred in one individual, 'neither formally by reason of their distinction, nor eminently and virtually, for then one should have power to produce the other, and that nature which is producible is not divine. But all acknomledge God to be absolutely and infinitely perfect, in whom all perfections imaginable, which are simply such, must be contained formally, and all others which imply any mixture of perfection, virtually.' "[5]

Sthenidas the Locrian says, "The first god is conceived to be the father both of gods and men, because he is mild to everything which is in subjection to him, and never ceases to govern with providential regard.

Nor is he alone satisfied with being the maker of all things, but he is the nourisher, the preceptor of everything beautiful, and the legislator to all things equally.

"The universal symbol by which this great Being was designated, viz., the point within a circle, it may be necessary to explain with some degree of minuteness, because it constitutes one of the most important emblems of masonry.

One of the earliest heathen philosophers of whom history gives any account was Hermes Trismegistus, and he describes the Maker of the universe as 'an intelligible sphere whose centre is everywhere, and whose circumference cannot be defined,' because the universe is boundless, and He existed from all eternity.

---

[5] Pearson on the Creed, Art. i

David expressed a similar sentiment when he said, 'Thou art the same, and Thy years will have no end.' We are told that the Persians, when they wished to pay a high respect to the Diety, ascended to the top of a high mountain, and expanding both hands, they prayed to Him in the name of the circle of heaven.

In like manner, the Jews entertained a belief that 'the heaven of heavens could not contain Him.' The Romans placed a circular target as a symbol of the Deity, because, as in the circumference there is but one point at its centre, and can be no more, so in the whole circumference of the universe there can be only one perfect and powerful God; nor is it possible there should be another.

"I have received a suggestion from a very intelligent brother respecting this symbol, which merits consideration.

He says: When the W.M. elect enters into the obligation of an Installed Master, the brethren form a circle round him, he being in the centre; and in this situation he is said to be the representative of Solomon, the son of David.

Now, as this is unquestionably a Christian degree, I understand this son David to be a figurative expression for the Redeemer of mankind.

The W. M. is then specially intrusted with the Holy Scriptures and invested with a jewel which is emblematical thereof, and it then becomes his duty to exhort his brethren to search those Scriptures, because they contain the words of eternal life, and testify to the divinity of Christ.

Searching implies something lost; and our ancient brethren, the early Christians, after they had lost, by an untimely death, their Lord and Master, remembered that while assembled together in Lodge here below, He promised, that when two or three were gathered together in His name, He would be in the midst of them; and cheered by the recollection, they were naturally led to hope that He would always be found in the centre of their circle, whenever regularly assembled together in a just and perfect Lodge dedicated to God and holy St. John.

In like manner, we are reminded by that sacred symbol that He is always in the midst of us - that His all-seeing eye is always upon us, and therefore exhorted to discharge our duty towards Him and our fellow-creatures with freedom, fervency, and zeal.[6]

---

[6] This refers to the Ancient Method of installing a worshipful Master. (W.R.S.)

"The Monad, amongst the Grecian philosophers, was a symbol of the hermaphrodite deity, or junction of the sexes, because it partakes of two natures.

In a mysterious passage of the Yajur Veda, Brahma is spoken of, after his emanation from the golden egg, as experiencing fear at being alone in the universe; he therefore willed the existence of another and instantly became masculo-feminine.

The two sexes thus existing in one god mere immediately, by another act of volition, divided in twain, and became man and wife.

This tradition seems to bave found its way into Greece; for the Androgyne of Plato is but another version of this Oriental myth.

If the Monad be added to an odd number, it makes it even, and if to an even number, it makes it odd.

Hence it was called Jupiter, because it stands at the head of gods and men; and also Vesta or Fire, because like the point within a circle, it is seated in the midst of the world.

It was also cadled the Throne of Jupiter, from the great power which the centre has in the universe being able to restrain its general circular motion, as if the custody of the Maker of all things were constituted therein

"Plutarch tells us that Numa built a temple in an orbicular form for the preservation of the sacred fire; intending by the fashion of the edifice to shadow out, not so much the earth as the whole universe; in the centre of which the Pythagoreans placed Fire, which they called Vesta and Unity.

The Persians worshipped the circumference, but it could only refer to the apparent course of the sun in the firmament, which is the boundary of common observation; for the real circumference is far beyond the comprehension of finite man.

And the sun, under the symbol of a point within a circle, was the great object of worship amongst the Dionysian artists who built the Temple of Solomon.

"The Monad further signified Chaos, the father of life, substance, the cause of Truth, reason, and the receptacle of all things.

Also in greater and lesser it signified equal; in intention and remission, middle; in multitude, mean; in time, now, the present, because it consists in one part of time which is always present.[7] The cabalists considered that the first eternal principle is magical, and like a

---

[7] "Macrob. in somn.," 1. i., s. 6

hidden fire, is eternally known in its colours, in the figure, in the wisdom of God, as in a looking-glass.

The magical centre of the first principle is fire, which is as a spirit, without palpable substance."

"The learned Aben Ezra, on the 11th chapter of Daniel, says that the number one is in a manner the cause of all numbers, and it is besides a complete number; it causes multiplication and remainder, but does not admit of either itself.

And in another place he says,

'Numbers are founded on the unit one.' The sage Latif observes the same.

According to Euclid, in his second definition of the seventh book, numbers are formed of many units; but unity being indivisible, has no composition, nor is it a number, but the fountain and mother of all numbers.

Being the cause of all numbers, they are formed by a plurality of units.

Thus 2 is twice 1; 3 is three units, etc.; so that all numbers require the Monad, where it exists by itself without requiring any other.

All which is to be considered of the first cause; for as one is no number, but the cause and beginning of number, so the First Cause has no affinity to creatures, but is the cause and beginning of them; they all stand in need of Him, and He requires assistance from none. He is all in all, and all are included in Him in the most simple unity.

The Jewish Rabbins agree that He is One, and there is no unity like His in the universe; the nearest idea that we can form of Him is symbolized by the unit or figure one.[8]

The Pythagoreans say, 'the Monad is the principle of all things.

From the Monad came the indeterminate duad, as matters subjected to the cause. Monad, from the Monad and indeterminate duad; Numbers, from numbers; Points, points; Lines, from lines; Superfices, from superfices; Solids, from these solid Bodies, whose elements are four, Fire, Water, Air, Earth; of all which, transmuted, and totally changed, the World consists.'[9]

But Freemasonry has a peculiar preference for the monad, which produces some very striking and remarkable coincidences in every nation under the sun.

In an old ritual of the Fellow-Craft's degree, used about the middle of the last century, we find the following passage in reference

---

[8] Manasseh ben Israel, "Concil.," vol., P. 105.
[9] "Laert in vit Pyth."

equally to the first step of the winding staircase, the Point, and the letter G: 'God, the great Architect of the Universe, whom it is at all times our duty to worship and obey.' In a ritual still more ancient, the same meaning is rather differently expressed, viz., 'the Grand Architect and Contriver of the Universe; or He that was taken up to the topmost pinnacle of the Holy Temple.'[10]

"This acknowledgment of the divine unity, or point within either a circle or a triangle, was common to all the systems of Spurious Freemasonry that ever existed, from India and Japan to the extremest West, including the Goths, the Celts, and the aborigines of America.

All acknowledge the unity of T.G.A.O.T.U., whether involved in the deepest ignorance, or refined by civilization and a knowledge of philosophy and science.

The sages of Greece, through a series of wire-drawn reasoning, came to the same conclusion as the uninformed savages of Britain, Scandinavia, Mexico, or Peru.[11]

"Zoroaster is sublime in his description of the Deity; but he had enjoyed the advantage of associating with the learned Jews at Babylon and from them, doubtless, he had acquired his knowledge. He taught that 'God is the first: incorruptible, eternal, unmade, indivisible, not like anything, the author of all good, the wisest of the wise, the father of justice, self-taught and absolutely perfect.' An-aximenes, the follower of Thales, like his master, was a bold and subtle reasoner, and called everything by its proper name.

He denominated the one God Zeus, by which he intended to intimate that, like the air we breathe, He is infinite, omnipresent, and eternal.

The Emperor Trajan, in a conversation with the Rabbi Joshua, hearing the latter say, that 'God is everywhere present,' observed, 'I should like to see Him.' 'God's presence is indeed everywhere,' replied Joshua, 'but He cannot be seen; no mortal eye can behold His glory.' The Emperor insisted.

'Well,' said Joshua, 'suppose we try first to look at one of His ambassadors.' The Emperor consented.

The Rabbi took him into the open at noonday, and bid him look at the sun in his meridian splendor.

'I cannot - the light dazzles me.' 'Thou art unable,' said Joshua, 'to endure the light of His creatures, and canst thou expect to behold the

---

[10] Oliver

[11] Oliver.

resplendent glory of the Creator? Would not such a sight annihilate you?"[12]

"Xenophanes, the principal leader of the Aleatic sect, entertained the same belief; and described that Great Being, whom they all admitted to be incomprehensible, as 'incorporeal, in substance, and figure globular; and in no respect similar to man.

That He is all sight and hearing, but does not breathe.

That He is all things; the mind and wisdom; not generate, but eternal, impassible, and immutable.' Parmenides held that 'the principle of all things is one; but that it is immovable.' Sophocles assures us that in his time, the belief in one God, who made heaven and earth, was prevalent among those who had been initiated into the Greater mysteries.

"Socrates and his pupil Plato maintained the same opinion.

By the name of God,' said they, 'we mean the parent of the world; the builder of the soul; the maker of heaven and earth; whom it is difficult to know by reason of His incredible power; and if known, it is impossible to clothe our knowledge in words.' Anaxagoras contended for the supreme government of one God, but acknowledged that he was unable to comprehend his nature.

His pupil, Euripides, however, was more fortunate, for he discovered the omnipresence of the Deity; and confessed it by asking whether it is possible to confine Him within the wall of a temple built with hands? Protagoras was banished by the Athenians for impiety in declaring that 'he knew nothing of the gods, because in so short a life it was impossible to acquire a knowledge of them.'

"Zeno taught the unity and eternity, of the Deity.

Plutarch, learned in all the rites and doctrines of the Spurious Freemasonry of Egypt and Greece, expresses himself plainly on this point in his treatise of Isis and Osiris.

Atistides believed and taught his disciples that 'Jove made all existing things, in the earth, the heavens, or the sea.'"

Thus was the doctrine of the Monad or unity, the first point in the Pythagorean Triangle, carried out in these early ages, and among an idolatrous people; for however they might worship an indefinite number of intelligences, they had discrimination enough to perceive that there could be only one Being of unbounded power, because a duplication of such beings would circumscribe the potency of each individual, and destroy his omnipotence and immutability. "It was idle," says Bryant, "in

---

[12] Goodhugh's "Lectures on Bibliographical Literature."

the ancients to make a disquisition about the identity of any god, as compared with another; and to adjudge him to Jupiter rather than to Mars, to Venus rather than Diana.

According to Diodorus, some think that Osiris is Serapis; others that he is Dionysus; others still, that he is Pluto; many take him for Zeus or Jupiter, and not a few for Pan."

"The twofold reason of diversity and inequality, and of everything that is divisible in mutation, and exists sometimes one way, sometimes another, the Pythagoreans called Duad, for the nature of the Duad in particular things is such.

These reasons were not confined to the Italic sect, but other philosophers also have left certain unitive powers which comprise all things in the universe; and amongst them there are certain reasons of quality, dissimilitude, and diversity.

Now these reasons, that the way of teaching might be more perspicuous, they called by the names of Monad and Duad, but it is all one amongst them if they be called biform, or equaliform, or diversiform."[13]

From such definitions and principles it will not be difficult to see that the Duad was sufficiently comprehensive to admit of a vast number of references; and therefore the prolific fancy of poets and philosophers assigned to it a variety of remarkable qualities.

Being even it was esteemed an unlucky number, and dedicated to the malignant genii and the infernal deities, because it conveyed to the mind ideas of darkness, delusion, versatility, and unsteady conduct."[14] For this reason, the Pythagoreans spoke of two kinds of pleasure, "whereof that which indulgeth to the belly and to lasciviousness, by profusion of wealth, they compared to the murderous songs of the Syrens; the other, which consists in things honest and just, comprising all the necessary indulgences of life, is quite as attractive as the former, and does not bring repentance in its train."[15] The Duad was considered indefinite and indeterminate, because no perfect figure can be made from two points only, which, if united, would merely become a right line; whence a notion was originated that it is defective in its principles, and superfluous in its application to the sciences.

It signified also misfortune, from a general belief in its unpropitious qualities; and discord, because in music that which renders dissonances grating, is, that the sounds which form them, instead of

---

[13] Porp., "Hist. Phil.," p. 32
[14] Porph., "Vit. Pyth.," p. 84
[15] Ibid., p. 25

uniting to produce harmony, are heard each by itself as two distinct sounds, though produced at one and the same time.

Brand tells us[16] that there is a little history extant of the unfortunate reigns of William II., Henry II., Edward II., Richard II., Charles II., and James II., entitled "Numerus Infaustus in the preface to which the author says, "Such of the kings of Enghnd as were the Second of any name, proved very unfortunate princes."

"The number two was referred to Juno, because she was the sister and wife of Jove;[17] and hence the Duad became a symbol of marriage. On this subject Hierocles says two things are necessary to all men in order to pass through life in a becoming manner, viz., the aid of kindred, and synmpathetic benevolence.

But we cannot find anything more sympathetic than a wife, nor anything more kindred than children, both of which are afforded by marriage.

And to produce these two beneficial effects, Callicratides gives the following excellent advice: 'Wedlock should be coadapted to the peculiar tone of the soul, so that the husband and wife may not only accord with each other in prosperous, but also in adverse, fortune.

It is requisite, therefore, that the husband should be the regulator, master, and preceptor of his wife.

The regulator, indeed, in paying diligent attention to her affairs; but the master, in governing and exercising authority over her; and the preceptor in teaching her such things as are fit for her to know.'

"But how unfortunate soever the Duad may have been esteemed as a general principle, it was not devoid of its share of beneficent properties to balance against those that were malignant or forbidding. 'The two principles,' said the Paracelsic Lectures of Continental Masonry, 'are not always at strife, but sometimes in league with each other, to produce good.

Thus death and anguish are the cause of Fire, but fire is the cause of Life.

To the abyss it gives song and fierceness, else there would be no mobility.

To the Light - World, essence, else there would be no production but an eternal Arcanum.

To the world it gives both essence and springing, whence it becomes the cause of all things.' The Duad was defined by the Pythagoreans, 'the only principle of purity; yet not even, nor evenly even,

---

[16] "Pop. Ant,," vol. iii., p. 145
[17] Mart. Capel., "Eulog. in somn. Scrip.

nor unevenly even, nor evenly uneven.' It was an emblem of fortitude and courage, and taught that as a man ought to do no wrong, neither ought he to suffer any, without due sense and modest resentment of it; and therefore, according to Plutarch, the 'Ephori laid a mulct upon Sciraphidas, because he tamely submitted to many injuries and affronts, concluding him perfectly insensible to his own interest, as he did not boldly and honestly vindicate his reputation from the wrongs and aspersion which had been cast upon it; under the impression that he would be equally dull and listless in the defence of his country, if it should be attacked by a hostile invader.'

"The Duad was elevated by the ancient philosophers of the Italic sect into a symbol of justice, because of its two equal parts.

Hence Archytas, who was a follower of Pythagoras, says, 'The manners and pursuits of the citizens should be deeply tinctured with justice; for this will cause them to be sufficient to themselves, and will be the means of distributing to each of them that which is due to him according to his desert.

For thus also the sun, moving in a circle through the zodiac, distributes to everything on the earth, generation, nutriment, and an appropriate portion of life: administering, as if it were a just and equitable legislation, the excellent temperature of the seasons.'[18]

"It signified also science, because the demonstration of an unknown number or fact is produced from syllogistic reasonings on some other number or fact which is known; and this is deducible by the aid of science.

It was further considered as a symbol of the soul, which is said to be divided into two parts, the rational and the irrational; the latter being subdivided into the irascible and the appetitive.

The rational part enables us to arrive at the truth by contemplation and judgment; while the irrational uniformly impels the soul to evil.

And it signifies Opinion, which must be either true or false; and Harmony, whence the ancients introduced music at their banquets along with wine; that by its harmonious order and soothing effect it might prove an antidote to the latter, which being drank intemperately, renders both mind and body imbecile."

"The Pythagorean philosophy," says Reuchlin,[19] "taught that the Monad and Duad were a symbol of the principles of the universe for

---

[18] "Fragments" of Archytas, p. 16.
[19] "A. Cabal.," I., ii., P. 2.

when we make inquiry into the causes and origin of all things what sooner occurs than one or two ? That which we first behold with our eyes is the same, and not another; that which we first conceive in our mind is Identity and Alterity - one and two.

Alcmaeon affirmed two to be many, which, he said, were contrarieties, yet unconfined and indefinite, as white and black, sweet and bitter, good and evil, great and small.

These multiplicitous diversities the Pythagoreans designed by the number Ten, as proceeding from the Duad; viz, finite and infinite, even and odd, one and many, right and left, male and female, steadfast and moved, straight and crooked, light and darkness, square and oblong.

These pairs are two, and therefore contrary; they are reduced all into ten, that being the most perfect number, as containing more kinds of numeration than the rest; even, odd; square, cube; long, plain ; the first uncompounded, and first cornpounded, than which nothing is more absolute, since in ten proportions four cubic numbers are consummated, of which all things consist."

"Categories, reducible in two, Substance and Accident, both springing from one essence; for ten so loves two, that from one it proceeds to two, and by it reverts into one.

The first Ternary is of one and two, not compounded but consistent; one having no position, makes no composition; an unit, whilst an unit, hath no position, nor a point whilst a point.

There being nothing before on, we rightly say, one is first; two is not compounded of numbers, but a coordination of units only.

It is therefore the first number, being the first multitude; not commensurable by any number, but by a unit, the common measure of all number; for one, two, is nothing but two; so that the multitude which is called Triad, arithmeticians term the first number uncompounded, the Duad being not an uncompounded number, but rather not compounded."[20]

"The Chinese philosophers entertained similar fancies about the color of blue, which is formed by a mixture of red and black.

This color, they say, 'being the color of heaven, represents the active and passive principle reunited in one; the male and female, the obscure and brilliant.

All corporeal beings are produced by inapprehensible nature, emanating from blue, which forms the origin of all subtile natures.' In

---

[20] Colebrook, "Philosophy of the Hindus," p. 21

the science of astrology, which was very prevalent half a century ago, the signs were invested with significant colors.

Thus it was said that Taurus was designated by white mixed with citron; Aries and Gemini, by white and red; Cancer, green and russet; Leo, red and green; Virgo, black speckled with blue; Libra, black or dark crimson; Scorpio, brown; Sagittarius, yellow or green; Capricorn, black or russet; Aquarius, a sky color or blue; and Pisces by a brilliant white."

"Nor were the Jews destitute of a respect for the number two which was indeed inculcated in the Mosaical writings.

Thus while the clean beasts were admitted into the ark of Noah by sevens, the unclean ones were allowed to enter by pairs.

The angels that were deputed to destroy Sodom were two; Lot had two daughters; the sons of Isaac and the daughters of Laban were each two in, number, as were also the sons of Joseph.

Moses was directed to make two cherubim; the Onyx-stones of remembrance on the high-priest's shoulders were two, to symbolize the Sun and Moon, as Josephus says; but Beda thinks they were emblematical of the faith and practice of the patriarchs and prophets, while others suppose, with greater probability, that the high-priest bore them on his shoulders to prefigure the manner in which Christ was to bear the sins of His people.

The Jewish offerings were frequently directed to be by pairs; as two lambs, two pigeons, two turtles, two kids, etc.

The wawe loaves were two; and the shewbread was placed on the table in two rows; the sliver trumpets to direct the march of the Israelites in the wilderness were the same number."

"Again, Joshua erected two monuments on passing the river Jordan, one in the bed of the river, and the other on its banks; the temples of Solomon and of Gaza were each supported on two pillars; Jeroboam made two golden calves, and set them up at Dan and Bethel; there were two witnesses against Naboth, as the Mosaic law required in cases affecting human life; and two bears were sent to vindicate the character of Elisha.

In the case of Naaman the Syrian, we find the use of this number fully exemplified in the two mules' burden of earth - two young men of the sons of the prophets - two talents - two changes of garments - two servants, etc.

In the visions of Daniel the ram had two horns; and in Zachariah we have two olive-trees, two anointed ones, and two staves called Beauty and Bands, an emblem of brotherhood.

Similar coincidences might be found in the Gospels, but the detail would be tedious, and the result without utility, as far as regards Freemasonry."[21]

"In our system, the principle of the duad is plainly enunciated (although two is not esteemed a masonic number) in the two Pillars of the porch of Solomon's Temple, which were placed in that situation by the wise and judicious monarch, to commemorate the remarkable pillar of a cloud and of fire; the former of which proved a light and guide to the Israelites in their escape from their Egyptian oppression; the other represents the cloud which proved the destruction of Pharaoh and his host in their attempt to follow them through the depths of the Red Sea.

Our noble and illustrious Grand Master placed them in this conspicuous situation, that the Jews might have that memorable event in their recollection, both in going in and coming out from divine worship."

In the spurious Freemasonry of some ancient nations, this principle of duality was extended to support the doctrine of a good and evil power, who possessed almost equal government in this lower world; and the prospeity or decadence of a nation was supposed to be produced by the superiority of one or other of these beings, which, however, was esteemed, in most cases, accidental.

In Persia the doctrine attained its climax.

Oromases was Light, and Ahriman, Darkness.

Hyde says, "The Magi did not look upon the two principles as co-eternal, but believed that light was eternal, and that darkness was produced in time;[22] and the origin of this evil principle they account for in this manner: Light can produce nothing but light, and can never be the origin of evil; how then was evil produced ? Light, they say, produced several beings, all of them spiritual, luminous, and powerful; but their chief, whose name was Ahriman, had an evil thought contrary to the light.

He doubted, and by that doubting he became dark.

From hence proceeded all evils, dissension, malice, and everything also of a contrary nature to the light.

These two principles made war upon one another, till at last peace was concluded, upon condition that the lower world should be in subjection to Ahriman for seven thousand years; after which space of time, he is to surrender back the world to the Light."[23]

---

[21] Oliver
[22] Darkness is the absence of light, cold is the absence of heat. - EDITOR.
[23] Hyde, " Rel. Ant. Pers.," c. ix., p. 163

In countries where the two principles were represented by two serpents, the solstitial colures were described under these symbols. Thus in the Egyptian hieroglyphics, two serpents intersecting each other at right angles, upon a globe, denoted the earth.

These rectangular intersections were at the solstitial points.[24] The Teutonic Masonry of the last century thus explained the two principles of Light and Darkness: "From the eternal centre is made the eternal substantiality as a body or weakness, being a sinking down, and the spirit is a springing up, whence comes motion, penetration, and multiplication; and when the spirit created the substantiality into an image, breathing the spirit of the Trinity into it, the whole essences, even and the whole eternity, it instantly blossomed and became the paradise or angelical world.

In the Darkness is the genetrix, in the Light is the wisdom: the first imaged by devils, the other by angels, as a similitude of the whole eternal being, to speak as a creature.

And Lucifer, imaging beyond the meekness of the Trinity, kindled in himself the matrix of Fire, and that of nature becoming corporeal, then was the second form of the matrix, viz., the meekness of the substantiality enkindled, whence water originated, out of which was made an heaven to captivate the fire, and of that Fire and Water came the Stars."

---

[24] Jablonski, "Panth. Eg.," I., i., c. 4, cited by Deane, p. 73.

CHAPTER IV

LEGENDS AND SYMBOLS IN THE SEVERAL DEGREES OF MASONRY

MOST Masonic writers of recent date have assumed that Speculative Masonry was founded upon the legends and symbols of antiquity.

Dr. A.G. Mackey, in the preface to his valuable work on Symbolism of Freemasonry, says: "Of the various modes of communicating instruction to the uninformed, the Masonic student is particularly interested in two; namely, the instruction by legends, and that by symbols.

It is to these two, almost exclusively, that he is indebted for all that he knows, and for all that he can know, of the philosophic system which is taught in the institution.

All its mysteries and is dogmas, which constitute its philosophy, are intrusted, for communication, to the neophyte, sometimes to one, sometimes to the other of these two methods of instruction, and sometimes to both of them combined.

The Freemason has no way of reaching any of the esoteric teachings of the Order except through the medium of a legend or a symbol."

It is greatly to be regretted that the most important legends of Masonry are so communicated and represented, when the degrees are conferred, as to impress upon the minds of the candidates the realisms, rather than the "allegories," which were originally designed as "veils" to conceal the "moral principles" of the system, and which are also "illustrated by symbols."

Legends have no documentary evidence of the truthfulness of the narrative or any authenticity.

Such are the legends in the Masonic degrees.

There is no authenticity whatever for the statements or representations.

In fact, strict adherence to authentic history as contained in the "Great Light" of Masonry itself, contradicts the details of all the Masonic legends; hence we arrive at the truthfulness of the allegorical system, which was originally designed to teach the morality contained in the Institution.

The first three degrees of Freemasonry are in themselves allegorical, representing certain important principles in their enumeration.

First, the introduction into Masonic Life and Light.

Secondly, the progress during life in instruction - the life-work - education in all branches of useful knowledge.

Thirdly, the decadence, death, and final disposition of the body, its resurrection, and the immortality of the soul.

In each of these degrees symbolisms are introduced, teaching important truths, which are calculated to impress upon the mind the value of the great moral principles thus visibly represented.

Step by step, as the candidate advances in each degree, he learns the value of the gradation in moral lessons, by which his future life is to be guided.

All of these are primarily referable to his first declaration of "Faith in God," "Hope in Immortality," and "Charity or Love to all Mankind."

In these we recognize the several "duties" incumbent upon all men, which were inculcated in every system of morality taught by the ancient patriarchs and philosophers - our duty to God, our duty to ourselves, and our duty to all men.

In these are found the realisms of Masonry, and not in our legends and allegoies, by which they are veiled and concealed.

Of what value to us, at the present day, are the representations of the manner in which the Craftsmen and Apprentices were distributed when the Temple of Solomon was under construction ? Or when and how they recoved their wages? Every step, from the first admission of a candidate to the ante-room of a regularly constituted lodge, until he has become an obligated Mason, has its moral lesson.

His preparation, admission, and subsequent progress is marked by a lesson, which it is intended shall be carefully studied by the candidate for his future guidance in life.

The following sections of that degree are lessons, explanatory and instructive, in the art of Masonry.

The first section of the second and third degrees are similar to that of the first; and the following sections are strictly instructive and allegorical.

The instructions in all three of these degrees is by symbols and emblematical representations.

The science of symbolism is perhaps as old as any other science - the learning of the ancient world was originally conveyed by symbolism.

At the present day philosophy treats only on abstract propositions.

Freemasonry, however, retaining its traditions, continues the ancient method as the best means of imparting its moral lessons - by symbols - which word, derived from the Greek; means to compare one thing by another.

This method of instruction, or "object teaching," is employed in schools at the present day.

It is the language of poetry.

The "legend" is a spoken symbol and is employed in Masonic teaching, in some countries is an acted drama, in others it is merely recited or react; in both, it is designed to convey to the mind important moral truths.

It is the province of the initiated candidate to investigate these symbols and allegories to draw out from them the philosophies and moral lesson concealed by them.

It has been well said that "Freemasonry is the Science of Morality, veiled in Allegory, and illustrated by Symbols." We personally do not claim for Freemasonry the title of a science, but we do insist that it comprehends all true philosophy.

Its fundamental principle is a belief in God, without which there can be neither morality or philosophy.

The second principle taught in Masonry is the immortality of the soul; and the third principle is the resurrection of the body.

These constitute the philosophy of Freemasonry.

It is upon these principles that all the ancient religions were founded.

In the belief of all the ancients in a Deity, we find a multiplicity of gods; yet, in all of them, there was a chief god, who was so far above all the others as to constitute a distinct Deity.

Most of these ancient religions contemplated a Triune God.

"The rites of that science which is now received under the appellation of Freemasonry, were exercised in the Antediluvian World; revived by Noah after the flood; practised by mankind at the building of Babel, conveniences for which were undoubtedly contrived in the interior of that celebrated edifice; and at the dispersion spread with every settlement, already deteriorated by the gradual innovations of the Cabiric Priests and modelled into a form, the great outlines of which are distinctly to be traced in the mysteries of every heathen Nation, exhibiting the shattered remains of one true system whence they were all derived.

The rites of idolatry were indeed strikingly similar and generally deduced from parallel practices, previously used by the true Masons; for idolatry was an imitative system, and all its ceremonies and doctrines were founded on the general principles of the patriarchal religion.

If the patriarch united in his own person the three offices of king, priest, and prophet, the secret assemblies of idolatry were also governed by a Triad, consisting of three supreme offices; if primitive Masonry was a system of Light, the initiated heathen equally paid divine honors to the Sun, as the source of light, by circumambulating in the course of that Sutninary, during the ceremony of initiation."[25]

Sammes, in his Britannia, says: "The Mysteries of the Cabiric rites were accounted so sacred and powerful that whosoever was initiated in them, immediately secured, as they thought, some extraordinary gifts of holiness, and that in all their dangers they had a present remedy and expedient about them to deliver and rescue them; but that which most affected the Pnwnicians was a confidence they had that those religious ceremonies preserved them from dangers by sea; therefore it is no wonder that, arriving in Britain, they taught the inhabitants that worship to which they held themselves most obliged for their safety."

In the above extract from Oliver reference is made to the rite of circumambulation.

Every Mason will recognize that rite as an essential one in every degree of Masonry, both ancient and those degrees invented since 1717. Pythagoras required his initiates to pass three years in silence and darkness before admission to the mysteries. In all the ancient rites of the Orient the candidate was conducted by devious ways over many rough and rugged paths, and encountered various obstacles, and had to pass through the cold air, and water, the fire, and at last the earth, which four elements were symbols of purification, and lustrations by these were

---

[25] Oliver's "Signs and Symbols," pp. 4, 5.

requisite before the postulant could receive the higher mysteries and become an epopt.

"The uniformity of practice which attended the progress of error in different nations is truly astonishing. They equally used the Ambrosice Petrae as vehicles of regeneration; they shrouded their rites under the impenetrable mask of secresy; they possessed the same mode of instruction by symbols, allegory, and fable; the same repugnance to committing their abstruse secrets to writing; the same system of morality; the same attachment to amulets, telesmans, and perhaps Magic; and equally inculcated the immortality of the soul, and a future state of rewards and punishments, which were alike pantomimically exhibited during the initiations."[26]

"The old Asiatic style, so highly figurative, seems, by what we find of its remains in the prophetic language of the sacred writers, to have been evidently fashioned to the mode of the ancient hieroglyphics; for, as in hieroglyphic writing, the sun, moon, and stars were used to represent States and empires, kings, queens, and nobility, their eclipse and extinction, temporary disasters, or entire overthrow, fire and flood, desolation by war and famine, plants or animals, the qualities of particular persons, etc.; so, in like manner, the holy prophets call kings and empires by the names of the neavenly luminaries; their misfortunes and overthrow are represented by eclipses and extinction; stars falling from the firmament are employed to denote the destruction of the nobility; thunder and tempestuous winds, hostile invasions; lions, bears, leopards, goats, or high trees, leaders of armies, conquerors, and founders of empires; royal dignity is described by purple or a crown; iniquity by spotted garments; error and misery by an intoxicating draught; a warrior by a sword or bow; a powerful man by a gigantic stature; and a judge by balance, weights, and measures. In a word the prophetic style seems to be a speaking hieroglyphic."[27]

Pythagoras expressed his mystical system by symbols which were explained to the initiated and were not comprehended by the rest of the world. His secrets were forbidden to be committed to writing and were communicated orally as ineffable mysteries. The Pythagoreans conversed with each other mostly by the sign language; instruction by symbols was found useful in impressing on the mind the most comprehensive truths, and it is said was adopted from Masonry into all the mystic associations: " The most ancient and such as were contemporary with, and disciples of Pythagoras, did not compose their writings intelligibly, in a common

---

[26] Ibid., p. 5
[27] Warburton's "Divine Legation," B. IV., s. iv

vulgar style, familiar to every one, as if they endeavored to dictate things readily perceptible by the hearer, but consonant to the silence decreed by Pythagoras, concerning divine mysteries, which it is not lawful to speak of before those who were not initiated; and therefore clouded both their mutual discourses and writings by symbols; which, if not expounded by those that proposed them, by a regular interpretation appear to the hearers like old wives' proverbs, trivial and foolish; but, being rightly explained, and instead of dark rendered lucid and conspicuous to the vulgar, they discovered an admirable sense, no less than the divine oracles of Pythian Apollo; and give a divine inspiration to the Philologists that understand them."[28]

The Druids used hieroglyphics which, with much reluctance, were communicated even to their initiates themselves. These symbols were imitated from natural objects. Of a man of enlarged mind it was said, "he is an oak," an irresolute and wavering person was an "Aspen-leaf," one who was deceitful was a "Reed."[29] The Druids used geometrical figures as lines, angles, squares, and perpendiculars as symbols. They did not use enclosed temples, as being thought by them inconsistent with the dignity and majesty of the gods; they did not employ carved images to represent deities, but employed the rude undressed stones, such as they found in the hills or on sides of mountains, which were erected in their circles for worship, which were marked out by rudse stone pillars surrounding an altar placed in the centre. They also constructed of similar stones long passages between two rows of such stones. Some of these passages were miles in extent.

In Egypt, in all probability, originated those passages, where we find the remains of them as sphinxes, obelisks, and catacombs, all of which no doubt were erected for the observance of their mystic rites. Clement of Alexandria says: " Sphynxes were erected in front of temples and places of initiation, to denote that all sacred truth is enfolded in enigmatical fables and allegories."[30]

In the Egyptian mysteries the candidate was instructed in this as an ineffable secret, that the mysteries were received from Adam, Seth, Enoch; and in the last degree the postulant, after the completion of his initiation, was called, from the name of the Deity, AL-OM-JAH; pronounced Allhawmiyah. In India, the completed initiate was instructed in the great word, A.U.M., pronounced OME (o long); we

---

[28] Stanley's "Life of Pythagoras," B. IV., ch. i.
[29] Davis. "Celt. Res.," p. 207.
[30] Clement of Alexandria, Lib. V., ch. iv

thus see that the same word was used in Egypt as the second word. It has been supposed by some that these were initials of three certain names of Deity, viz. ,- Agni, Fire; Ushas, Dawn; and Mitra, Mid- day Sun, all of them referring to " Light" in its different degrees of intensity. In the higher degrees in Freemasonry these letters appear, having a deep significance, which we are not at liberty here to say more of. We may here quote from Dr. Oliver: "It is an extraordinary fact that there is scarcely a single ceremony in Freemasonry but we find its corresponding rite in one or other of the idolatrous mysteries; and the coincidence can only be accounted for by supposing that these mysteries were derived from Masonry. Yet, however they might assimilate in ceremonial observances, an essential difference existed in the fundamental principles of the respective institutions. The primitive veneration for Light accompanied the career of Masonry from the creation to the present day, and will attend its course until time expires in eternity; but in the mysteries of idolatry this veneration soon yielded its empire over men's minds, and fell before the claims of darkness; for a false worship would naturally be productive of impure feelings and vicious propensities." It is true, indeed, that the first Egyptians worshipped ON (A. U. N. in Hebrew, but pronounced Own) as the chief deity, who was supposed to be the eternal Light; and hence he was referred to the Sun as its great source and emanation. Thus it was said that God dwelt in the Light, his Virtue in the Sun, and his Wisdom in the Moon. But this worship was soon debased by superstitious practices. The idolaters degenerated into an adoration of Serpents and Scorpions, and other representatives of the evil spirit; and, amidst the same profession of a profound reverence for Light, became most unaccountably enamoured of Darkness; and a Temple near Memphis was dedicated to Hecate Scotia,[31] which was styled the Lord of the Creation, and in some respects deemed oracular. The superstition of Egypt which gave divine honors to Darkness spread throughout the world of idolatry, upon the principle that Darkness of Night, which existed in Chaos before the Creation of Light, was of superior antiquity. They therefore gave precedence to Night; and hence to signify the revolving of the earth they said a night and a day. Even the Jews began their time with the evening or commencement of darkness, as in Genesis i. 2, 3. Moses said God created Light out of Darkness. (I Kings viii. 1 2, 2; Chron. vi. I; Psalms xviii. 9.) Darkness was considered the incomprehensible Veil of Deity.

---

[31] "Diod. Sic. ," B.I., ch. vii

In the Orphic Fragments Night is celebrated as the parent of gods and men and the origin of all things. In all the rites of initiation. Darkness was saluted with three distinct acclamations; hence we may see that before the Aspirant could participate in the "higher mysteries" he was placed in a coffin, bed or pastos, or was subjected to confinement for a period of time, in seclusion and darkness for reflection, which custom is still employed in some secret societies. This was a representation of the symbolic death of the mysteries; when he was released from that ceremony, it was to indicate his deliverance, and represented the act of regeneration or being born again, or bezels raised from the dead.

We learn from Clement of Alexandria that in the formulary of one who had been initiated he was taught to say, "I have descended into the bed-chamber." Dr. Oliver says: "The ceremony here alluded to was, doubtless, the same as the descent into Hades; and I am inclined to think that when the Aspirant entered into the Mystic Cell, he was directed to lay himself down upon the bed, which shadowed out the tomb or coffin of the Great Father. This process was equivalent to his entering into the infernal ship; and while stretched upon the holy couch, in imitation of his figurative deceased prototype, he was said to be wrapped in the deep sleep of death. His resurrection from the bed was his restoraztion to life, or his regeneration into a new world; and it was virtually the same as his return from Hades, or his emergence from the gloomy cavern, or his liberation from the womb of the ship-goddess."[32]

The time required for this ceremony or imitation of death was generally for the space of three days and nights; but was varied in different localities. Nine days in Great Britain were required for the solitary confinement. In Greece three times nine days. In Persia it extended to fifty days and nights of darkness, want of rest and fasting. The remains in Great Britain of the places where the ceremonies were observed by the Ancient Druids are very numerous and well known at the present day, and have been referred to in a former part of this sketch. Among these are the remains of the celebrated Kit's Cotti House, near Maidstone. "This was a dark chamber of probation, for Kit is no other than Ked, or Ceridwen, the British Ceres; and Cotti or Cetti meant an Ark or Chest; and hence the compound word referred to the Ark of the diluvian god Noah, whose mysterious Rites were celebrated in Britain; and Ceridwen was either the consort of Noah, or the Ark itself symbolically the great Mother of Mankind. The peculiar names which

---

[32] Fab. Paz. Idol in Oliver's "Signs and Symbols," p. 79

these monuments still retain throughout the kingdom, are a decisive proof that they were appropriated, almost exclusively, to this purpose."[33]

Near a village in Somersetshire called Stanton Drew, or Druid Stones, there are the evidences of a rude structure which originally consisted of three circles of stones and an Adytune or a Pastos. There were various other similar structures in different parts of Britain, evidences of the prevalence of these ceremonies, religious in their character.

The initiation into the mysteries was a most important part of the religious worship; and all those who held any important place as priest or legislator, must pass through all their religious ceremonies, as indispensable preliminaries to their advancement, by the solitary confinement in the darkened Pastas. "The religionists of those days considered initiation as necessary as the Christians do baptism."[34]

We have referred, in a former page, to the several steps in the progress of initiation in the mysteries of the several degrees in Freemasonry, and that all of these were symbols by which the various principles sought to be inculcated were thus illustrated.

Each individual item was emphasized as the candidate progressed; when he was prepared in the ante-room, viz., his raiment, which should always be pure white, to represent that he was a candidate, from the Latin candidus, which means white. The peculiar arrangement of this raiment, in each degree, is explained in the lecture appertaining to each, as also the Zennaar[35] which accompanies the raiment of each degree, which is in Freemasonry denominated a Cable-tow. The different degrees require a different disposal of this cable-tow; in each there is a distinct symbolism, known only to the initiated. The candidate thus prepared is in darkness as to what he is to encounter, ignorant of what will be revealed to him in his progress in the various steps of his initiation; he is to be regenerated, born again into a new world of mysteries; as he was originally born into the world of physical light, so now he is to be born again into the moral and intellectual Light of Freemasonry. The following preliminary steps are purely ritualistic, and each Mason who has passed through them can for himself apply the

---

[33] Oliver, "Signs and Symbols," p. 80.
[34] Warburton, "Divine Legation," B. II., s. iv.

[35] The Zennaar in Hindostan was a cord composed of nine threads twisted into a knot at the end, and hanging from the left shoulder to the right hip. The Masonic scarf takes the place of the Zennaar

symbols to their appropriate significations. It would be well for us just here to call to mind what has been said by others on this method of instruction in the Church. In the Explanation of the Symbolism of the Mass, Bishop England said that in every ceremony we must look for three meanings. " The first, the literal, natural, and it may be said, the original meaning; the second, the figurative or emblematic signification; and thirdly, the pious or religious meaning; frequently the last two will be found the same; sometimes all three will be found combined." Bro. A. G. Mackey, in quoting the above extract from the "Churchman," makes the following just comment: "The Roman Catholic Church is, perhaps, the only contemporaneous institution which continues to cultivate, in any degree, the beautiful system of symbolism. But that which, in the Catholic Church, is, in a great measure, incidental, and the fruit of development, is, in Freemasonry, the very life-blood and soul of the institution, born with it at its birth, or rather, the germ from which the tree has sprung, and still giving it support, nourishment, and even existence. Withdraw from Freemasonry its symbolism, and you take from the body its soul, leaving behind nothing but a lifeless mass of effete matter, fitted only for a rapid decay."[36]

The candidate, after his admission to the lodge-room, follows the ancient custom of all the mysteries in a perambulation, which is a symbol of the Sun in his annual course through the twelve signs of the Zodiac, as also his diurnal course from east to west by way of the south. The candidates in the mysteries were said to as imitate the Sun and follow his beneficent example." This symbolism referred to the custom of Pythagoras, who required his candidates to pass three years in silence and in darkness. The various obstructions met with in this "circumambulation" were in imitation of those encountered in the Ancient Mysteries, but of quite a different character, as in the Ancient Mysteries these obstructions were to severely test the courage and persistence of the candidate, and often resulted in the death of the individual; and in some of their underground passages which have been explored in modern times, evidences have been discovered that many persons thus lost their lives.

After the most solemn and impressive ceremonies, whereby the postulant becomes a Mason, he is brought to Light in Masonry by a symbolism, faint indeed, but highly significant of a great event in the history of creation. All that follows is instruction in the science and morals of Masonry. Each degree in Masonry is divided into "Sections" -

---

[36] Mackey, "Symbolism of Freemasonry," p. 74

the first section is always the Rite of Initiation. The other sections are for the instruction of the Neophyte, the second section being a rehearsal of the various steps in the first section, and exoteric reasons for these. The following sections contain the morals and dogmas in the several different degrees appertaining to each. In the Fellow-Craft's degree the second section is a pure allegorical representation; no Intelligent Mason can for a moment accept it other than an Allegory. As such there is nothing more impressive than the important lessons in each part of the representations. The American Rite differs from all others in the arrangement and number of the steps, and in some particulars there are other differences along the whole line. That this legend of the second degree is an allegory we have simply to consult the only history of King Solomon's Temple as found in the "Great Light" and we will find that there was no possibility of adapting our Masonic ritual to that structure. In the sixth chapter of the First Book of Kings we read: "The door for the Middle Chamber was in the right side of the house; and they went up with winding stairs into the Middle Chamber and out of the Middle Chamber into the third." Dr. Mackey, in commenting on this passage, says:[37] "Out of this slender Material has been constructed an Allegory, which if properly considered, in its symbolical relations, will be found to be of surpassing beauty. But it is only as a symbol that we can regard this whole tradition; for the historical facts alike forbid us for a moment to suppose that the legend as it is rehearsed in the second degree of Masonry is anything more than a magnificent philosophical myth."

In addition to what Dr. Mackey has said, we would say that the middle and third chamber mentioned in the text referred to were the chambers on the north and south sides of the Temple mentioned in the same chapter of First Kings and fifth and sixth verses: Fifth, "And against the wall of the house, he built chambers round about, the walls of the house about, of the temple and the oracle;[38] and made chambers round about." Sixth, "The nethermost chamber five cubits broad, and the middle six cubits broad, and the third seven cubits broad: for without of the house he made narrowed rests round about that the beams should not be fastened in the walls of the house."

Then followed in the eighth verse, same chapter, as to where the door was to these three tiers of chambers, in the "right side of the house," viz., at the east end, inside of the porch or vestibule. We take occasion at this place to say that in all of our rituals our lodge-rooms are diametrically opposite in their Orientation" to that of the Temple, which

---

[37] "Symbolism of Freemasonry," p. 215
[38] Sanctum Sanctorum.

it is supposed we copy, viz.: the east of a Masonic lodge-room is at the end opposite to the "entrance." Now the entrance to the Temple was at the east end, and the if "Oracle," or Holy of Holies, was at the west end, where we now place the presiding officer, and all Masonic bodies claim it to be the "East" or "Orient."

The situation of Solomon's Temple, on Mount Moriah, on the eastern side of the City of Jerusalem, now occupied by several mosques of the Mohammedan worship, the central building being the mosque of Omar; the topography of that part of the city militates against every legend and myth in our Masonic rituals in all the various rites, and thus is destroyed any attempt at realism in our degrees, which many very excellent Brethren still adhere to in their firm belief in the "Masonry of the Temple." We again refer to Dr.

Mackey for his comments on this point: "Let us inquire into the true design of this legend and learn the lesson of symbolism which it is intended to teach. In the investigation of the true meaning of every Masonic symbol and allegory, we must be governed by the single principle that the whole design of Freemasonry as a speculative science, is the investigation of divine truth. To this great object everything is subsidiary The Mason is from the moment of his initiation as an Entered Apprentice, to the time at which he receives the full fruition of Masonic light, an investigator - a laborer in the quarry and the temple - whose reward is the Truth. All the ceremonies and traditions of the order tend to this ultimate design. Is there light to be asked for? It is the intellectual light of wisdom and truth. Is there a word to be sought? That word is the symbol of Truth. Is there a loss of something that has been promised? That loss is typical of the failure of Man, in the infirmity of his nature, to discover divine truth. Is there a substitute to be appointed for that loss? It is an allegory, which teaches us that in this world, man can only approximate to the full conception of truth."[39]

The proper lesson in the Allegory of the Fellow-Craft's degree is to teach the Seeker after Truth that the intellectual faculties must be cultivated and educated by a regular course of instruction in the liberal arts and sciences. In the Entered Apprentice degree the candidate has been instructed in the moral and fundamental principles so essentially necessary for the proper and due performance of his several duties in life, to God, his neighbor, and himself.

All Speculative Masonry must be philosophical. No man can become truly a Speculative Mason without a knowledge of the liberal arts

---

[39] Mackey, "Symbolism of Freemasonry," p. 216.

and sciences. It is in the second degree that the postulant learns of Operative and Speculative Masonry, and these two divisions are simply described in the lecture. The candidate must apply himself diligently to those seven arts and sciences enumerated and symbolized by the seven steps in order to appreciate Speculative Freemasonry. Does anyone imagine that the eighty thousand craftsmen at the building of the Temple were instructed in those seven liberal arts and sciences? That there was among them all, or in that day anyone, who understood the mechanics of the heavens or who did believe that the Sun was the center of the solar system, and that the Earth was in annual revolution around the sun, and diurnal rotation on its own axis? And yet these two principles are the foundation of astronomy.

In our rituals of the United States, the winding stairs are divided into three sets of odd numbers. The ancient temples were all approached by steps, odd in number; and Vitruvius, the most ancient writer on architecture, assigns the reason to be that, commencing with the right foot at the bottom, the worshipper would find the same foot foremost when he entered the temple, which was considered a fortunate omen. Dr. Mackey thinks, however, that Masonry derives the use of odd numbers from Pythagoras, in whose system of philosophy it plays an important part, and in which odd numbers were considered as more perfect than even ones. Tracing boards of the 18th century show only five steps, delineated, and in some there are seven. The lectures used in England in the commencement of the present century, according to Preston, make as many as thirtyeight, in sums of one, three, five, seven, nine, and eleven.

After the union of the two Grand Lodges in 1813, Dr. Hemming, the Senior Grand Warden, in his new lectures corrected the error in having an even number (38), by striking out the eleven. In the United States these numbers were changed to three, five, and seven, making fifteen. Like all intellectual acquirements there must be a gradual increase in knowledge. The postulant at his approach to the ascending scale of knowledge is primarily instructed in the lessons of the three steps; having acquired these, he advances to the next ascent of five, wherein he is instructed in the human senses, so essentially necessary for the apprehension of all physical knowledge of the objective world. Now, inasmuch as the comfort and happiness of mankind is greatly added to in the best methods of construction of our dwellings, as also all public structures, the science of building is taught by showing the fundamental principles of architecture as illustrated in the five Orders derived from the three original Orders of the Greeks. In the next steps the candidate rises to the highest position of intellectual cultivation in the liberal arts and sciences. Having attained to this elevation, he is entitled to his reward, which is denominated "wages." Here is introduced another allegory, which is derived from a scriptural passage, and is designed to prove the value of a secret pass-word, all of our Masonic degrees, which is to distinguish a friend from a foe, and by which is proved the right of a member to admission to the lodge, and should always be given before opening the lodge, and by every member or visitor before admission. This is often entirely neglected in some jurisdictions

King Solomon's Temple as a Masonic Symbol.
   Prior to 1860 - many writers on Masonry held to the opinion that Speculative Masonry dates its origin from the building of King Solomon's temple by Jewish and Tyrian artisans, and, no doubt, general assent was given to the proposition; but subsequent authorities in Masonic history do not now concur therein.
   Speculative philosophy existed prior to the construction of the Temple, but we may conjecture that in the formation of the rituals of the three degrees of Symbolic Masonry, the authors took the Temple and its construction as symbols, whereby the instructions in the moral principles, which formed the foundation of Speculative Masonry, were conveyed to the initiates. The very spirit of all of our lectures proves conclusively that when they were formulated they were designed to teach pure trinitarian Christianity, and while the Jewish scriptures did forecast the intermediary of a Christos, as all the ancient heathen mysteries did also, yet Jesus Christ as shown and demonstrated in the writings of the New Testament, was not understood by the Jewish writers of the Old Testament, nor by but very few of that faith since. The first three degrees taken in connection with the Holy Royal Arch, as they have always been with our Brethren of England, certainly show pure Christianity, as taught throughout the writings of the New Testament scriptures. It is possible that the investigations which for many years have engaged the earnest and serious attention of students of the Quatuor Coronati Lodge of London, may result in determining the period when our Masonic lectures were definitely formulated. We know historically that, commencing with the formation v the Grand Lodge, of England in 1717, the separation of Masonic "Work" into distinct degrees did not occur earlier than 1719.[40] From that date, those who aided in the progressive movement were, first, Dr. Anderson and Dr. Desaguliers; by

---

[40] Chaps. xxxiii.-xxxvi., Part II. of this work

whom, principally, the "work" was divided into the three degrees of Apprentice, Fellow of the Craft, and Master; second, Entick, by whom, perhaps, the lectures of the degrees were first clearly divided; the third one who made important and valuable improvements in the lectures was Hutchinson; and about the same period Dunckerly made many additions and subsequently united with Hutchinson, in the improvement of the work and lectures of the three degrees. The fourth attempt to improve the lectures was by William Preston. He entered the door of Masonry in a Lodge of the Ancients, but subsequently became a member of a Lodge of the Moderns. Preston's lectures recommended themselves at once to the more literary class of Masons, and toward the close of the 18th century were the prevailing lectures, and were introduced into all the English working lodges in the Colonies except in Pennsylvania, where we have understood the work and lectures of the ancients continued to prevail and are more or less the work and lectures of the present day.

When the two rival Grand Lodges of England united in 1813 and became the "United Grand Lodge," Dr. Hemming, the Senior Grand Warden of the new Grand Lodge, was intrusted with the work of preparing a new set of lectures and arranging the floor work of the three degrees and reconciling any discrepancies. This was the last change in the English work and lectures in England. About the close of the 18th century in the last decade Thomas Smith Webb, who became very conspicuous as a Masonic scholar in the northern part of the United States, made many changes in the work and lectures of all the several degrees in Masonry as far as they had been introduced into the country.

Jeremy L. Cross, of Vermont, became his scholar, and about 1816 he too " took a hand" at the lectures and made changes in Webb's work; so that now, in all the States of the Union except, as before said, in Pennsylvania, the Webb-Preston work and lectures prevail.

The first section in all the degrees in Masonry is the initiatory rite. So soon as the candidate in any degree has been obligated he is essentially a Mason of that degree, and as such is entitled to all the secrets and mysteries appertaining to that degree; hence every following section in any degree comprises instructions and explanations of the several steps in the initiatory section of the degree.

In the third degree, the second section is a dramatical representation of the "Legend." To ordinary minds, unaccustomed to allegorical representations, it is received as a true representation of a real occurrence. Scholars who have critically examined and compared all the circumstances of the allegorical representation, are well satisfied that such an occurrence could not have happened in the locality represented. The situation of the Temple and the surrounding topographical features all forbid any such circumstances as are related in the Legend. Hence we must assume that our authors of the legend intended it to be the culminating Symbol of Ancient Craft Masonry. In that legend is carried out to its ultimate extent the grand idea which prevailed and dominated every one of the Ancient Mysteries of the Oriental religious rites, and when we carefully "read between the lines" we learn how very near to the fundamental principles of "Christianity" all of those religious rites approached, even in their ignorance of what Dr. Oliver and Dr. Mackey have denominated "true Masonry." True Masonry, as originally designed, was intended to be strictly "Trinitarian Christianity," and every step taken in Masonry prior to the organization of the Grand Lodge of England, in 1717, was Christian, and no one could be a Mason who was not such, and was true to "Mother Church," as all the Ancient Manuscripts prove, and in some Grand Lodges in Europe this test is still required and a Jew or an infidel is excluded. Perhaps the change made in this direction, after 1717, admitting only those who professed a belief in God as being the only test of eligibility, has done good, by spreading abroad all the valuable principles involved in our several lectures, founded, as they all are, upon Faith in God, and having no other dogma. To this end was the legend of the third degree invented, and the secret mysteries of the whole of Masonry are concealed in the substitute when properly interpreted, as that should be, and not as now generally explained, which has no meaning whatever. When properly explained, it agrees precisely with that for which it was substituted.[41]

  Notwithstanding the conclusion reached by Dr. Mackey in the Chapter XXXI. referred to, we do not fully agree with him, but believe that the origin of the Mysteries involved in the third degree were invented some time subsequent to the organization in 1717; and that, perhaps, Chevalier Ramsay may have been the author, or, with the priests in the College at Clermont, have concocted those secrets, and invented the Royal Arch degree, which he brought with him into England, and endeavored to introduce into the work of the Grand Lodge of England. We know that the degree was finally introduced into the work of the "Ancients" of

  Dermott, and subsequently, by Dunckerly, into the old Grand Lodge of England, of which he was a very conspicuous and distinguished member. Through him the third degree was so altered that to obtain the

---

[41] See in this work ch. xxxi., p. 290 et sequiter

original essential secrets of that degree it became requisite to take the Royal Arch degree. Now, in the Ancient and Accepted Rite the degree of "Mason of the Royal Arch," which is essentially the same as the Ramsay degree, is so nearly like the English Royal Arch degree that we may say they are both from the same original source. Everyone who is familiar with these several degrees must confess there is a family likeness, and they all concur, in their essential features, in demonstrating that the religious elements are the same.[42]

In reference to the occult science in India, we take the following extract from Louis Jacolliot, as translated by Willard L. Felt:

"Remember my Son, that there is only one God, the Sovereign Master and Principal of all things, and that the Brahmins should worship him in secret; but learn also that this is a mystery, which should never be revealed to the vulgar herd: - otherwise great harm may befall you. [Words spoken by the Brahmins upon receiving a candidate for initiation according to Vrihaspati.]

This triangular arrangement of the great name, AUM, recognized as the WORD in the higher Mysteries in India, as the One God referred to in the above extract, represents the Triune God of all the Ancient Mysteries of the Oriental religions.

Under the head of Freemasonry, Chapter II., page 484, Dr. Mackay says:

"Krause gives ample proof that the Colleges of Artificers made use of symbols derived from the implements and usages of their craft. We need not be surprised at this, for the symbolic idea was, as we know, largely cultivated by the ancients. Their mythology, which was their religion, was made up out of a great system of symbolism. Sabaism, their first worship, was altogether symbolic, and out of their primitive adoration of the simple forces of nature, by degrees and with the advancement of civilization, was developed a multiplicity of deities, every one of which could be traced for his origin to the impersonation of a symbol. It would, indeed, be strange if, with such an education, the various craftsmen had failed to have imbued their trades with that same symbolic spirit which was infused into all their religious rites and their public and private acts."

In plates 1 and 2 (pages 1718 and 1720) we have shown a very few of the symbols used by the Ancients in their mythologies, and which are copied from Calmet, and herewith is a short description of each.

---

[42] See in this work ch. xxii., pp. 135 to 139; also ch. xxxvi., p. 178

Figure 1, plate 1, is an Indian representation of Vishnu, the second person of the Trimurti - the semblance of the God, is seated on a lotus-plant having four arms, and in each hand a peculiar emblem is displayed. The stem is supported by Vishnu, represented as an immense turtle. A huge serpent encircles the pillar; the gods hold the tail part and the daityas or demons hold the opposite end. By pulling the serpent alternately the sea was converted into milk, and then into butter, and from this was obtained the Amrita or water of life which was drank by the Immortals.

Figure 2 represents Brahma seated on a lotus flower after the deluge. Calmet supposes it to represent Noah and his three sons. The connection between numbers one and two may be seen in the conch shells shown in the hands, and the chains of pearls around the necks.

Figure 4 represents the Sun-God and Deus Lunus.

Figures 3, 5, and 6 are different forms of Nergal. The word Ner-Gal divides into two parts: Ner signifies light, or luminary, etc., and gal signifies to roll, revolve, a revolution, a circuit, the two together implies the revolving or returning light. If this be truly descriptive of Nergal, there is nothing improbable in considering the cock as allusive to it, since the vigilance of the cock is well known, and that he gives due notice of the very earliest reappearance of light morning after morning. There are different senses in which lightt may be taken, besides its reference to natural light.

"1st. Deliverance from any singular danger, or distress. Esth. Viii. 16.

"2dly. Posterity; a son, or successor. I Kings xi. 36; 2 Chron. cxi. 7.

"3dly. Resurrection, or something very like it. Job xxxiii. 28, 30; Psalm xcvii. II."

In the figures 3, 5, and 6 there is no allusion to the first of these principles, but they have a strong reference to the second, Posterity, and the idea of fecundity is expressed in the adaptation of the figure of a cock, which signifies the returning of light. In figure 5, which is taken from a gem in the Gallery at Florence, Italy, two cocks are yoked to the car of Cupid, and driven by one Cupid and led by another; and not merely as if harnessed to a common car, but as if they had been in a race and had come off victorious; as the driving Cupid carries a palm-branch, which is the reward of victory, obtained by these his emblematical coursers.

In figure 3 we have a car with a cock standing in the attitude of crowing and flapping his wings; which is the custom of this bird on certain occasions. The star shown is the Star of Venus, and distinguishes this equipage as the consecrated vehicle of that supreme goddess of love and beauty. At a short distance in the background sits Hymen, the god of marriage and conjugality; his torch brightly blazing; at his feet is a cock crowing, etc., in a manner and attitude very like the other; and with precisely the same allusions. The indication of this allegory is the influence of Venus and Hymen, the genial powers of vitality, on the renovation of life, in human posterity.

As the extinction of lamps, or torches, indicated utter desolation, deprivation of children and misery, so on the contrary we are led to imply the joy of connubial engagements.

The figure 6 represents a cock holding in his bill two ears of corn; he is attended by Mercury, having a Caduceus in one hand, and a bag of money tithe other. This gem has puzzled the learned. Montfaucon[43] E says: "To see Mercury with a cock is common enough; but to see him walking before a cock larger than himself, is what I have never noticed, except in this representation. It may denote that the greatest of the qualities of Mercury is vigilance. The cock holding the corn in his bill, may, perhaps, mean that vigilance only can produce plenty of the productions necessary to the support of life." Ancient Mythology adopted various representations of the human form.

Figure 7 is an Abraxas, taken from Montfaucon. It represents a man with two faces having on his head the bushel or sacred Calathus, two wings are on his shoulders and two wings on his hips, and a scorpion's tail and a staff in each hand.

Figure 8 evidently represents Neptune.

Figure 9 represents Ashtaroth or Astarte, which is the same as Venus. She holds a long cross in her hand and has the sacred Calathus on her head. This is a Medal of Zidon, which was a city of great antiquity; St. Ambrose, in writing to Symmachus, implies that Venus is the Metrane of Persia, and though worshipped under different names yet is constantly the same power. In this connection we must enlarge somewhat upon the names of Ashtaroth, Astarte, and Venus, as in the description of several of the following figures the subject will be better understood.

Venus represented with a dove is referred to Askelon, and yet we know that Egypt had her Venus and dove, as shown in a medal when she stands with a staff in one hand and a dove supported by the other hand extended. This medal was struck in Tentyra, a city of Egypt. This

---

[43] Vol. i.. pp. 123, 128

shows that the worship of the dove was very prevalent in these countries. The etymology of Askelon is derived from weight, or balance, shekel.

Another origin is suggested; Ash in Hebrew denotes fire; Kel denotes activity, briskness, and heat, even to wasting; lun denotes to reside, to stay, to remain. These ideas combined, mean, "the residence, or station, of fire, in activity or heating." To explain this the following Hindoo story is found in Aszatic Researches, vol. iv., p. 168, which agrees with this etymology. "The Puranas relate that, Sami Rami, in the shape of a dove, came and abode at Asc'halanorthan, which is obviously Askelon; here Samiramis was born, according to Diodorus Siculus, and here she was nursed by doves. She was, says he, the daughter of Derketos. Here, say the Indian Puranas, she made her first appearance. Now, by doves, we are to understand priestesses; by her birth, the institution or establishment of her worship, as daughter, i.e., immediate successor or offspring of Derketas. Sami is the Hindoo word for fire, and Rama signifies the fir-tree; 'Sthan is station, residence, dwelling. By uniting these ideas, we find they also signify 'the residences,' 'Sthan, of fire, Sami, in perfect conformity to the Hebrew name, as above explained."[44]

Figure 10 represents Dagon, properly Dag-Aun. We must anticipate the description of this figure by reference to another figure, not shown, viz.. There is a gem in the Florentine Gallery which is probably of Grecian workmanship; it shows the progress of those variations by which in process of time Art relinquished the truly ancient representation of Dagon. This figure exhibits a union of the human and fishy parts; but this union is contrary to the original idea of the emblem, which was that of a person coming out of a fish, not making a part of the fish, but issuing from it. (As will be seen in figure 10.) Shall I be thought fanciful in referring the figures of this plate to traditional memorials of Noah, his wife, and three sons? All of them having human upper parts, but piscine lower parts; i.e., all of them originally considered as having issued from a fish; though by lapse of time the import of that allegorical representation was forgot.

N.B. The original Merman and Mermaid of our heraldry supporters.[45] In figure 10, instead of the male and female, and three children, all having piscine lower parts, there is one person allied to a fish; but this one person has four arms, or governing powers.

---

[44] Calmet, Fragment 269, p. 373.

[45] Ibid., p.133

Now I take the fact to be this: when the male personage was used as a type of the event commemorated in this emblem, then the original allusion was to Noah and his three sons; but when a female personage was used, as an emblem of the very same event, then the allusion was to the wife of Noah. On the same principle genealogies were reckoned, and are still in the East, only by the male sex; we have no genealogy by women in Scripture; but this rule was departed from, speciali gratia, when the universal mother of the second race of mankind was to be commemorated. Vide figure 2 for the picture of a man with four heads and four arms, that is, four governing powers, Mental and Corporal; or in this Indian emblem, the four states and conditions of life, or the four castes and distinctions among the inhabitants, which castes are, on the Indian system, equally attributable to Noah as the father, or to his wife as the mother of succeeding generations. The four bearded heads may be those of the four fathers of mankind united into one; signifying legislative government, morals, etc. The four arms to the female figure, No. 10, may signify executive government. Still they represent government in some manner or other; and wherefore four? unless four persons had originally their respective departments in conducting the general welfare of the community, their descendants.

Figure 10, plate 2, is from Maurice's History of India.[46] It represents a female, crowned, having four arms, each holding its proper symbol, coming out of a great fish; as if this great fish was casting forth this personage, after the tempestuous ocean was calmed, the evil demon destroyed, and the verdant meadows were again clothed with cheerful herbage, as appears in the background of the original.

This emblem is called in Indian one of the appearances of Avartas of Vishnu.

There is an ancient fable that Oannes, who was said to be half a man and half a fish, came to Babylon and taught several Arts; and afterward returned to the sea . . . there were several of these Oannes . . . the namer of one was Odacon, i.e., o Dagon [the Dagon]. Berosus, speaking of Oannes, says he had the body and head of a fish; and above the head of the fish he had a human head, and below the tail of the fish he had human feet. This is the true figure of Dagon, who was the God of the Philistines, i.e., the most of the inhabitants of Palestine, long prior to the time when Joshua led the children of Israel across the river Jordan and took possession of the whole country and divided it among the twelve tribes. Etymologists say that Dagon was Saturn; others say he was

---

[46] Plate VII., p. 507, per Calmet, vol. iii., p. 183.

Jupiter; others say Venus, whom the Egyptians worshipped under the form of a fish; because in Typhon's war against the gods, Venus concealed herself under this shape.[47] Diodorus Siculus says,[48] that at Askelon the goddess Derceto, or Atagatis, was worshipped under the figure of a woman, with the lower parts of a fish (see figure 18, plate 2), and Lucian, de Dea Syr: describes that goddess, or Venus, as being adored under this form.

There is an ancient fable, that Oannes, a creature half man, half fish, rose out of the Red Sea, and came to Babylon, where he taught men several arts, and then returned again to the sea. Apollodorus reports that four such Oannes, in several ages, had arisen out of the Red Sea, and that the name of one of them was Odacon: whence the learned Selden derives Dagon.[49] The worship of Dagon continued in Palestine until the change in the mythology of early days to the Greek nomenclature, after the days of Alexander the Great. The temple of Dagon was pulled down by Sampson at Gaza. The Philistines deposited the ark in the temple of Dagon at Azoth.

Figure II, plate II, represents Succoth Benoth, and is a companion to the Deity Nergal; which the Babylonians selected as their favorite object of worship (2 Kings xvii. 30).

This representation is evidently Venus rising from the sea, attended by Tritons, who regard her with veneration and triumph united; but this is not the original Venus; it is the story poetically treated, varied by the looser imagination of the Greeks, from the ancient emblem; retaining the idea, but changing the figures, etc., as seen they did in Dagon, and as they were accustomed to do in all their Deities; from whence the Egyptians, etc., thought them impious; and indeed their images became hereby altogether desecrated. To this incident of Venus rising from the Sea ought to be referred all that the poets have written on the birth of the goddess of beauty from the briny wave, from the froth or foam of the sea, etc., of which enough may easily be met with among the classic writers, Greek or Latin.

The Hebrew word Succoth is usually rendered booths, i.e., temporary residences, as tents, etc. The Rabbins translate it "tents of the young women": it is literally "the tabernacles of the daughters, or young women," that is, "if benoth be taken as the name of a female idol, from Bench to build up, procreate children, then the words will express, The tabernacles sacred to the productive powers feminine."

---

[47] Ovid, " Met.," lib. v., fab. 5
[48] Lib. ii., p. 65
[49] Calmet's Dictionary Dagon

The dove, when used as an insignia or as a token, referred primarily to the dove at the deluge; and the double-faced Jason referred primarily to Noah; who looked backward on one world, ended, and forward on another, beginning. In the illustrations connected with Succoth Benoth the head of Venus on one side of a medal with a dove for its reverse, and a head of Janus with a dove also for its reverse, must originally have referred to the same event; and this event was what the figure of Derketos, who was the Syrian goddess, commemorated; in other words, Venus rising from the Sea.

Derketos issuing from a fish; 1st, Noah, as the great progenitor of mankind, restored to light and life; 2dly, the prolific powers again in exercise, to 3dly, the revival of human posterity, etc., after a temporary residence in that floating womb of mankind, the ark of preservatlon.[50]

The composition of a woman with the form of a fish is seen in a medal of Marseilles representing Atergatis, Derketos, the Syrian goddess Venus. Marseilles was settled by a colony of Phoenicians from Syria. They, like the Men of Babylon, carried their country worship and gods with them to their distant settlement.[51]

In figure 12 is a representation of the eighth Avatar of Vishnu, in which he represents the Good Black Shepherd treading upon the head of the Serpent Calanach. The promise made to Adam and Eve when they were turned out of the garden of Eden, was that their seed should bruise the head of the Serpent. Now, this figure of Vishnu, the second person of the Indian Trimurti, was called Krishna - the Anointed one - and some have thought that this myth was to illustrate the promise made to Adam and Eve, as above stated.

Figure 13 is a representation of Ashtaroth, the same as Astarte or Venus. The horns are not united to form a crescent as in other pictures but are more natural; around the beautiful head are the Seven stars by three and four, and two figures of lightning to show her authority as regent of night.[52]

Figure 14 represents another form of Abraxas which has more emblems than figure 7.

This figure has on its head the lotos; it has four wings; and connected with each wing an arm; and in each of its four hands different destructive emblems. It has on its feet what might be taken for a third pair of wings; but these are very imperfect, if they be wings.

---

[50] Calmet, vol. ii., p. 283.
[51] Ibid p. 234.
[52] Ibid., p. 375

Figure 15 is Dea Luna or Deus Lunus. This represents a man with a Phrygian bonnet on his head, clothed in a short dress, a sword in his right hand, in his left a man's head, which he has recently cut off from the body lying by him, whose flowing blood spirts upward. Marcrobius says "the Moon was both male and female;" and adds one particular from Philocorus, that the male sex sacrificed to him in the female habit, and the female sex in the male habit. Though Spartian speaks of Carhoe as a place famous for the worship of Lunus, the reader must not think this worship was confined to that place and to Mesopotamia; for it was spread all over the East. This worship was established in Phoenicia long before the empire of Caracalla; a medal published by Vaillant hath Antoninus Pius on one side and the god Lunus on the others with his Syrian cap on, and holding a spear with a great star on one side of him, and a crescent, which signifies the moon, on the other. The medal was struck at Gaba, near Caesarea in Palestine, by the borders of Phoenicia.[53]

Figure 16 represents the Egyptian Venus. This medal was struck in Tentyra, a city of Egypt, as appears by the legend upon it. Strabo mentions a temple of Venus at Tentyra. This is a reverse of a medal of Adrian; it represents Venus holding her dove in one hand, in the other a staff. On the whole, this has a strong similitude to medals of Askelon, and shows that the worship of the dove was very prevalent in these countries, and in their respective adjacencies.[54]

Figure 17 is a representation of a four-horned goat, which is said to be from Spain, with two upright and two lateral horns. This animal was alive in London about 1769. It is a symbol of the goat of Mendes.

Figure 18 represents the figure of a woman united to the form of a fish, and is similar in composition and shape of Atergatis-Derketos, the Syrian goddess.

Figures 19 and 20 represent two appearances of Baal. They are human heads with symbols of an ox added to them.

Observe in No. 19 the stars which accompany the head; if these stars, or if a single star, be referred to the Deity it accompanies, then we see how easily the Israelites might "take up the Star of their God" (Amos v. 26), i.e., portrayed on medals, or small figures, whether images or coins, etc., carried about them; and secured from detection by their smallness and readiness of concealment. This figure has the bull's or cow's horns and ears on its head.

---

[53] Calmet, vol. ii., p. 375.
[54] Ibid., P 374

No. 20 has only the ears of a bull or cow; but has on its head a garland of vine-leaves and grapes, whereby it is allied to Bacchus; with two apples on the front of the head, whereby it is allied to Ceres, or to Pomona, i.e., it indicates a fruit-bearing divinity, perhaps Isis fructifera.[55]

We have selected the foregoing examples of the very earliest symbols employed by the Ancient Nations to express their ideas of the Deities whom they worshipped; these all coalesce at last in the Sun and Moon. What was Fortune ? Baal Gad, the Luna Dea which presided over favorable times; where then is the wonder that the Israelites should be tempted to solicit favorable seasons from this goddess, instead of entreating them from the Lord ? as he complains; or that they should offer propitiatory incense to the queen of heaven? (Jer. xliv. 17) or that the question be asked,

Can any of the deities of the heathen give rain? which is so necessary to fertility; and an act of true divinity alone. We see, too, how Gad and Meni terminate in the Sun and Moon.[56]

We now revert to quite a different class of symbols, which we find prevailed in Egypt, Persia, Assyria, and was employed by the Almighty himself when he revealed his worship to the children of Israel. We allude to the Cherubim. The first authentic reference which we have in history we find in Genesis, ch. iii., v. 24, and in Exodus, ch.

xxv., vs. 18, 19, and 20, which we quote, viz.: "And thou shalt make two Cherubims of gold, of beaten work shalt thou make them, on the two ends of the Mercy Seat. And make one Cherub on the one end, and the other Cherub on the other end; even of the Mercy Seat[57] shall ye make the Cherubims on the two ends thereof. And the Cherubims shall stretch forth their wings on high, covering the Mercy Seat with their wings, and their faces shall look one to another; toward the Mercy Seat shall the faces of the Cherubim be."

It would seem from the directions here given by the Almighty to Moses, that the cherubic form was well known to him, from his familiarity with the Cherubim so common in Egypt. We must therefore look to the Cherubim of Egypt to understand the subject and appreciate the Cherubim of the first Ark of the Covenant carried by the children of Israel in their forty years of "Wanderings in the Wilderness," and into the "land of Promise" and the great Miracle wrought by it in the midst of the river Jordan. (Joshua, ch. iii., vs. 15, 16, 17.)

---

[55] Calmet, vol. ii., p. 122. 2
[56] Ibid., p. 124
[57] Another rendering may be, "of the matter of the Mercy Seat."

In all the different nations, where the cherubic forms were employed, they were compound animals. The various authors on this subject have employed many articles.

Mr. Parkhurst, in his Dictionary, uses no less than sixty; and M. Calmet has many pages and numerous illustrations, some of which we will use. In these articles Calmet proceeds by giving a description of the various parts, separately entering into the compound animal.

I. He first takes the Cherubim described in the Bible, of their heads or countenances.

Each Cherub has four: 1st, that of a man; 2d, that of a lion; 3d, that of an ox; 4th, that of an eagle. In what manner were they placed? Were they four heads attached to four necks rising from the trunk of the body; or four faces attached to one head? He thinks they were four faces attached to one head.

II. Of their bodies, i.e., from the neck downward. This was human., the "likeness of a man," which extended below the navel and to the lower rim of the stomach.

III. Of their wizzgs. Ezekiel describes them as having four wings; Isaiah describes the Seraph as having six wings, viz.: two on the head, two on the shoulders, and two on the flanks.

IV. Of their arms. The translations say hands, but certainly imply arms at length; their number was four, one on each side.

V. The lower part. It must have been 1st, either human thighs, legs, and feet to which was appended at the posteriors the body and hind legs of an ox; or, rather, 2d, the body and four legs of an ox, out of which the human part seemed to rise, so that all below the rim of the belly was in the form of an ox, and all above that was human.

VI. Their services, or, what they appeared to do. The vision seen by Ezekiel, and also by Isaiah, was the resemblance of a movable throne or chariot, of prodigious dimensions, on which the sovereign was supposed to sit; that the wheels were annexed to it in much the same manner as to the royal traveling or military thrones of the Persian Kings; and that the four Cherubims occupied the places of four horses to draw this capacious machine.

Did our limits permit, we could extend this examination into the subject of the Cherubim with great profit; but our object will have been obtained if we can succeed in showing how almost universal was the idea of compounding different animals into one for the purpose of illustrating the general ideas of the different attributes of their deities among all the nations of antiquity.

We copy from Calmet's Dictionary the following description of the Cherub.

CHERUB - derived from the Chaldee, signifies as a child, from the adverb ki; as, and rabia, a young man, a child; otherwise, as multiplying, or as combating, from rahab, or abundance, or multitude of knowledge; from tab, a multitude, and Nacar, to know, otherwise, in Hebrew, rahar signifies to grow great, to nourish, to bring up; in Syriac, to labour.

This term in Hebrew is sometimes taken for a calf or an ox. Ezekiel i. 10 mentions the face of a Cherub, as synonymous to the face of ar ox. The word Cherub in Syriac and in Chaldee signifies to till or plough, which is the work of oxen. Cherub also signifies strong and powerful, possessing the strength of an ox. Grotius says the Cherubim were figures like a calf. Bochart thinks they were nearly the figure of an ox. So does Spencer. Josephus says they were extraordinary creatures of a figure unknown to mankind. Clemens of Alexandria believes that the Egyptians imitated the Cherubim of the Hebrews in their Sphinxes and hieroglyphical Animals.[58]

The descriptions, in various parts of Scripture, of the Cherubim differ, but agree in a figure composed of various creatures except in the first description in Exodus. The others an ox, a lion, a man, and an eagle, as in Ezekiel i. 5, and x. 2. Those placed in the Temple by Solomon were probably similar to these. (I Kings vi. 23.) We can readily see that those on the Original Ark could not have been like those in the Temple, for there evidently was but one head on each one from the expression "and their faces shall look one to another; toward the mercy seat shall the faces of the Cherubim be." (Ex. xxv. 20.) There could only be one head and face to each of the two Cherubim.

Calmet's own conclusion on this difficult question is as follows:

"So great obscurity has hitherto overwhelmed this figurative representation, notwithstanding it has been the theme of many very learned men, that I cannot flatter myself with succeeding at once in explaining it. I think, however, that this opens a new way for attaining some conception of its real forms; and I feel some satisfaction in the idea that these symbols were not unknown in kingdoms and countries independent of Judea."

The Cherubic or compound form was common to most of the nations of the Orient. In Egypt, the sphynx and other examples are extant at the present day; in Assyria, all the Temples had such

---

[58] Calmet Dictionary, Cherub

compound figures at their entrances, and we show some of these in figures 21, 22, 23, 24.

If In regard to these Cherubic forms, there were two extreme opinions: 1st. That it pleased God to compose the Jewish religious rites, ceremonies, and symbols, of materials as unlike as possible to those of the countries around them, especially of Egypt, in order to establish a total dissimilarity, and to exclude idolatry. 2d. That a close resemblance, especially to Egyptian manners, was established, in order to accommodate the services to the temper and habits of a people who had been used to such in Egypt. This was the hypothesis of the learned Spencer. The truth, I apprehend, lies between these opinions.

"The Jews considered the Cherubim as of the utmost important under the Levitical priesthood; yet they have lost their true representation. If the flame placed to keep the way to the tree of life was a Cherub, then this emblem is extremely ancient. Mr. Parkhurst finds resemblance to this symbol in the West Indies; in the Temple of Elephanta, in the East Indies; in Diana; in Proserpine; in Rhadigust, an ancient German idol; in Mithras, a Persian Deity; in the gryphon, or griffion, of Cochin-China; in Yahuthana Nasr, Arabian idols resembling a lion and an eagle; and in many other parts of the world. The opinion of this writer seems to be sufficiently established to warrant the inference, that this emblem was not borrowed by the Jewish ritual from Egypt only, but was known among many other nations in its principle at least."[59]

When we reflect that at the very earliest ages, when religious rites were new among all the nations of the earth, it does seem probable that they all derived their ideas from one original stock; and in time the varieties of manners and customs, and also following these, the methods of worshipping their gods with the same central and general ideas; the variations were like branches of an original stock. The fact that in the vast number of cherubic forms, found in any part of the original heathen and idolatrous world, the common symbols have a great likeness to those symbols used by the Jewish people and described in the Jewish sacred books.

The Cross.

When the Cross became a symbol is lost in the remotest antiquity, and there is no mention of it, historically, at any period, or to the country, or the people who were the first to make use of it as a

---

[59] Calmet.

symbol; nevertheless, it is found at a very early period, by which certain forms have been recognized by certain names having specific meanings.

There are principal forms of the cross which are used as symbols, and others frequently employed in ornamentation having no special signification There are a great many forms of the cross. Among these we call attention to the Swastika which is the usual form of the Swastika, or Svastika, a symbol which has recently excited very much attention among archaeologists. In 1894, the Smithsonian publication contained a very lengthy paper of 221 pages, giving the most complete history with full illustrations and examples of this symbol by Professor Thomas Wilson, Curator Department of Prehistoric Anthropology, U.S. National Museum. He says: "The swastica has been called by different names in different countries, though nearly all countries have in later years accepted the ancient Sanskrit name of Swastika; and this name is recommended as the most definite and certain, being now the most general and, indeed, almost universal. It was formerly spelled s-u-a-s-t-i-c-a and s-w-a-s-t-i-k-a, but the later spelling, both English and French, is s-w-a-s-t-i-k-a. The definition and etymology of the word is thus given in Littre's French Dictionary:

"' Svastica, or Swastika, a mystic figure used by several (East) Indian sects.'

"It was equally well known to the Brahmans as to the Buddhists. Most of the rock inscriptions in the Buddhist caverns in the West of India are preceded or followed by the holy (sarramentelle) sign of the Swastika. (Eugene Burnouf, Me Lotus de la tonne loi; Paris, 1852, p. 625.) It was seen on the vases and pottery of Rhodes (Cyprus) and Etruria.

"Etymology: A Sanskrit word signifying happiness, pleasure, good luck. It is composed of Sa (equivalent of Greek ev), 'good,' and asti, 'being,' 'good being,' with the suffix ka (Greek Ka, Latin co)."

In the Revue a'Ethnographie (IV., 1885, p. 329), Mr. Dumoution gives the following analysis of the Sanskrit swastika:

"Su, radical, signifying goad, well, excellent, or suvidas, prosperity.

"Asti, third person, singular, indicative present of the verb as, to be, which is sum in Latin.

"Ha, suffix forming the substantive."

The Century Dictionary says, Swastika - [Sanskrit, lit., "of good fortune." Svasti (su,, well, + astz; being), welfare], Same as fylfot.

Compare crux ansata and gammadion.[60]

In Ilizos (p. 347), Max Muller says:

"Ethnologically, svastika is derived from svasti and svasti from su, 'well,' and as, 'to be.' Svasti occurs frequently in the Veda, both as a noun in a sense of happiness, and as an adverb in the sense of 'well' or 'hail!' It corresponds to the Greek xxxxx. The derivation swastika is of later date, and it always means an auspicious sign, such as are found most frequently among Buddhists and Jainas M. Eugene Burnouf defines the Mark Swastika as follows:

"A monogrammatic sign of four branches, of which the ends are curved (or bent) at right angles, the name signifying, literally, the sign of benediction, or good augury."

The foregoing explanations relate only to the present accepted name "Swastika."

The sign Swastika must have existed long before the name was given to it. It must have been in existence long before the Buddhist religion or the Sanskrit language.

In Great Britain the common name given to the Swastika from Anglo-Saxon times by those who had no knowledge whence it came, or that it came from any other than their own country, was Fylfot, said to have been derived from the Anglo-Saxon fower fot meaning four-footed, or many-footed.[61]

"Many theories have been presented concerning the symbolism of the Swastika, its relation to ancient deities and its representation of certain qualities. In the estimation of certain writers it has been respectively the emblem of Zeus, of Baal, of the Sun, of the sungod, of the sun-chariot, of Agni the fire-god, of Indra the rain-god, of the Sky, of the sky-god, and finally the deity of all deities, the Great God, the Maker and Ruler of the Universe. It has also/been held to symbolize light or the god of light, of the forked lightning, and of water. It is believed by some to have been the oldest Aryan symbol. In the estimation of others it represents Brahma, Vishnu, and Siva, Creator, Preserver, Destroyer. It appears in the footprints of Buddha, engraved upon the solid rock on the Mountains of India. It stood for the Jupiter Tonans and Pluvius of the Latins, and the Thor of the Scandinavians. In the latter case it has been considered - erroneously, however - a variety of the Thor hammer. In the opinion of at least one author it had an intimate relation to the Lotus sign of Egypt and Persia. Some authors have attributed a phallic meaning to it; others have recognized it as representing the generative

---

[60] Smithsonian Report, 1894, p. 769
[61] R. P. Greg per Smithsonian Report, 1894, p. 769.

principle of mankind, making it the symbol of the female. Its appearance on the person of certain goddesses, Artemis, Hera, Demeter, Astarte, and the Chaldean Nana, the leaden goddess from Hissarlik, has caused it to be claimed as a sign of fecundity."[62]

Commenting upon the theories of the various writers quoted, Professor Wilson says:

"In forming the foregoing theories their authors have been largely controlled by the alleged fact of the substitution and permutation of the Swastika sign on various objects with recognized symbols of these different deities. The claims of these theorists are somewhat clouded in obscurity and lost in the antiquity of the subject. What seems to have been at all times an attribute of the Swastika is its character as a charm or amulet, as a sign of benediction, blessing, long life, good fortune, good luck. This character has continued into modern times, and while the Swastika is recognized as a holy and sacred symbol by at least one Buddhistic religious sect, it is still used by the common people of India, China, and Japan as a sign of long life, good wishes, and good fortune."

Whatever else the sign Swastika may have stood for, and however many meanings it may have had, it was always oSamental. It may have been used with any or all of the above significations, but it was always ornamental as well.

"Dr. Schliemann found many specimens of Swastika in his excavation at the site of ancient Troy on the hill of Hissarlik. They were mostly on spindle whorls. . . . He appealed to Professor Max Muller for an explanation, who, in reply, wrote an elaborate description, which Dr. Schliemann published in Ilios."

He commences with a protest against the word Swastika being applied generally to the sign Swastika, because it may prejudice the reader or the public in favor of its Indian origin. He says:

"I do not like the use of the word Swastika outside of India. It is a word of Indian origin and has its history and definite meaning in India. . . . The occurrence of such crosses in different parts of the world may or may not point to a common origin, but if they are once called Swastika the vulgas profanum will at once jump to the conclusion that they all come from India, and it will take some time to weed out such prejudice.

"Very little is known of Indian art before the third century B.C., the period when the Buddhist sovereigns began their public buildings.

---

[62] Smithsonian Report, 1894, p. 771.

"The name Svastika, however, can be traced (in India) a little farther back. It occurs as the name of a particular sign in the old grammar of Panani, about a century earlier.

Certain compounds are mentioned there in which the last word is karma, 'ear.' one of the signs for marking cattle was the Svastika, and what Pinani teaches in his grammar is that when the compound is formed, saastika-karna, i.e., having the ear marked with a sign of a Svastika, the final a of Svastika is not to be lengthened, while it is lengthened in other compounds, such as datra-karna, i.e., having the ear marked with the sign of a sickle."

"It (the Swastika) occurs often at the beginning of Buddhist inscriptions, on Buddhist coins, and in Buddhist manuscripts. Historically, the Svastika is first attested on a coin of Krananda, supposing Krananda to be the same king as Xandrames, the predecessor of Sandrokyptos, whose reign came to an end in 315 B.C. (See Thomas on the identity of Xandrames and Krananda.) The paleographic evidence, however, seems rather against so early a date.

"In the foot-prints of Buddha the Buddhists recognize no less than sixty-five auspicious signs, the first of them being the Svastika; the fourth is the Suavastzka, or that with the arms turned to the left; the third, the Nandydvarta, is a mere development of the Svastika. Among the Jainas the Svastzka was the sign of their Seventh Jina, Suparsva."

"In the later Sanskrit literature, Svastika retains the meaning of an auspicious mark; thus we see in the Ramayana, that Bharata selects a ship marked with the sign of the Svastika. Varapamihira in the Brihat-samhita mentions certain buildings called Savastika and Nandyavarta, but their outline does not correspond very

exactly with the form of the sign. Some Sthupas, however, are said to have been built on the plan of the Svastika.... Originally, Svastika may have been intended for no more than two lines crossing each other, or a cross. Thus we find it used in later times referring to a woman covering her breast with crossed arms, Svahastasvastika-stanti, and likewise with reference to persons sitting cross-legged."[63]

Max Muller continues:

"Quite another question is, why the sign should have an auspicious meaning, and why in Sanscrit it should have been called Svastika. The similarity between the group of letters sv in the ancient Indian alphabet, and the sign of Svastika is not very striking, and seems purely accidental.

---

[63] Smithsonian Report, 1894, p. 772

"A remark of yours [Schliemann] (Troy, p. 38) that the Svastika resembles a wheel in motion, the direction of the motion being indicated by the crampons, contains a useful hint, which has been confirmed by some important observations of Mr. Thomas, the distinguished Oriental numismatist, who has called attention to the fact that in the long list of the recognized devices of the twenty four Jaina Tirthankaras the sun is absent, but that while the eighth Tirthankara has the sign of the half-moon, the seventh Tirthankara is marked with the Svastika, i.e., the sun. Here, then, we have clear indications that the Svastika, with the hands pointing in the right direction, was originally a symbol of the sun, perhaps of the vernal sun as opposed to the autumnal sun, Suavastika, and, therefore, a natural symbol of light, life, health, and wealth.

"But, while from these indications we are justified in supposing that among the Aryan nations the Svastika may have been an old emblem of the sun, there are other indications to show that in other parts of the world the same or a similar emblem was used to indicate the earth. Mr. Beal . . . has shown . . . that the simple (+) occurs as a sign for earth in certain ideographic groups. It was probably intended to indicate the four quarters - north, south, east, west -

or, it may be, more generally, extension in length and breadth.

"That the cross is used as a sign for 'four' in the Bactro-Pali inscriptions (Max Muller, Chips fram a German workshop, Vol. II., p. 298) is well known; but the fact that the same sign has the same power elsewhere, as, for instance, in the Hieratic numerals, does not prove by any means that the one figure was derived from the other. We forget too easily that what was possible in one place was possible also in the other places; and the morale we extend our researches, the more we shall learn that the chapter of accidents is larger than we imagine."[64]

In the Smithsonian Report (Annual) for 1897 we find an article by Marquis De Nadaillac on the "Unity of the Human Species," who, in concluding one part of the subject, says:[65]

"The accumulated proof renders it incontestable that the funeral rite of cleaning the bones and coloring them red was practised in different countries widely separated by sea or desert. Thucydides says the history of a people is to be sought in their tombs. In the cases cited, the tomb has responded and has thrown a clear light on the earliest origin of the rite, and at the same time on the common origin of man. A question arising from these facts is, whether they relate to religious or funeral

---

[64] Smithsonian Report, 1894, p. 773.
[65] Ibid., 1898, pp. 563 to 569

rites. But this is comparatively of small importance. It was surely a custom of the unknown ancestors of these peoples, transmitted from generation to generation. These facts do not allow us to say that primitive life was everywhere the same, nor that if the productions of men are everywhere the same, they are always to satisfy the same needs. In the strange rite that we have recounted, a rite which has required much thought and multiplied cares and which one can believe was strange to barbarous and nomadic races, it is not a question of similar needs growing out of similar creations. In order to find a solution it is necessary to seek higher and farther; it is the identity of the genius of man in all times and in all regions that should be inquired of, and it is only there that it can be found.[66]

"The mysterious Swastika sign born in undefined regions and rapidly extended over the entire world, goes to support this hypothesis. We will seek the lessons it teaches.

"For a long time the Swastika (the croix gammee, a Greek cross, with arms bent to the right at right angles) has been regarded as an Aryan sign, even the Aryan sign par excellence. From this, or from its apparent place of origin, the name Indian (East Indian) has been given it; a name difficult at present to maintain because of the daily discoveries of its diffusion or spread among absolute strangers to the Aryan race.[67]

"It appears from the researches made during late years that the origin even of the Swastika sign appears to be contested. Thus we read in the work of Count Goblet d'Alviella,[68] one of those who has best studied the question:

"'The croix gammee (Swastika) appears from prehistoric times among the peoples originating in the valley of the Danube, who have

---

[66] J. McGuire, Classification and Development of Primitive Implements. "Amer. Anthrop.," July, 1896.

[67] The literature upon the Swastika has increased in late years until it has become a library. In 1889 Count Goblet d'Alviella made a communication to the Royal Academy of Belgium entitled "La croix gammee, or Swastika." It has since been enlarged and published under the title "La migration des Symboles," Paris, 1891. An English translation appeared with an introduction and note by Sir G. Birdwood. Among recent publications were those of Michael Zmigrodzki. "Zur Geschichte der Swatika," Brunswick, 1890, and Thomas Wilson, "The Swastika," Washington, 1896. Eminent savants in all countries have been occupied with the question of its origin and signification, but it appears, nevertheless, that it is not yet entirely cleared, for Dr. Brinton writes: "It is easy to read into barbaric scratches the thoughts of later times, and we must acknowledge that something more than the figure itself is needed to prove its symbolic sense."

[68] La migration des Symboles. "Revue des deux Mondes," May 12, 1889.

respectively colonized the Troad and the north of Italy. It extends with the products of this antique culture, on one side, among the Greeks, Etruscans, Latins, Gauls, Germans, British, and Scandinavians; on the other side, to Asia Minor, Persia, the Indies, and to China and Japan.'

"Such is also the opinion of M. Salomon Reinach.[69] According to him the sign of the Swastika already represented in the city of Hissarlik, prior, according to all probabilities, to the thirteenth century.[70] He continues that one does not find the symbol in Egypt,[71] nor in Phoenicia, nor Assyria; while, on the other hand, it is frequent in northern Italy, in the valley of the Danube, in Thrace, in Greece, and on the western shores of Asia Minor. Thence comes his conclusions that we should seek in Europe for its origin.[72]

"I do not pretend to contradict this, but the first discovery of the Swastika on the hill of Hissarlik determines that this was not its place of origin. When came this mysterious sign which we see at Troy ? To what rite does it belong ? Where did it originate ? These are questions we would like to have answered. In the present state of our knowledge, the question is insoluble. One point excites my interest, that is the long persistence of the Swastika and its rapid diffusion throughout such different regions. I see in this an important argument in favor of the unity of the human species. This argument should be further presented and such facts produced as justify it.

"An infant, the child of a savage, might amuse himself by tracing in the sand or on stone, or on the first object that came under

---

[69] Le mirage oriental. " L'Anthropologie," 1895
B.C., did not penetrate the Indies until after that period.
[70] M. Reinach afterward recognized that the Swastika mentioned by Goblet d'Alviella on certain ingots of silver in the form of dominoes, serving as money, and also those with inscriptions in honor of Acoka, belonged to the third century B.C. - "L'Anthropologie," 894, p. 248.
[71] Flinders Petrie has found at Naukratis certain vases ornamented with the Swastika (Third Memoir Egyptian Exploration Fund), but this pottery appears to have been imported from Caria or from Cyprus. Stuffs ornamented with the same sign have also been discovered at Panopolis, Upper Egypt, but these have been attributed to Greek workmen who were numerous at Coptos, a neighboring village where Clermont Ganneau has recently discovered a Greek inscription. - "Acad. des Inscriptions," March 5, 1897 (Forrer, "Die Graber und Textilfunde von Achmin Panopolis ").
[72] "As for India, everything induces the belief that the Swastika was there introduced from Greece, from the Caucasus, or from Asia Minor, by routes as yet unknown." - Goblet d'Alviella. " La migration des symboles," p. 107

his hand, squares and circles and crosses, and lines, making all imaginable angles; with progress the child can reproduce the images of his mind, the scenes that strike him most, even to bizarre figures which are due only to his imagination. He will not produce a sign as complicated as the Swastika unless he has it or has had it before his eye, or unless it shall have been transmitted to him by his ancestors. It is puerile to explain its presence in so many and such widely separated regions by the theory of the identity of the psychologic state among human races which have the same rudimentary culture

"The mysterious Swastika[73] figured on the idols and spindle whorls[74] of the ancient Dardania, on the diadem of the daughters of Priam, and on the numberless objects from the early cities on the hill of Hissarlik,[75] in the sacred temples of India as on the bas relief of Ibriz, attributed to the Hittites,[76] on Celtic funeral urns, and on the hut urns of Albano or Corneto, a curious imitation of the habitations of the living wherein they have piously deposited the ashes of the dead.[77]

"We see the Swastika on the balustrades of the porticos of the temple of Athena at Pergamos, on the sculptured ceiling of the Treasury at Orchomenos, on the vases of Milo and Athena, those of Bologna, the ancient Felsina of the Etruscans,[78] of Caere (Cervetri),[79] Cumes,[80]

---

[73] Sometimes the arms of the Swastika turn to the left, to which Professor Max Muller says has been given the name Suavastika. (Mr. Virchand R. Gandhi reports that while studying an ancient Sanscrit philosophy, in the British Museum library, he found the word Suavastika in connection with Swastika - T. W.)

[74] The number of these objects casts a doubt upon their use as spindle whorls only. They have been religious objects, a sort of ex-voto, for example.

[75] Schliemann, "Ilios," Figs. 1873, 1911, and others.

[76] S. Reinach, Le mirage oriental. "Anthropologie," 1893.

[77] Dennis, "Cities and Cemeteries of Etruria," vol. i., p. 69; vol. ii., p. 457. Dennis regards these urns as anterior to the Etruscan civilization. See also " Annali Dell' Inst. Romano," 1871, pp. 239, 279. Professor H. W. Haynes, of Boston, is of opinion that these belong to the " Iron Age " (Nation, January 24, 1889). Professor Heilbig, " Guide to the Collection of Classic Antiquities in Rome," vol. ii., p. 267; Pigorini, "Bulletino Ethnologia Italiana," vol. xii., p. 262; Chantre, "Necropoles Halstattiennes de Italie et de l'Autriche, Materiaux," vol. xviii., pp. 3, 4.

[78] Gozzadini, " Scavi Archaeologici," Plate IV.

[79] In a tomb at Caere there has been found a golden fibula with engraved Swastika Greffi, "Monumenti di Caere," Plate VI., No. 1.

[80] At Cumes has been found the sign (Swastika) on pottery, buried at great depth, which mark the establishment of sepulchres at the most ancient periods,

Cyprus,[81] and on the pottery gathered at Konigswalde on the Oder; on a golden fibula of the Museum of the Vatican, and a copper fibula of the Royal Museum of Copenhagen.

"It is encountered in the most ancient paintings of the catacombs of Rome, on the tunic of the Bon Pasteur,[82] and on the archbishop's chair of St. Ambrose at Milan, where it is associated with the Latin cross and the monogram of Christ; on the ancient sacred books of Persia, as well as on the coins of Arsacides and the Sassanides; on the most ancient Christian monuments of Scotland and Ireland, often accompanied with Ogam inscriptions;[83] on the Scandinavian runic books; in the Halstattien sepulchres of San Margarether or de Rovische,[84] and in the necropolis of Koban.[85]

"Schliemann found it at Tiryns and at Mycenae;[86] Cartailhac in the citanias, those strange fortified towns of Portugal, some of which date from Neolithic times;[87] Chantre in the tombs in Caucasus,[88] and the Russian archaeologists on the bronze objects from their country in the Museum of Moscow.

"The Swastika has been found in France, in the Tumuli (mounds) of Haguenau, engraved on the cinctures of bronze.[89] It is perpetuated on objects posterior or strange to the Roman domination. For example, on those taken in the Frankish tombs opened at Colombe (Loire-et-Cher), on a funeral stele at the Museum of Toulouse, on a vase at the Museum of Rouen,[90] on the tinctures, Gallo-Roman or

---

beneath the tombs of the Hellenic epoch, they in turn being under those of the Roman epoch. Alex Bertrand ("Arch. celtique et gauloise," p. 45).
[81] "Cesnola, Cyprus, its Ancient Cities, Tombs and Temples," Plates XLIV. and XLVII.
[82] Roller, "Les Catacombes de Rome," Plates VI., X.. XXXII., XXXIX., LIV., LXXXVII., XCIV
[83] Dr. Graves, Bishop of Limerick, "Proceedings Roy. Irish Acad." Ludvig Muller reports the same.
[84] "Materiaux," 1884, pp. 137, 139, 466, and Fig. 84.
[85] Ibid., 1888, p. 352.
[86] "Mycene," p. 193.
[87] "L'Espagne et le Portugal prehistoriques," Figs. 410-412. Recently M. da Veiga has recognized the Swastika in the compartments of a mosaic found in Algarve. " L'Anthropologie," 1891, p. 222.
[88] M. Chantre assimilates these burials to those of Villanoba, Halstatt, and Bismen tovia in upper Italy. " Materiaux," 1881, pp. 164, 165.
[89] De Mortillet, " Album prehistorique," pp. 98, 99, 100.
[90] Ibid., Figs. 1247, 1257.

Merovingian, near La Fere.[91] The Swastika also is found on a Celto-Roman altar erected at Ambloganna, in England by a Dacian legion in honor of Zeus or Jupiter,[92] on the right and left are two circles, rayed after the fashion of stars, which Gaidoz believes to be a representation of the sun.[93] The Laplanders still engrave the Swastika on their drums intended to be used in Magic rites.

"The Chinese decorate with it their standards, instruments of music, and their cannon.[94]

"The Japanese employ it as a mark on their pottery, and the Hindus paint it in red on their houses at the beginning of the New Year, and make it with flour or sacred rice upon a table or stand when entering a house or church as a sign of good luck or good wishes, or the occasion of a Wedding or fete.[95]

"The diffusion of a sign so complicated as the Swastika throughout all time and in all countries is something to be remarked, and of which we should recognize the importance. Our astonishment is doubled when we find the same symbol among the Ashantes on the Western coast of Africa,[96] and see it figured in America among the most ancient civilization of which we have any knowledge. By what migration has it crossed the Atlantic, by what migrations has it penetrated such distant countries and appeared among races of men so different ? And if, as we believe, all these representations are due to an indigenous art, either Indian or African, where did they obtain their model ? Our ignorance on these points is complete, and the most we can do is to give a resume of the principal known facts.

---

[91] Moreau, "Album de Caranada."

[92] Goblet d'Alviella, " La migration des symboles," p. 65.

[93] "Le dieu gaulois du soleil et la migration des symboles."

[94] The Letter of Gordon to Schliemann. " Ilios," p. 352.

[95] It has been contended by some persons that the triskelion was an evolution from or to the Swastika - the triskelion of three human legs bent at the knee and joined at the thigh. It is found on the Lycian coins about 480 B.C., and thence was carried by Agathocles to Sicily. (Barclay Head, "Coins of the Ancients," Plate XXXV.) It is also found on a vase from Agrigentum. (Waring, "Ceramic Art in Remote Ages," Plate XLII.) Newton explains how the symbol (triskelion) is found on the arms of Sicily, and also those of the Isle of Man. ("Athenaeum," September, 1892.) The Duke of Athol, proprietary of the Isle of Man, sold in 1765 his right to the Crown of England, but because he had been its sovereign he kept the triskelion in his coat of arms.

[96] "It is not possible to admit," says Count Goblet d'Alviella ("Migration des symboles," p. 108), "that this has been spontaneously conceived and executed. Of all a priori hypotheses, this is certainly the most difficult to accept."

"The Swastika has been found engraved on a shell from a mound in Tennessee which contained thirty-two human burials,[97] on plates (five) of copper from the mounds of Chillicothe, Ohio,[98] a stone hatchet from Pemberton, N. J., on an Arkansas vase in the National Museum, on a silver ornament, the authenticity of which appears incontestable, and which was shown in 1887 at the reunion at the Association Fransaise at Toulouse.[99]

"Nordenskiold cites numerous examples of the Swastika, now engraved in straight lines, other times indicated by dots, among the cave dwellers of Mesa Verde, and the same is done by Max Mullet in Yucatan and Paraguay, while other savants have found it among the Huacas of Peru and among savage tribes of Brazil, where the triangular pieces of pottery, sometimes bearing the mysterious Swastika sign, often form the only dress of the women.[100]

"We find it in the paintings of the Navajos[101] and on the ornaments of the Pueblo Indians, while the Sac Indians of the Southwest wear it on their collars and garters on occasion of their religious fetes, although it is not possible that they should know the sense which is attached to it,[102] and the Wolpis paint it on their dance rattles.[103]

"I have omitted to treat of numerous figurines ornamented with the Swastika in the hope to find an explanation of this mysterious symbol. We find it engraved on a figure of Buddha in the United States National Museum,[104] on the base of a bronze Buddha from Japan, and on a vase in the Kunsthistorische Museum of Vienna where it figures on the breast of Apollo.[105] Astarte bears it on her arms and shoulders,[106] Adonis on his arms, a follower of Aphrodite, on her robe,[107] a centaur

---

[97] "Third Annual Report," Bureau of Ethnology, Fig. 140.
[98] "Twelfth Annual Report," Bureau of Ethnology. Other similar discoveries have been made in Ohio.
[99] "Comptes rendus," i., p. 284
[100] Wilson, Swastika, "Report U. S. Nat. Mus.," 1894, Plate XVIII.

[101] Ibid., Plate XVII.
[102] Ibid., Plates XV. and XVI. (Nevertheless these Indians recognize it as a sign of good luck and give it a corresponding name. - T. W.)
[103] "Rev. d'Ethnographie," 1885, No. 1.
[104] Wilson, 1. c., Plate 1.
[105] Goblet d'Alviella, 1. c., Plate 1.
[106] "Bul. Soc. d'Anth.," 1888, p. 676.
[107] This statuette was found in 1887 in a Greek tomb. "Bul. Soc. d'Anth.," 1888, p. 677

from Cyprus on his right shoulder.[108] In a rude representation of Apollo directing the car of the sun it is found on the wheels of the chariot.[109] A female statue in lead found at Troy wears a triangular covering over the ulva, the center of which bears a Swastikas Numerous cinctures or girdles worn by women bore this same Swastika sign. Does this not indicate that it may have been regarded as an emblem of the generative forces of nature?

"But we will not venture further in our researches for the signification of a sign so obscure as is the Swastika. Probably (and the figurines just mentioned give this hypothesis a semblance of truth)[110] it was a religious emblem, an amulet consecrated by the varied superstitions of man, as is the hand with the fingers raised a survival of an ancient Chaldean symbol which is worn to-day by the Italians, as is the little pig by the Parisians.[111] Was it dedicated to the living sun; to Zeus or Baal; to Astarte or to Aphrodite; to Agni, the god of fire; or to Indra, the god of rain; or, still further, to Vishnu or to Siva, the Hindu representatives of creation and destruction? All these hypotheses are possible; more than this, all of them are probable, for the signification of Swastika has singularly varied according to the time and to tradition.[112] Those persons who in the actual state of our knowledge pretend to formulate general conclusions are sadly in error.

"I approach the end of my task. By the side of the similarity of the anatomic structure of man in all times and of all races, I have sought to place the similarity of his genius, as proved by the identity of his conceptions. The ossuaries which contain the remains of his predecessors, the custom of coloring his bones red after they had been denuded of their flesh, the mysterious sign to which we have given the name Swastika, and other conceptions, other almost universal creations, which it would be easy to add, all tend toward the confirmation of the knowledge given to us by the earliest arms, the first tools and implements of flint, and the most ancient pottery. We believe it impossible to misapprehend or mistake the multiplied proofs that flow

---

[108] Cesnola, "Salaminia," p. 243.
[109] Ibid.
[110] Schliemann, "Ilios," Fig. 226.
[111] W. W. Rockhill ("Diary of a Journey through Mongolia and Tibet," 1891-92) cites the Tibetan who had a Swastika tattooed on his hand.
[112] Sewell ("Indian Antiquary," July, 1881) presents innumerable hypotheses to which the Swastika has given rise. To cite but one: Mr. Cunningham, a distinguished savant, believes the Swastika to have been a monogram.

from modern researches, all of which affirm with an irrefutable eloquence the unity of the human species."

Among the very ancient symbols of the Orient we find the Pentalpha, or five-pointed star. In one of the illustrations in the Iconographic Encycpoedia of the late Professor Baird, President of the Smithsonian Institution, who succeeded Professor Henry, we observe that the Pentalpha occupies the most conspicuous place. That picture represents the universe, viz., the great celestial serpent forms a circle having the tail in its mouth, at the top; diametrically opposite, at the bottom the serpent twists the body in a large coil; upon this coil is a huge tortoise; on the back of the tortoise stand four elephants occupying the four cardinal points; on these elephants rests the earth, which is flat on the bottom and hemispherical on the top; above the earth are represented concentrically the seven heavenly spheres; immediately above the uppermost sphere, and suspended from the junction of the tail and mouth of the serpent, is the Pentalpha.

The Pentalpha has been so called, because the five (pence) points each represented the Greek letter Alpha (A). It was called Hygeia or symbol of health by Pythagoras.

We refer our readers to Book IV., Chapter IV., pages 1755 to 1783 - and especially on pages 1781 to 1783 - wherein we have shown the connection between some of the symbols now employed in our modern Masonic system, with those of the remotest antiquity, and have made frequent references to Dr. Mackey and to his predecessor, Dr. Oliver, from whose works on symbolism we have freely quoted such passages as would demonstrate our subject.

The writer of this treatise on Symbolism has endeavored to place before the reader the intimate relation between all the forms of language, as displayed by man, from the earliest ages, in the crudest efforts to convey his ideas to others, down to the perfected forms of animal life, as displayed in the unnatural compositions in the cherubim, which was shown first to Moses, and subsequently to the prophets Ezekiel and Isaiah, as described in the text.

We can give no further explanations than those taken from ancient writers, as, down to the present day, they are as mysterious as they have always been in every age of the world, like the image of the veiled Isis in her temple on the island Philae in Egypt, with the following inscription: " I am that which was, which is, and which is to come, and no mortal hath lifted my veil."

PART FIVE

ANCIENT AND ACCEPTED SCOTTISH RITE
ROYAL ORDER OF SCOTLAND
ANCIENT AND ACCEPTED SCOTTISH RITE
THE EARLY HISTORY OF THE SCOTTISH RITE

IN Chapter LI of this work will be found a "History of Christian Knighthood," and in the following chapter, LII, "Knight Templarism in America." In pages 1332 to 1336, Chapter LI, is given the history of the suppression of the "Templar Order," the death of the last Grand Master, Jacques De Molay, and the dispersion of the "Order."

There is no need to repeat in this place the account of the destruction of the greatest of the three great military orders, the "Poor Fellow-soldiers of Christ and Solomon's Temple" as they officially described themselves. On March 11, 1314, the Grand Master, Jacques de Molay, was burned to death in Paris, declaring with his last breath that the confessions wrung from him and other knights by torture were untrue, and that the order was innocent. The Papal Bull, issued by Clement V. the year before, had suppressed the order and transferred its estates to the Knights Hospitallers, or Knights of St. John of Jerusalem, for centuries the bitter foes of the Templars. The Templars who escaped the cruelty of the French King, Philip the Fair, fled to other countries.

From this period until the invention of printing there was a slow but gradual increase in learning, which was mostly confined to the priesthood; very few, even of the nobility, could read or write; hence they employed as chaplains the learned class of the clergy, who conducted all of their business affairs, and became domesticated in their families.

After the invention of movable type and the increase of books, "learning" became more popular, and by the political changes in the kingdoms of Europe there were important improvements in science and the arts brought about, so that from the close of the 14th century to the death of Charles II. of England, very important events had taken place and an entire revolution of society had occurred, growing out of the "Reformation" in religion. The great fire in London - although a local affair - had its effects upon other parts of Europe. The reconstruction of the city of London - and particularly of the religious edifices - produced a revolution in architecture under the supervision of Sir Christopher Wren, who was appointed by Charles II. as superintendent of all the public buildings after the great fire. Under the sanction of the King, Wren visited the continent and became familiar with the classic orders of architecture, of which there were few examples in England. There is no doubt that the great cathedral of St. Paul's in London, in its order of architecture, was a copy of St. Peter's in Rome.

Sir Christopher Wren has often been called by Masonic writers a Grand Master of Masons, but there is no evidence whatever that he was even an Apprentice Mason when he became the government architect or " Superintendent."

Lessing, the German critic, goes so far as to describe Wren as the inventor of Speculative Masonry, but later investigators affirm that while Inigo Jones, the great architect of so many noble buildings in England, is claimed to have held a place in the Masonic order, yet Sir Christopher Wren is only mentioned in a professional capacity.

As the first code of Masonic laws and the first items of Masonic history were published by authority, it may justly be inferred that the triumvirate of compilers had no knowledge of his having ever been a member of the Society. The English Freemasons of the period of the so-called revival of 1717 seemed to have found no reason to believe in Wren's connection with the Society. Wren was one of the most eminent men of the time, "a prodigy of universal science," President of the Royal Society, the builder of the new cathedral of St. Paul's, London, and numerous colleges and other buildings, and, more than all, the rebuilder of London after the Great Fire, and it would be strange that the initiation or affiliation of such a distinguished man as the King's Architect should have been forgotten by the lodges of Masons subsisting when the revival of 1717 took place.

The invention of new degrees was continuous, in the countries of Europej during the middle portion of the 18th century, but most of them were worked to a limited extent only and soon passed into oblivion. The three degrees of Entered Apprentice, Fellow Craft, and Master Mason were the source from whence this prolific development of degrees sprang, and these three degrees were selected, with twenty-two others, to compose a Rite which was destined to retain its vitality, and to spread its influence, throughout the world. This Rite was known as the "Ancient and Accepted Rite."

There have been various accounts of the manner in which these degrees were selected and arranged in the so-called "Rite of Perfection." The most reasonable statement is as follows:

The Chevalier de Bonneville established a chapter of twenty-five degrees of the so- called High Degrees in the College of Jesuits of Clermont, in Paris, in 1754. The adherents and followers of the House of the Stuarts had made the College of Clermont their asylum, they being mostly Scotchmen. One of these degrees being the "Scottish Master," the new Body organized in Charleston, S.C., in 1801, gave the name of "Scottish Rite" to these degrees, which name ever since that time has characterized the Rite all over the world, of which more anon. The name previously given to these degrees was the "Rite of Perfection," or the Ancient and Accepted Rite.

The Marquis de Lernais carried these degrees to Berlin in 1758 and they were introduced into and adopted by the Grand Lodge of the Three Globes. The Rite was revived in Paris that year under the authority of the "Council of Emperors of the East and West." In consequence of the interference of the Jesuits, who, finding that their former efforts had not succeeded in finally suppressing the Rite, again forced themselves into the Rite and "sowed seeds of dissension," the result was that a new organization was formed called the "Council of the Knights of the East;" and as a consequence a rivalry sprung up between these two bodies and the Grand Orient of France. In 1781, however, both of these bodies became incorporated with that Grand Body which held the Rite of Perfection within itself.

In 1762 it is asserted that Frederick the Great, who had taken under his patronage all of Masonry in Germany, formed and promulgated what have been known ever since then as the Grand Constitutions of 1762.

The "Rite of Perfection," which for a quarter of a century, with many struggles, had not fully accomplished the work proposed for it by its authors, was improved, it is said, by Frederick himself, by a reorganization and reconstruction which placed it on a higher standard in its philosophy and in its teachings; that eight other degrees were added to it, and the name was changed to "The Ancient and Accepted Scottish Rite of Freemasonry," and that the Grand Constitutions of 1786 were ratified and signed by Frederick in Berlin, in May of that year.

By these Constitutions of 1786, Frederick the Great resigned the authority he had held from 1762 as Grand Commander of the Order of Princes of the Royal Secret, and Supreme Chief of the Scottish Rite or of Perfection. His Masonic prerogatives were by the same document deposited with a council for each nation, to be composed of Sovereign Grand Inspectors-General of the Thirty-Third and last degree of legitimate Freemasonry, limited in numbers to that of the years of Christ on earth.

The Grand Constitutions formed in 1762 were ratified in Bordeaux, October 25th of that year, and were proclaimed as the governing laws for all the several Bodies of the "Rite of Perfection" over the two Hemispheres.

Prior to this, in 1761, Stephen Morin was invested with power by the Grand Consistory of Sublime Princes of the Royal Secret in Paris, on the 27th of August, 1761, to carry the "Rite of Perfection" to America. He received a Patent, as his credential, of which the following is a copy:

Morin's Patent.

To the glory of the G. A. O. T. U., etc., and by the good will of H. S. H. the very illustrious Brother Louis de Bourbon, Count de Clermont, Prince of the Blood Royal, Grand Master and Protector of all Lodges.

At the Orient of a most enlightened place where reign Peace, Silence, and Concord, Anno Lucis 5761, and according to the common style, 27th August, 1761.

Lux ex tenebris. Unitas, concordia fratrum.

We the undersigned, Substitutes General of the Royal Art, Grand Wardens and Officers of the Grand and Sovereign Lodge of St. John of Jerusalem, established at the Orient of Paris; and we, Sovereign Grand Masters of the Grand Council of the Lodges of France, under the sacred and mysterious numbers, declare, certify, and decree to all the very dear Bros., Knights, and Princes scattered throughout the two hemispheres, that being assembled by order of the Substitute General, President of the Grand Council, a request was communicated to us by the worshipful Bro. Lacorne, Substitute of our very illustrious G. M., Knight and Prince Mason, and was read in due form.

Whereas our dear Bro. Stephen Morin, Grand Perfect Elect (G. elu parfait) and Past Sublime Master, Prince Mason, Knight and Sublime Prince of all orders of the Masonry of Perfection, member of the Royal Lodge of the "Trinity," etc., being about to depart for America, desires to be able to work with regularity for the advantage and aggrandisement of the Royal Art in all its perfection, may it please the Sovereign Grand Council and Grand Lodge to grant him letters of constitution. On the report which has been made to us, and knowing the eminent qualifications of Bro. S. Morin, we have, without hesitation, accorded him this slight gratification in return for the services which he has always rendered this Order, and the continuation of which is guaranteed to us by his zeal.

For this cause and for other good reasons, whilst approving and confirming the very dear Brother Morin in his designs, and wishing to confer on him some mark of our gratitude, we have, by consent, constituted and invested him, and do by these presents constitute and invest him, and give full and entire power to the said Bro. Stephen Morin, whose signature is in the margin of these presents, to form and establish a Lodge in order to admit to and multiply the Royal Order of Masons in all the perfect and sublime degrees; to take measures that the statutes and regulations of the Grand and Sovereign Lodge, general or special, be kept and observed, and to never admit therein any but true and legitimate brothers of sublime Masonry.

To rule and govern all the members who shall compose his said Lodge, which he may establish in the four quarters of the world wherever he may arrive or shall sojourn, under the title of Lodge of St. John, and surnamed In Perfect Harmony; "we give him power to choose such officers as he may please to aid him in ruling his Lodge, whom we command and enjoin to obey and respect him; do ordain and command all Masters of regular Lodges of whatsoever dignity, scattered over the surface of land and sea, do pray and enjoin them in the name of the Royal Order, and in the presence of our very illustrious G. M., to acknowledge in like manner as we recognise our very dear Bro. Stephen Morin as Worshipful Master of the Lodge of Perfect Harmony, and we depute him in his quality of our Grand Inspector in all parts of the New World to reform the observance of our laws in general, etc., and by these presents do constitute our very dear Bro. Stephen Morin our G. M. Inspector, authorising and empowering him to establish perfect and sublime Masonry in all parts of the world, etc., etc.

We pray, consequently, all brothers in general to render to the said Stephen Morin such assistance and succour as may be in their power, requiring them to do the same to all the brothers who shall be members of his Lodge, and whom he has admitted and constituted, shall admit or constitute in future to the sublime degree of perfection which we grant him, with full and entire power to create Inspectors in all places where the sublime degrees shall not already be established, knowing well his great acquirement and capacity.

In witness whereof we have given him these presents, signed by the Substitute- General of the Order, Grand Commander of the Black and White Eagle, Sovereign Sublime Prince of the Royal Secret, and Chief of the Eminent Degree of the Royal Art, and by us, Grand Inspectors, Sublime Officers of the Grand Council and of the Grand Lodge established in this capital, and have sealed them with the Grand Seal of our illustrious G. M. His Serene Highness, and with that of our Grand Lodge and Sovereign Grand Council. Given at the G. O. of Paris, in the year of light, 5761, or according to the Vulgar Era, 27th August, 1761. (Signed) Chaillon de Jonville, Substitute-General, W. M. of the first lodge in France called "St. Thomas," Chief of the Eminent Degrees, Commander and Sublime Prince of the Royal Secret. Bro. the Prince de Rohan, Master of the Grand Lodge "Intelligence," Sovereign Prince of Masonry. Lacorne, Substitute of the Grand Master, W. Dep. M. of Lodge "Trinity," Grand Perfect Elect, Knight and Prince Mason. Savalette de Bucheley, Grand Keeper of the Seals, Grand Elect, Grand Knight and Prince Mason. Taupin, etc., Prince Mason, Brest-dela-Chaussee, etc., W.

M. of the Lodge "Exactitude," Grand Elect Perfect Master, Knight Prince Mason. Count de Choiseul, etc., Prince Mason Boucher de Lenoncourt, etc., W. M. of the Lodge "Virtue," Prince Mason.

By order of the Grand Lodge. Daubertin, Grand Elect Perfect Master and Knight Prince Mason, W. M. of the Lodge "Saint Alphonse," Grand Secretary of the Grand Lodge and of the Sublime Council of Prince Masons in France, etc.

APPRENTICE'S PILLAR
Roslyn Chapel, Edinburgh

The first soil which Morin touched on his mission to America was San Domingo, and afterward, on his arrival at Kingston, Jamaica, he appointed Henry Francken a Deputy Inspector-General Later on other appointments were made by him to this office, and these Deputies he supplied with copies of the Grand Constitutions, which had been adopted in 1762. Soon after his appointment Francken visited the North American Colonies, where he gave an appointment of Deputy Inspector-General to Moses M. Hayes, at Boston, Mass. Francken established under his commission from Morin a lodge at Albany, N. Y. This was a Lodge of Perfection of the 14th Degree. On December 20, 1767, he conferred the degree of Sublime Prince of the Royal Secret, the 25th Degree of the Rite, on several Brethren of the order. This lodge seems not to have prospered, and was nearly forgotten when in 1822 Giles Fonda Gates, one of the most active Brethren of the Northern Masonic Jurisdiction, discovered the original Warrant, together with some patents of the Brethren of the body, and its books of record.

This was, no doubt, the very first body of the "Rite of Perfection" ever planted on the Continent of North America, and there were, doubtless, several such bodies in the Islands of the West Indies.

Those Masons who have progressed beyond the Blue Lodge degrees, and are familiar with the Capitular and Cryptic Rites, as also the degrees of the Commandery and those of the A.'. A.'. A.'. S.'. R.'. can readily perceive how Thomas Smith Webb was able to manufacture the degrees attributed to him, after his residence in Albany, and his connection with the Masons of that city

(1) The date is not known, but it must have been between 1762 and 1767

Brother Da Costa was made Deputy Inspector-General for South Carolina by Hayes in 1781; he also appointed Solomon Bush Deputy for Pennsylvania, and B. M. Spitzer Deputy for Georgia.

Da Costa established in Charleston in 1783 a Sublime Grand Lodge of Perfection.

A Council of Princes of Jerusalem was duly constituted in Charleston, and Meyers, Spitzer, and Frost were present and installed the Officers. The Council of Knights Kadosh was organized in Philadelphia in 1796 by refugees from San Domingo. When France again assumed authority over San Domingo, these Brethren returned home and the council became dormant if not entirely extinct.

In New York City a chapter of Rose Croix (18th Degree) was established in 1797, the Grand Constitution of 1786 and the ritual of the eight added degrees having been received in Charleston at that time. The bodies already established in Charleston accepted the new regime and adopted the new degrees, and in 1801 a convention was held and preliminary steps inaugurated to form a Supreme Council of the 33d and Last Degree of the Ancient and Accepted Scottish Rite of Freemasonry.

The name of this new body was "The Supreme Council of Sovereign Grand Inspectors- General of the Thirty-third and Last Degree for the United States of America." It was formed and organized by John Mitchell and Frederic Dalcho, and during the year the full number of members, nine, was admitted.

This new body recognized the Constitutions of 1762, the Secret Constitutions, and the much-discussed Constitutions of 1786.

These latter constitutions are believed to have been approved and ratified by Frederick the Great of Prussia, as Supreme Head and Governor of the Rite, and, as already stated, provide for the government of the Rite, after his death, by a council in each nation. Although these constitutions claim to have been recognized as the Supreme Law of the Rite in 1786, they were not published till 1832, when a French version appeared. A Latin text was published two years afterward which, while agreeing with the French book in essentials, differs in many of the details. It may be broadly stated that the Latin version is more precise, more complete, more in legal form, and, hence, some students have arrived at the conclusion that the Latin constitutions, thus written in a language universally understood, were the original, while the French version was really an adaptation for the use of the Brethren in France.

But the question whether the French or Latin text is the original is a mere trifle of little importance compared with another vital one, namely: "Were the Constitutions of 1786 ever seen or sanctioned by Frederick the Great? Were they not forged in Charleston? Those who asserted the falseness of the constitutions made no attempt to demonstrate the commission of forgery at Charleston, but confined themselves to denying that they were ever sanctioned Dy Frederick. The reasons alleged for this opinion were that in 1786 Frederick was mentally and physically incapacitated for business, and, furthermore, that the names subscribed to the Latin version were fictitious. The injurious suspicions as to the veracity of numerous Masonic statements, caused by the injudicious zeal and the uncritical methods of many Masonic writers, led to the general acceptance of the belief that the constitutions as contained in the Latin version were like many of the stories invented by the arch-impostor, Cagliostro, and others, simply stupid forgeries by men ignorant or careless of historical facts and historical probabilities. This belief, it may be repeated, was held not only by men not affiliated to any Masonic order, but by many Masons of good standing. It was reserved for an American Mason, of the highest degree, Brother Albert Pike, to refute this theory. That eminent Mason, in his Historical Inquiry, showed from documents of the period that in 1786 Frederick the Great, while undoubtedly suffering from physical ailments, was still in the habit of attending to business. Brother Pike likewise showed that the names appended to the Constitution of 1786 were those of men who were connected with the Court of Berlin. The result of his investigations, after an extensive and impartial study of all accessible sources of information, was to the effect that the aforesaid constitutions were drawn up at Berlin and duly ratified by Frederick in the year assigned to them. As such they were recognized by the Southern Supreme Council. This refers to the Latin version of the constitutions. Another student of the history of the Rite considers the French version the original, and this is the version which is recognized by the Northern Supreme Council.

Without quoting at length from Bro. Pike's Historical Inquiry, it may be advisable to give some of his conclusions. He shows that when Francken in 1767 introduced the Rite into the American Colonies it was generally understood that the supreme governing power was in Berlin, and that in 1770 the Lodge of Perfection at Albany was directed to transmit reports to Berlin, while, still earlier, a tracing-board made by one of its members displays the double eagle of Prussia as a symbol of the head of the order.

Moreover, in 1785, the Lodge of Perfection at Philadelphia drew up an address to be presented to Frederick as head of the order.

The Ancient and Accepted Scottish Rite of 33d, the title of which heads this chapter, like all the so-called Scottish Masonry, has nothing whatever to do with the Grand Lodge of Scotland. No portion of it, except perhaps the Royal Order of Scotland, ever originated in Scotland, nor were any of these so-called Scottish degrees at any time practiced in Scotland. Gould, in his history, applies the word Scots as distinguished from Scottish to show these additions to Freemasonry made on the Continent. These so-called Scottish or Scots degrees seem to have originated about the year 1740 in France. The statement that Irish chapters existed in Paris from 1739, holding their constitutions from the Grand Chapter of Dublin, cannot be accepted. There is no evidence to support it, and Masonic authorities reject it, holding that a much later date must be assigned to all these Irish degrees. Nor must we confuse the "Orient de Bouillon" with these so-called Scots Masons, for that was simply a Grand Lodge established in Luxemburg, years afterward.

What these Scots lodges taught nobody knows and nobody need care. Rituals exist in lamentable profusion, but unfortunately they do not agree. They are, however, all permeated with one notion, the absurdity of which will show the absurdity of the system.

They state that some Scottish crusaders found in a vault the long-lost ineffable word, and that in their search they worked "with the sword in one hand and the trowel in the other." This expression is taken from the Hebrew account of the building of the Second Temple of Zerubbabel, and while natural enough as applied to builders; is quite out of place in the case of men rummaging in some subterranean passage.

The story of the "long lost, ineffable word" we meet with in the Arabian Nights, where we learn that the knowledge of it made Solomon, the King of Genii, able to perform all kinds of marvels.

The Arabian Nights is the fit place for the story. It must be remembered, too, that the temple that the Crusaders saw was not Solomon's nor Zerubbabel's, but Herod's, erected a little before the birth of Christ.

At any rate, relying on this fable, the Scots Master claimed to be in possession of the true secrets of Freemasonry, the true history and the real designs of the order. He claimed also to be in every way superior to the Master Mason, and to hold various peculiar privileges.

In utter contempt for the great principle on which Freemasonry is founded, the perfect equality of all its members with a governing body elective and representative, the Scots Masters claimed to rank before the W.M. of any lodge even when they were only present as visitors. They claimed the right to wear a distinctive dress and to remain covered even in a Master's Lodge. They claimed to impart the secrets of the E.A., F.C., and W. M. degrees, personally and either with or without ceremony as the whim seized them. They would not, if they were members of a lodge, permit anyone but other Scots Masons to sit in judgment upon them. Matters became still worse when the Scots Lodges were "grafted on the ordinary Lodges," and increased in number and in arrogance. In these cases the W.M., instead of being elected by the lodge, was nominated by the Scots Lodge, and as was inevitable, he was almost always one of themselves. All questions of ritual and doctrine were decided by the Scots Lodge, all the finances were managed by the Scots Lodge, in fact all the governing powers were usurped by the Scots Lodge. Nay, the Scots Lodge went so far as to arrogate to itself all the powers of a Grand Lodge, and as such to issue Warrants of Constitution. From the exercise of these powers arose the so-called Scots Mother Lodges which became so numerous in France, each Mother Lodge claiming and exercising the right of granting constitutions and warrants to other lodges, and of developing systems of degrees peculiar to themselves, and worked in chapters all independent of each other.

France, it has been said, was the inventor of all these novelties, and the most important of its Scots Mother Lodges was the one established in Marseilles in 1751 under the title of St. John of Scotland. To give it some ground for calling itself Scots, it professed to he founded by a traveling Scotsman, and proceeded to grant warrants to a large number of lodges in France and elsewhere. From it descended another so-called Mother Lodge, the Mother Lodge of the county of Venaissin, with its seat at Avignon, which in turn became the mother of the Scottish Philosophic Rite. In all these new systems not only was the true original and beautiful simplicity of the Craft overlaid and disfigured by foolish legends and childish ceremonies, but to quote Br. Gould, "the governing power is autocratic and irresponsible, a hierarchy is formed, the highest class rules all the others, and directs the lower classes without appeal from those below it." France, we have seen, may be considered as the inventor of what a German historian of Masonry calls "the lying fictions" of the so-called High Degrees, and in the 18th century, as in the present, set the fashion to Europe. The arch impostor Balsamo, who called himself the Count Cagliostro, was in the height of his reputation, preaching the doctrines of his Egyptian Masonry, of which he made himself the Grand Cophta; his dupes were persons of the highest rank, and speedily a flood of imbecile mysticism overwhelmed most of the lodges on the Continent of Europe. From France it spread to Germany, and the name of its introducer into the Empire is given as a Count von Schmettau. In Berlin the members of the lodge entitled the Three Globes erected a Scots Lodge in 1741, Hamburg followed with a Scots Lodge or two in 1744, and the Saxon city of Leipzig in 1747, and the Free City of Frankfort followed suit in 1753. It is stated that between 1742 and 1764 no fewer than forty-seven such lodges were erected in Germany. These Scots Lodges, however, were soon absorbed by the Clermont system with its low chapter degrees, which system in its turn was absorbed by the Templar system of "Strict Observance." Even now, some of these Scots Lodges, according to Mr. Gould, form the basis of the German Grand Lodge Systems, styled the "Inner Orient."

To France and to the Scots Lodges in France must be assigned the manufacture of those new degrees which connected the Scots Masons with the Knights Templars and thus gave life to the whole system of Templarism. It was an age of disbelief and credulity, of sensuality and mysticism, of the hardest common-sense and the wildest tomfoolery. It was an age of unrest, of decay, and a longing for a new birth, and the teachings of history were scorned, and every fable - the more improbable the better - was eagerly accepted, till men really believed that there was some foundation for the legend that the Military and Religious Order of the Temple, in spite of its having perished in fire and blood, had in some unknown way, preserved a germ of vitality for some four hundred years. In 1741 a degree called the Kadosh degree, representing the Vengeance of the Templars, was invented by the Masons of Lyons, and henceforth all the new rites of French origin contain Knightly and almost all Templar degrees, the connection being in all instances formed by some of the Scots degrees. The German Handbook enumerates over sixty-eight such degrees in various rites, and it is probable this list could be extended. The name Scottish, too, is assumed by many rites to designate the whole system, for instance the Scottish Philosophic Rite. The above- mentioned system of the chapters of Clermont was a Templar continuation of the Scots degrees, and grew into the so-called Emperors of the East and West, and finally developed into the "Ancient and Accepted Scottish Rite 33d."

It was on the Continent of Europe that these innovations on the simple ceremonies and beneficial doctrines of the Craft spread out most luxuriantly. Under the assumption that the Scots lodges could issue warrants of constitutions, whole swarms of irresponsible lodges were formed, in which the principles of the Craft were little considered. From this period may be dated the enmity of the Church and the Kings of Europe to any association that bore the name or claimed any affiliation with the Freemasons. There is no doubt that most of these lodges became political centers of social and political conspirators. In the hierarchy of these rites, each class is self-elected, and thus admits only those it pleases, while the lower classes have no voice in the management of their affairs or in the election of their rulers.

Our limits will not permit any very extended reference to the varied changes in these so-called is High Degrees "prior to the full establishment of the Ancient and Accepted Rite; but we must mention the most important events, that the reader may appreciate the subsequent and final establishment of the Ancient and Accepted Scottish Rite, which took its origin, as such, in Charleston, S.C., in 1801, and the formation of the very first "Supreme Council of Grand Inspectors General of the 33d degree, in South Carolina," with Colonel John Mitchell Sov. Grand Commander.

From all the authorities which have been examined, in respect to the Chapter of Clermont, the system of Masonry therein practiced gives no definite information. Thory, who wrote sixty years subsequently, states that Chevalier de Bonneville founded a chapter on November 24, 1754. Brother Gould, in his history of this chapter, denies the statement of Thory, that Von Hund took the Templar degrees in that chapter, as he had left France for the last time in 1743, or eleven years previously, and erected his first Templar Chapter in Unwurde in 1751.

Thory also says: "The Chapter was based on the three degrees of Freemasonry, and the Scots or St. Andrew degree, and worked three higher, 5d, the Knight of the Eagle or Select Master; 6d, the Illustrious Knight or Templar; 7d, the Sublime Illustrious Knight."

The Chevalier de Bonneville, mentioned above, is probably the same person as the Count de Bonneville who founded in 1760 a lodge in the Nouvelle France, near Paris, which is described as being brilliantly conducted and frequented by persons of high rank. The difference in the titles given to Bonneville can be explained by the old French system by which a younger son was styled Chevalier until by the death of older members of the family he attained the higher rank of Count, and such deaths may have occurred between the two dates of 1754 and 1760. Not much information can be found respecting the doings of this lodge created by M. de Bonneville, and it is probable that Kloss's opinion of it referring to the "Emperors of the East and West" is the nearest to the truth. As to the "Emperors of the East and West," an account will be given later.

While the history of the Rite, as far as France is concerned, is obscure, its history in Germany is more important.

We will now briefly state the Masonic affairs of Germany in connection with this "Chapter of Clermont." In 1742 the members of the "Three Globes" erected the Scots Lodge "Union" to work the fourth or Scots degree. The Baron Von Printzen was, in 1750-54 and 1757-61, W.M. of the Mother-Lodge "Three Globes" of Berlin; i.e., he was ex-officio Grand Master of all the lodges of is "Three Globes." In 1757 the French Marquis Gabriel Tilly de Lernais came to Berlin as a prisoner of war, and in 1758, with Printzen, founded a chapter of the three Clermont degrees, grafted upon the Mother- Lodge of the "Three Globes," and the Scots Lodge "Union." On June 10, 1760, this chapter constituted the chapter "Sun" at Rostock; and on July 19, 1760, took the title of "Premier Grand Chapter of Clermont in Germany." Philip Samuel Rosa was appointed to travel over the north of Germany, to bring the lodges under the control of the "Three Globes" and to institute chapters. A fourth chapter was constituted by Rosa at Stettin, March, 1762; he then, subsequently, instituted eight others, in different cities, until in June, 1763, his career was terminated by being expelled from the Craft; his successor, Schubart, instituted the last and fifteenth German chapter of Clermont, at Magdeburg, November 27, 1763.

It has been thought by some writers that the name of Clermont was derived from the College of Jesuits of that name. Brother Gould, however, does not concur therewith, and says: "I am unable to believe that the Jesuits could have consented to glorify the Knights Templars, nor can I see anything new in these degrees, being, as they were, merely amplifications and rearrangements of previous ones. I prefer to consider the title a delicate compliment to the Duke of Clermont, Grand Master of French Masonry from 1743 to 1770.[113]

Inasmuch as the "Knights of the East" was a body of "improved" Masonry about that period, it becomes proper to give some account of that organization, and we are again indebted to Brother Gould above all other authors for his very impartial examination into the history of not only this particular body, but also in that connection all of those systems which flooded the Continent about the middle of the 18th century and toward the close of it.

The only real attempt to arrive at the facts, in regard to this early system, was made by Dr. Kloss. Other writers had overlooked the separate existence of Masons, who were called "Sovereign Princes of Masonry," "either confusing them with certain special degrees of other systems, or treating them as an offshoot of the Emperors of the East and West." Even the usually diffuse Handbuch is excessively meager in the information which it supplies. Yet if Kloss's extensive and minute researches are to be given their just weight, it is to the rivalry between the Knights and the Emperors that must be attributed the sorrowful picture of discord presented by the Grand Lodge of France, 1760-80.

In 1754 the Grand Lodge of the members of the Chapter of Clermont had been founded, and in the following year the Grand Lodge of France acknowledged the privileges which were claimed to be possessed by the so-called Scottish Masons. This action may probably have been with a desire to counterbalance the influence of the Chapter of Clermont. This chapter seems to have been decidedly of an aristocratic order, and to have enrolled as its members only the high nobility, members of the Court circle, high officers in the military and other professions reserved to nobles, while all less favored individuals were refused admission to it. It was a period in French history when the lower noblesse, and the noblesse of the robe, as the highest lawyers or judges were entitled, as distinguished from the noblesse of the sword, the designation of the old feudal nobility, with its military traditions, were striving to obtain great influence and higher recognition in the social hierarchy. It was from this class of the lower nobility and less highly placed officials that the association of "Knights of the East, Princes and Sovereigns of Masonry" was formed in 1756. Its separate subdivision took the name of colleges, each of which bore the name of its president. The chief college was that of Valois of Paris. If this college followed the usage of its fellow colleges, Valois must have been a man who as yet

---

[113] Gould, vol v., p. 95

remains undiscovered. Under these circumstances, it is more probable that the name is taken from the province of the Valois, adjoining the Isle of France, in which Paris is situated, and which gave its name to the royal family that sat on the throne of France from Francis I. to Henry III. Be this as it may, some names of these Knights of the East survive, and they clearly show that the association was recruited mainly from the lower nobility and the upper middle class.

The occurrence of a name like Baron Tschadi is no objection to this view. In the first place, the name shows he was not a Frenchman, and in the second place the title baron was that reserved to the richer members of the mercantile or financial class.

The statutes of the Rite are elaborate; one article provides that the position of Sovereign shall be held for the space of one year by each member in turn. Another article, No. 7, decrees that the Knights of the East are the born princes of the complete order, just as the Scottish Masters are the Grand Superiors of the Masonic Order. The next article lays down the doctrine that if a Knight of the East comes in his travels to a place where no lodge of the Rite exists, he may dispense the light of the first six degrees to a Master Mason. The term "first six degrees" implies that the degrees were more than that number, and that therefore there were at least seven degrees beyond that of Master, or ten degrees in all, thus working three degrees higher than the Chapter of Clermont.

The dominant position of the College of Valois in the Knights of the East was lost in 1762, as the result of an intestine quarrel. Its place evas taken by a Sovereign Council of the Knights of the East, of which the following officers of the Grand Lodge of France were members: The Grand Keeper of the Seal, Brest de la Chaussee; the President, one of the Wardens; the Grand Orator, the Secretary General and the Grand Secretary. The prime mover of this resolution is said to have been a Parisian tailor named Poilet, but this is improbable, as in 1764 we find a Poilet acting as a leading member of the rival Emperors, and his humble profession would certainly have excluded a tailor from the aristocratic Emperors. There is reason, however, to believe that from this period the aristocratic Emperors of the East and West lost much of their influence in Grand Lodge, while the lower class Knights gained power. The old rivalry still went on and in 1766 the Knights sustained a defeat from the Emperors and many of their members were expelled. The Sovereign Council of the Knights of the East retaliated by a circular in which it requested all lodges to cease working Templar degrees. The Knights evidently did not do so. The Emperors of the East and West, as they were an offshoot and continuation of the Chapter of Clermont, certainly did so.

The quarrels of the Emperors and the Knights continued and grew more bitter, till it became necessary in 1767 for the Government to issue an edict dissolving the Grand Lodge. From that the Knights of the East, as a body, sank into insignificance.

CHAPTER II

THE ORIGINAL SUPREME COUNCIL

THE very first Supreme Council of which we have any knowledge whatever, either by tradition or history, was the one organized by John Mitchell, Frederic Dalcho, Emanuel De La Motta, Abraham Alexander, Major T. B. Bowen, and Israel Delieben, at Charleston, S. C., May 31, 1801. This was a transformation of the former in "Rite of Perfection," or Ancient and Accepted Rite.

The Brethren who constituted this new Rite were all members of the several Constituent Bodies, which derived their Masonic life, and constituted authority from Morin through his Deputies duly appointed by him to propagate the Rite on the American Continent, or more extensively the Western Hemisphere.

The pedigree is as follows: Morin commissioned Francken, and Francken commissioned Moses M. Hayes; Moses M. Hayes commissioned Barend M. Spitzer, and the latter, on April 2, 1795, commissioned John Mitchell as Deputy Inspector-General, reciting in his patent of commission that he does so by authority of the Convention of Inspectors held in Philadelphia, June 5, 1781. This new Rite, which came into the world apparently fully developed, was really a transformation of the Rite of Perfection.

To show conclusively as to when the Supreme Council of the 33d and last degree was organized, we are permitted to furnish herewith a fac-simile copy of the "Register" of the several bodies of the A.'. A.'. A.'. S.'. R.'. which met in the city of Charleston, S. C., in 1802. The original is in the Archives of the Supreme Council of the Southern Jurisdiction in Washington, D. C

ANNUAL REGISTER OF THE BRETHREH WHO COMPOSE THE SUBLIME GRAND LODGE OF PERFECTIONW OF SOUTH-CAROLINA, ESTABLISHED AT CHARLESTON, ANNO LUCIS 5783 ALSO, THE LIST OF THE OFFICERS OF THE GRAND COUNCIL OF PRINCES OF JERUSALEM: OFFICERS OF THE SOVEREIGN CHAPTER OF ROSE CROIX DE HERODEN; OFFICERS AND MEMBERS OF THE GRAND CONSISTORY, AND GRAND INSPECTORS GENERAL OF THE 33d DEGREE,Hoc maxime officii, ut quisque masume opis indigeat, ita ei potissumum opitulari.

TULL REGISTER FOR THE YEAR 5802.

CHARLESTON (SOUTH CAROLINA) PRINTED BY T.B. BOWEN, NO 3, BROAD-STREETBY THE GLORY OF THE GRAND ARCHITECT OF THE UNIVERSE

Officers of the SUBLIME GRAND LODGE of PERFECTION of South Carolina

Sublime Grand Master
FREDERICH DALCHO, native of Maryland, Doctor of Medicine, Member of the Medical Society of South Carolina, Honoury Member of the Chemical and Medical Societies of Philadelphia, and one of the Physicians of the Charleton Dispensary, &c. &c. aged 32 years, R.' *.'. K.H. - P. R. S. Sov. Grand Inspector General of the 33d degree, and Lieutenant Grand Commander for the United States.

Sublime Deputy Grand Master.

JOSEPH JAPAN, native of Montargisa en Gatinois, Planter of Saint Domingo, aged 43 years, Master of the Lodge la Candeur, N. 12, Past Sublime Grand Master, R.' *.'. K.H. - P. R. S.

Sublime Senior Grand Warden.

ISAAC AULD, native of Pennsylvania, Doctor of Medicine, Member of the Medical Society of South-Carolina, Honorary Member of the Medical and Chemical Societies of Philadelphia. and one of the Physicians of the Charlston Dispensary. &c. aged 32 years, R.' *.'. K.H. - P. R. S. Sov. Grand Inspector General of the 33d degree.

Sublime Junior Grand Warden

WILLIAM PORTER, native of Ireland, Commission Merchant, aged 37 years, Prince of Jerusalem.

Grand Orator and Keeper of Seals.

JAMES MOULTRIE, native of South Carolina. Doctor of Medicine Port Physician, Vice- President of the Medical Society of South-Carolina, and one of the Physicians of the Charleston Dispensary, &c. aged 38 years, R.' *.'. K.H. - P. R. S. Sov. Grand Inspector General of the 33d degree.

Sublime Grand Treasurer.

JAMES ALLISON native of North Britain, Cooper, aged 46 years, R.' *.'.

Sublime Grand Secretary.

JOHN PETER PROYS, native of Hanovser. Accountant, aged 33 years, Prince of Jerusalem.

Grand Master of Ceremonies.

ALEXANDER PLACIDE, native of Bourdeaux, Manager of the Charleston Theatre, agent 45 years, R.' *.'. K.H. - P. R. S.

Captain of the Guards

PIERRE RIGAUD, native of Nantz, Planter of Saint-Domingo, aged 31 years, R.' *.'. K.H. - P. R. S. Grand Tyler. DAVID LABAT, native of Hamburgh, Storekeeper, aged 42 years, Perfection.

Members

JOHN MITCHELL, native of Ireland, Justice of the Quorum and Notary Public, late a Lieutenant-Colonel in the American Army, Member of the Cincinnati; and Past Sublime Grand, Master, aged 60 years. R.' *.'. K.H. - P. R. S. Sov. Grand Inspector General of the 33d Degree and Grand Commander for the United States.

THOMAS BARTHOLOMEW BOWEN, native of Ireland, Printer, late a Major in the American Army and Member of the Cincinnati; Past Sublime Grand-Master, aged 60 years, R.' *.'. K.H. - P. R. S. Sov. Grand Inspector General of the 33d Degree and Ill.

Grand Master of Cereomies.

ARAHAM SASPORTAR, native of Bourdeaux, Merchant, ageds 56years, R.' *.'. Knight of the Sun.

PIERRE BOUYSSOU, native of Cape Francois, Plantet, late Captain of Gendarmerie, and Orator of the Lodge la Candeur, aged 48 years. R.' *.'. K.H. - P. R. S

ISRAEL DELIEBEN, native of Bohema, Commission Merchant, aged 61 years, R.' *.'. K.H. - P. R. S. Sov. Grand Inspector General of the 33d degree.

MICHEL FRONTY, native of Saint- Martial, en Limodn, Doctor of Medicine, aged 50 years. R.' *.'. K.H. - P. R. S.

EMANUEL DE LA MOTTA, Native of Santa Croix, Commission Merchant and Auctioner, aged 42 years, R.' *.'. K.H. - P. R. S. Sov. Grand Inspector General of the B. Empire

ROBERT L'ALLEMAND, native of Post Republican, Planter of St Domingo, aged 53 years R.' *.'. K.H. - P. R. S.

JOSEPH BEE, native of South Carolina, Planter, aged 56 years R.' *.'. - Grand Pontiff.

ETIENNE DUBARRY, native of Jarbes, en Bigore, Planter of St Domingo, aged 49 years, R.' *.'. K.H. - P. R. S..

PETER SMITH, native of South-Carolina, Factor, aged 53 years, Prince of Jerusalem.

JOSEPH CLARET, native of Narbonne, Master of Lodge No. 45, aged 36 years, R.' *.'.

SOLOMON HARBY, native of London, Commission merchant and Auctioneer, aged 40 years, R.' *.'. K.H. - P. R. S..

JEAN ANDRE PELLETANT, native of Planter of St. Domingo aged years, R.' *.'.

THOMAS BAKER, native of England Insurance Broker, aged 27 years, Secret Master.

JEAN REIGNE, native of Castillon, near Bourdeaux, aged 30 years. R.'∴.

JOSEPH DICKINSON, native of South Carolina, Inspector of Exports, late a Captain of Infantry, aged 33 years, Intimate Secretary.

JEAN JACQUES THOMAS, native of London,. Merchant, aged 42 years, R.'∴.

JACOB DELEON, native of Jamaica, Commission Merchant and Auctioneer, aged 38 years, Intendant of the Building.

JEAN DESBEAUX, native of Buzet, Cooper, aged 37 years, R.'∴.

FRANCIS LOUVRIER SAINT MARY, native of Nevers, aged 39 years, Intimate Secretary.

PIERRE JOSEPH MORE, native of Fonttaine, en Franche Comte, Surgeon, aged 50 years, Knight of the East and West.

JEREMIAH WILCOX, native of Rhodes Island, Painter; aged 33 years, Provost and Judge.

GEORGE ESTILLET, native of New Orleans, aged 28 years, Intimate Secretary.

ISAAC CANTER, naiive of Santa Croix, Auctioneer, aged 33 years, Knight of the East.

JOHN HINCKLEY MITCHEL, native of South Carolina, Justice of the Peace, and Notary Public, aged 33 years, Secret Master.

WILLIAM ALEXANDER, native of South-Carolina, Factor, aged 26 years, Secret Master.

LEWIS T. RAYNAL, native of South Carolina, Accountant, aged 24 years, Elected of Nine.

JOHN BANKS, native of England, Accountant, aged 30 years, Intimate Secretary.

MORRIS GOLDSMITH, native of London. Merchant, aged 21 years, Secret Master.

JOHN BILLEAUD, native of Saint Sezaire, en Xaintonge, aged 30 years, Elected of Fifteen.

THOMAS NAPIER, native of North-Britain, Merchant aged 30 years, Knight of the East.

EMANUEL CANTOR, native of Santa Croix, Merchant, aged 30 years, Intimate Secretary.

Honorary Members

His Royal Highness CHARLES, Hereditary Prince of the Swedes, Goths and Vandals, Duke of Sudermania, Heir of Norway, Duke of Sleswick, Holitein, Stormarric and Dittmarche, Count of

Oldenburg and Delmeahorst. Grand Admiral of Sweden, Vicar of Solomon of the 7th and 9th Province, and National Grand Master of the Kingdom of Sweden, R.' *.'. K.H. - P. R. S.

Count ALEXANDER FRANCOIS AUGUSTE DE GRASSE, native of Verfailles, Planter of Saint Domingo, aged 36 years, R.' *.'. K.H. - P. R. S.. Sov. Grand Inspector General of the 33d degree, Grand Commander for the French West Indies, and Representative of the Sublime Grand Lodge of South-Carolina in and to the Sublime Lodge in Saint Domingo.

JEAN BAPTISTE MARIE DELAHQGUE, native of Paris, Planer of Saint Domingo, aged 58 years, R.' *.'. K.H. - P. R. S..Sov. Grand Inspector General of the 33d degree, and Lieutenant Grand Commander for the French West Indies.

JOHN SUCKLEY, native of London, Merchant of Saint Domingo, aged 24 years, R.' *.'. K.H. - P. R. S.

NICOLAS SAMSON PANEL, native of Normandy, Merchant of Porto Rico, aged 28 years, R.' *.'.

JONATHAN BAYARD SMITH, native of Pennsylvania, aged 50 years, late Grand Master of the State of Pennsylvania, R.' *.'. K.H. - P. R. S.

SAMUEL MYERS, native of New York, Merchant of Virginia, aged 43 years, R.' *.'. K.H. - P. R. S..

MOSES MICHAEL HAYES, native of Merchant, of Boston R.' *.'. K.H. - P. R. S.

ADDRESS:
TO DOCTOR FREDERICK DALCHO,
East- Bay Charleston, (South Carolina)

The Sublime Grand Lodge, meets at the Ineffable Lodge Room, Meeting-Street, every other Saturday evening at six o'clock, from the Autumnal to the Vernal Equinox, and on the first Saturday in every month at Seven o'clock, in the evening, from the Vernal to the Autumnal Equinox.

(XV - & XVI)
BY THE GLORY OF THE GRAND ARCHITECT OF THE UNIVERSE.
LUX E TENEBRUS
HEALTH, STABILITY AND POWER,

Officers of the Grand Council of Princes of Jersalem, in South Carolina A.L. 5802.

ILL. Bro.: Col˜ JOHN MITCHELL - Most Equitable
DR. FREDERICK DALCHO - Senior Most Enlightened
DR. ISAAC AULD - Junior Most Enlightened
ABRAHAM ALEXANDER - K.D.
SOLOMON HARBY - Grand Orator and Keeper of the Seals
ISRAEL DELIEBIN - Grand Treasurer
JOSEPH BEE - Grand Secretary.
ALEXANDER PLACIDE - Master of Ceremonies
Representative in St Domingo
AUGUSTUS DE GRASSE - K. H - P. R. S. Sov. Grand Inspector General of the 33d Degree.

Conventions are held on the first Sundays of February, May, August and November, at 12 oclock, M. at the Ineffable Lodge Room.

XVIII. IN THE NAME OF THE MOST HOLY AND UNDIVIDED TRINITY.
SS.
SS.
SS.

Officers of the Sovereign Chapter of Rose Croix de Hereden, in South Carolina, A.D. 1802
BRO. COL . JOHN MITCHELL - E. M. Perfect Soverign.
Dr. FREDERICK DALCHO - M.E.P. Senior Warden
DR. ISAAC AULD - M.E.P. Junior Warden
EMANUEL DE LA MOTTA Grand Treasurer
ABRAHAM ALEXANDER Grand Secretary
Major T.B. BOWEN Grand Master of Ceremonies.
Grant Tyler (vacant)
Assemblages of the Knights are held in the Ineffable Lodge Room at Meridian, on the day of the Annual Feast,
Shrove Tuesday, Tuesday after Easter, the day of Ascension, the day of Penticost, all Saints day and the two festivals of St John.

AD GLORIAM DEI Knights of K. H. and Members of the Grand Consistory of Princes of the Royal Secret in South Carolina, A. L. 5802.

COL. JOHN MITCHELL - T. Ill. Grand Commader.

DR. FREDERICK DALCHO - T. E Lieutenant Grand Commander.
JOSEPH JAHAN - T. L Lieutenant Grand Commander.
DR. JAMES MOULTRIE - Minister of State and Grand Orator
DR. MICHAEL FRONTY - Grand Chancellor
EMANUEL DE LA MOTTA - Grand Treasurer
ABRAHAM ALEXANDER - Grand Secretary
PIERRE BOUYSSOU - Grand Master Architect and Engineer
DR. ISAAC AULD - Physician General
ISRAEL DELIEBEN - Keeper of the Seals and Archives
MAJOR T. B. BOWEN - Grand Master of Ceremonies
PIERRE RIGAUD - Captain of the Guards
(S. Tyler vacant)
(J. Tyler vacant)
SOLOMON HARBY ETIENE DUBARRY ROBERT L ALLEMAND.
ALEXANDER PLACIDE MOSES C. LEVY
Representative in St. Domingo.
AUGUSTUS DE GRASSE - K. H - P. R. S.
Sov. Grand Inspector General of the 33d Degree.
Consistories are held at M. at the Ineffable Lodge Room, on the 21st March, 25th June. 21st September and 27th December (XVII - to - XXXIII inc) Universi Terrarum Orbis Architectonis gloris ab ingentis.
DEUS MEUMQUE JUS.
ORDO AB CHAO.
Supreme Council of Grand Inspectors General of the 33d degree, in South-Carolina.
COLONEL JOHN MITCHEL - Sov. Grand Commander.
DR. FREDERICK DALCHO - Lieutenant Grand Commander.
EMANUEL DE LA MOTTA - Ill. Treasurer General of the the H. Empire.
HIS MAJESTY, KING EDWARD VII.
P.G.M. And Protector of Masons of England
ABRAHAM ALEXANDER - Ill. Secretary General of the H. Empire.
MAJOR T. B. BOWEN - Ill Grand Master of Ceremonies.
ISRAEL DELIEBEN - Sov. Grand Inspector General.

DR. ISAAC AULD - Sov; Grand Inspector General
MOSES C LEVY - Sov. Grand Inspector General.

DR. JAMES MOULTRIE - Sov. Grand Inspector General.
Ill. Capt. of the Life Guards (vacant)
Representative in Saint Domingo
AUGUSTUS DE GRASSE - Sov. Grand Commander for the French West Indies

Councils are held at the house of the Grand Commander at Meridian, every third new Moon, reckoning from the new Moon in May.

CHAPTER III

THE SCOTTISH RITE IN THE UNITED STATES

COUNCIL of Princes of Jerusalem was duly constituted in Charleston, February 20, 1788, and Brothers Joseph Meyers, Behrend M. Spitzer, and A. Forst installed the Officers.

Notwithstanding that in planting the Scottish Rite, or, as it was then known, the "Rite of Perfection," in many States, by the appointment of Inspectors, who had only received what was at that early date recognized as the 25th Degree or "Prince of the Royal Secret," the Rite was only worked in Charleston. In consequence of the zeal of the Brethren in that city and their devotion to the Rite, we owe the foundation of the first bodies, as shown in the fac-similes given, the last one being the "Supreme Council of the 33d and last degree of the Ancient and Accepted Scottish Rite, Mother-Supreme Council of the World." A council of Knights Kadosh was organized in Philadelphia in 1796, by Masons who were refugees from San Domingo, during the negro insurrection on that island. This body soon ceased to exist, in consequence of the return of the Brethren to that island very soon after its organization

In New York, in 1797, a chapter of Rose Croix was instituted.

In 1792 it is said a Lodge of Perfection was formed at Baltimore, Md., by Henry Wilmans.[114] There is no certainty as to his authority for such establishment. Brother Edward T. Schultz gives a list of seventy-six members. There was also a Lodge of Perfection at Albany, N.Y., which was in accord with the symbolic lodge, and at one time had the same Brother for Master; and we notice also that the symbolic lodges

---

[114] "History of Masonry," by Edw. T. Schultz, vol. vi., p. 1555.

in Philadelphia were in union with the Lodge of Perfection in that city.[115]

A circular, which we give in part below, was issued by the Supreme Council at Charleston (adopted October 10, 1802), under date of December 4, 1802, and copies were sent to every Grand Lodge then in existence in the United States and also in other countries.

"Circular"

"As Society improved, and as discoveries of old records were made, the numbers of our degrees were increased, until, in progress of time, the system became complete.

"From such of our records as are authentic, we are informed of the establishment of the Sublime and Ineffable degrees of Masonry in Scotland, France, and Prussia, immediately after the crusades. But from some circumstances, which to us are unknown, after the year 4658 they fell into neglect until the year 5744, when a nobleman from Scotland visited France and re-established the Lodge of Perfection in Bordeaux.

"In 5761 the Lodges and Councils of the Supreme degrees being extended throughout the Continent of Europe, his Majesty the King of Prussia, as Grand Commander of the Order of Prince of the Royal Secret, was acknowledged by all the Craft as the head of the Sublime and Ineffable degrees of Masonry throughout the two hemispheres. His Royal Highness Charles, Hereditary Prince of the Swedes, Goths, and Vandals, Duke of Sudermania, Heir of Norway, was, and still continues the Grand Commander and protector of the Sublime Masons in Sweden; and his Royal Highness Louis of Bourbon, Prince of the Blood, Duke de Chartres, and the Cardinal Prince and Bishop of Rouen, were at the head of these degrees in France.

"On the 25th of October, 5762, the Grand Masonic Constitutions were finally ratified in Berlin and proclaimed for the government of all the Lodges of Sublime and Perfect Masons, Chapters, Councils, Colleges, and Consistories of the Royal and Military art of Free-Masonry, over the surface of the two hemispheres. There are Secret Constitutions, which have existed from time immemorial, and are alluded to in these instruments.

"In the same year the Constitutions were transmitted to our illustrious Brother, Stephen Morin, who had been Appointed[116] on the

---

[115] There is an old volume in the archives of the Supreme Council of the Southern Jurisdiction, which contains the history of "Sublime Free-Masonry in the United States of America. Being a Collection of all the Official Documents which have appeared on both sides of the question with Notes and an Appendix. By Joseph McCosh, Charleston, S. C., 1823."

27th of August, 5761, Inspector-General over all Lodges in the new World, by the Grand Consistory of Princes of the Royal Secret convened in Paris, at which presided the King of Prussia Deputy, 'Chaillon de Joinville, substitute General of the Order, Right Worshipful Master of the first Lodge in France, called St. Anthony's, Chief of the Eminent degrees, Commander and Sublime Prince of the Royal Secret,' etc.

"The following Illustrious Brethren were also present: The Brother Prince of Rouen, Master of the Grand Intelligence Lodge and Sovereign Prince of Masonry, etc.

"La Coine, substitute of the Grand Master, Rignt Worshipful Master of the Trinity Lodge, Grand Elect, Perfect, Knight and Prince of Masons.

"Maximillian de St. Simon, Senior Grand Warden, Grand Elect, Perfect and Knight and Prince of Masons.

"Savalette de Buchelay, Grand Keeper of the Seals, Grand Elect, Perfect Knight and Prince of Masons.

"Duke de Choiseuil, Right Worshipful Master of the Lodge of the Children of Glory, Grand, Elect, Perfect Master, Knight and Prince of Masons.

"Topin, Grand Embassador from his Serene Highness, Grand, Elect, Perfect Master, Knight and Prince of Masons.

"Boucher de Lenoncour, Right Worshipful Master of the Lodge of Virtue, Grand, Elect, Perfect Master, Knight and Prince of Masons.

"Brest de la Chausee, Right Worshipful Master of the Exactitude Lodge, Grand, Elect, Perfect Master, Knight and Prince of Masons. The Seals of the Order were affixed and the Patent countersigned by

"Daubertiny, Grand, Elect, Perfect Master, Knight and Prince of Masons, Right Worshipful Master of the Lodge of St. Alphonso, Grand Secretary of the Grand Lodge and Sublime Council of Princes of Masons, etc.

"When Brother Morin arrived in St. Domingo, he, agreeably to his patent, appointed a Deputy Inspector General for North America. This high Honor was conferred on Brother M. M. Hayes, with the power of appointing others, where necessary. Brother Morin also appointed Brother Frankin Deputy Inspector-General of Jamaica and the British Leeward Islands, and Brother Colonel Provest for the Windward Islands and the British Army.

---

[116] A copy of his commission is in the archives of the Supreme Council, Southern Jurisdiction, and is given in chapter I of A.A.S.R

"Brother Hayes appointed Brother Isaac Da Costa Deputy Inspector General for the State of South Carolina, who, in the year 5783, established the Sublime Grand Lodge of Perfection in Charleston. After Brother Da Costa's death, Brother Joseph Myers was appointed Deputy Inspector-General for his State, by Bro. Hayes, who, also, had previously appointed Brother Colonel Solomon Bush Dep. Insp. Gen. for the State of Pennsylvania, and Bro. Barend M. Spitzer to the same rank for Georgia, which was confirmed by a Convention of Inspectors when convened in Philadelphia, on the 15th of June, 5781.

"On the 1st of May, 5786, the Grand Constitutions of the Thirty-Third Degree, called the Supreme Council of Sovereign Grand Inspectors General, was ratified by his Majesty the King of Prussia, who as Grand Commander of the Order of Prince of the Royal Secret, possessed the Sovereign Masonic power over all the Craft. In the New Constitution this Power was conferred on a Supreme Council of Nine Brethren in each nation, who possess all the Masonic prerogatives in their own district that his Majesty individually possessed, and are Sovereigns of Masonry.

"On the 20th of Feb., 5788, the Grand Council of Princes of Jerusalem was opened in this City (Charleston, S. C.), at which were present Bros. J;. Myers, D.I.G. for South Carolina, B.M. Spitzer, D.I.G. for Georgia, and A. Forst, D.I.G. for Virginia. Soon after the opening of the Council, a letter was addressed to his Royal Highness, the Duke of Orleans, on the subject, requesting certain records from the Archives of the Society in France, which in his answer through Col. Shee, his Secretary, he very politely promised to transmit, but which the commencement of the French Revolution most unfortunately prevented.

"On the 2nd of Aug., 5795, Brother Colonel John Mitchell, late Dep. Quarter Master Genl. in the Armies of the United States, was made a Dep. Ins. Genl. for this State by Bro. Spitzer, who acted in consequence of Bro. Myers' removal out of the Country.

"Bro. Mitchell was restricted from acting until after Bro. Spitzer's death, which took place in the succeeding year.

"As many Brethren of eminent degrees had arrived from Foreign parts, consistories of Princes of the R. S. were occasionally held, for initiations and other purposes.

"On the 31st of May, 5801, the Supreme Council of the Thirty-third degree for the United States of America was opened with the high honors of Masonry, by Brothers John Mitchell and Frederick Dalcho, Sov: Gr: Insp: Genl:; and in the course of the present year the whole number of Grand Inspectors General was completed, agreeably to the Grand Constitutions.

"On the 21st of January, 5802, a Warrant of Constitution passed the Seal of the Grand Council of Princes of Jerusalem for the establishment of a Master Mark Mason's Lodge in this City (Charleston, S. C.).

"On the 21st of February, 5802, Our Illustrious Brother, Count Alexandre Francois Auguste Degrasse, Deputy Inspector General, was appointed by the Supreme Council a Grand Inspector General, and Grand Commander of the French West-Indies; and our Illustrious Brother, Jean Baptiste Marie De La Hougue, Dep. Insp. Genl., was also received as an Insp. Genl. and appointed Lieut. Grand Commander of the same Islands.

"On the 4th of December, 5802, a Warrant of Constitution passed the seal of the Grand Council of Princes of Jerusalem, for the establishment of a Sublime Grand Lodge in Savannah, Georgia

THE NAMES OF THE MASONIC DEGREES ARE AS FOLLOWS, VIZ.:

1st degree, called Entered Apprentice.
2nd Fellow Craft
3rd Master Mason
4th
"
Secret Master 5th
"
"
Perfect Master 6th
"
"
Intimate Secretary 7th
"
"
Provost and Judge 8th
"
"
Intendent of the Building 9th
"
"
Elected Knights of 9 10th "
"

Illustrious Elected of 15 11th " "

Sublime Knight elected 12th " "

Grand Master Architect 13th " "

Royal Arch 14th " "

Perfection 15th degree, called Knights of the East.
16th "
        "

Prince of Jerusalem.
17th "
     "

Knight of the East and West 18th "
                                 "

Sovereign Prince of Rose Croix de Heredom.
19th "
     "

Grand Pontiff.
20th "
     "

Grand Master of all Symbolic Lodges.
21st "
     "

Patriarch Noachite, or Chevalier Prussian.
22d "
    "

Prince of Libanus.
23d "
    "

Chief of the Tabernacle.
24th

"
"

Prince of the Tabernacle.
25th
"
"

Prince of Mercy.
26th
"
"

Knight of the Brazen Serpent.
27th
"
"

Commander of the Temple.
28th
"
"

Knight of the Sun.
29th
"
"

Knight of St. Andrew.
30th
"
"

K-H.
31st
"
"

Grand Inquisitor Commander.
32d
"
"

Sublime Prince of the Royal Secret Prince of Masons.
33d
"
"

Sovereign Grand Inspectors General. Officers appointed for life
"Besides the degrees, which are in regular succession, most of the inspectors are in possession of a number of detached degrees, given

in different parts of the world, and which they generally communicate, free of expense, to those brethren who are high enough to understand them. Such as Select Masons of 27 and the Royal Arch as given under the Constitution of Dublin. Six degrees of Maconnerie D'Adoption, Compagnon Ecossais, Le Maitre Ecossais and Le Grand Maitre Ecossais, making in the aggregate 52 degrees.

"The Committee respectfully submit to the consideration of the Council the above report on the principles and establishment of the Sublime degrees in South Carolina extracted from the Archives of the Society. They cannot, however, conclude without expressing their ardent wishes for the prosperity and dignity of the institution over which this Supreme Council preside; and they flatter themselves that if any unfavorable impressions have existed among the Brethern of the Blue degrees, from a want of a knowledge of the principles and practices of Sublime Masonry, it will be done away, and that harmony and affection will be the happy cement of the Universal Society of Free and Accepted Masons. That as all aim at the improvement of the general condition of Man-kind by the practice of Virtue, and the exercise of benevolence, so they sincerely wish that any little differences which may have arisen, in unimportant ceremonies of Ancient and Modern, may be reconciled, and given away to the original principles of the order, those great bulwarks of Society, universal benevolence and brotherly love, and that the extensive fraternity of Free-Masons, throughout the two Hemispheres, may form but one band of Brotherhood. 'Behold how good and how pleasant it is for Brethren to dwell together in Unity.'

"They respectfully Salute your Supreme Council by the Sacred Numbers. Charleston, South Carolina, the 10th day of the 8th Month, called Chisleu 5553, A.L. 5802, and of the Christian Era, this 4th day of December, 1802.

"FREDERICK DALCHO.

"K-H.P.R.S., Sovereign Grand Inspector General of the 33d, and Lieutenant Grand Commander in the United States of America.

"ISAAC AULD

"K-H. P.R.S., Sovereign Grand Inspector General of the 33d.

"E. DE LA MOTTA.

"K-H.P.R.S., Sovereign Grand Inspector General of the 33d, and Illustrious Treasurer General of the H. Empire.

"The above report was taken into consideration, and the Council was pleased to express the highest approbation of the same.

"Whereupon, Resolved, That the foregoing report be printed and transmitted to all the Sublime and Symbolic Grand Lodges, throughout the two Hemispheres.

"JNO. MITCHELL

"K-H . P. R. S., Sovereign Grand Inspector General of the 33d. and Illustrious Secretary General of the H. Empire."

The major part of this circular recites the history of Masonry, as generally understood at that early day, and which we omit, confining our extracts to that part which refers only to the A:.A:.A:.S:.R.

The Supreme Council, having been thus established and made known to the whole world of Masonry, is the mother of all the other regular Supreme Councils which have since been organized either immediately or mediately by her authority.

The council in Charleston conferred the 33d Degree on Count de Grasse Tilley, Hacquet, and de la Hogue; and through these Brethren by the authority of letters patent dated February 21, 1802, were established the Supreme Councils of France and also of the French and English West India colonies. Illustrious de Grasse Tilley installed the Supreme Council of France on December 22, 1804, at Paris. This was the first and only Supreme Council established in France; many years subsequently it was divided into two branches, in consequence of the dissension heretofore mentioned; one was called the Supreme Council of France, and the other the Supreme Council of the Grand Orient of France. Both of these bodies are still in existence; the former only, however, is in relations of comity with the Mother Supreme Council, and all the other regular Supreme Councils of the world. The Supreme Council of the Grand Orient is not so.

The Supreme Councils of Italy, Naples, Spain, and the Netherlands were also established by de Grasse Tilley.

Only one Supreme Council of the 33d Degree can exist in each nation or kingdom (by Article V. of the Grand Constitution of 1786); two in the United States of America, as far as possible one from the other; one in the British Islands of America, and one also in the French colonies.

The first Supreme Council at Charleston, S. C., began its labors on May 31, 1801, as hereinbefore stated, and its jurisdiction covered all of the United States of America, until August 5, 1813, at which date the " Supreme Council of the Ancient and Accepted Scottish Rite of Freemasonry for the Northern Jurisdiction of the United States" was established by special Deputy Emmanuel de la Motta at New York. This Supreme Council was substituted for the Grand Consistory of

Sublime Princes of the Royal Secret, 32d Degree. Brother D.D. Tompkins, Vice-President of the United States of America, was M.P.S. Grand Commander.

At a later period the seat of the Northern Supreme Council was changed to Boston. The jurisdiction of the Northern Supreme Council included all the northern and northeastern States east of the Mississippi River, viz.: Maine, New Hampshire, Vermont, Massachusetts, Rhode Island, Connecticut, New York, New Jersey, Pennsylvania, Michigan, Ohio, Indiana, Illinois, and Wisconsin. The other States and Territories were reserved for itself by the Supreme Council for the Southern Jurisdiction of the United States.

The Supreme Council of England and Wales was created by the Northern Supreme Council in March, 1846, and that body created the Supreme Councils of Scotland and of the Canadian Dominion. The Supreme Council for Ireland was established by the Supreme Council of the Southern Jurisdiction.

From August 5, 1813, Article V. of the Constitutions of 1786 has been complied with, and there have been consequently in the United States of America but two legitimate Supreme Councils, which have ever endeavored to preserve and enforce their authority: and they have always discountenanced all attempts against that authority which rightfully, according to the Grand Constitutions, belongs to them.

A third Supreme Council could not be established in the United States of America, without a violation of the Constitutions of 1786. Neither the 33d Degree nor a Supreme Council can exist without a compliance with that constitution. The establishment of a second Supreme Council in the United States was not a wise measure, although the constitutions provided for it, as subsequent events demonstrated. It was a remarkable coincidence that in the very year when the two Grand Lodges of Blue Masonry in England were consolidated into one, Scottish Masonry in the United States was amicably divided into two organizations, in consequence of which each Supreme Council altered and amended its own constitutions and statutes, and changed and made material alterations in the rituals, and thereby destroyed the harmony and uniformity of the work.

The injurious and pernicious consequences of this division were soon manifested and both Supreme Councils were called upon to make their defense against the invasion of illegitimate bodies, which not only affected Scottish Rite Masonry, but also all the other Grand Bodies of Masonry, from the Grand Lodges to the Grand Commanderies of

Knights Templars, illegitimate bodies of which were soon established, as well as of the Scottish Rite, by these unauthorized parties.

On October 7, 1856, Foulhouze formed a new Supreme Council and commenced making Masons at sight, and manufacturing Thirty-thirds. Pursuing the same system of misrepresentation as in 1850-51, he succeeded in causing two lodges to withdraw their allegiance from the Grand Lodge of Louisiana. This rebellion was short-lived; in 1858-59 these lodges memorialized the Grand Lodge to be reinstated on its register, and with difficulty obtained their request. On February 4, 1859, the Grand Orient of France expelled Foulhouze, and his so-called Supreme Council soon became dormant. In the early part of 1867 an attempt was made to revive it, and it obtained recognition from the Grand Orient of France; that recognition, however, failed to give it vitality, and in a short time it either became dormant or ceased to exist.

It would be useless to waste valuable time in tracing out all these irregular bodies; yet it would be unwise not to acknowledge that they have had an existence, and that some still continue to the detriment of Freemasonry.

We quote from a letter of the late Ill. Bro. Dr. Henry Beaumont Leeson, the Sovereign Grand Commander of the Supreme Council of England and Wales and their Dependencies, to the Grand Commander of the Southern Supreme Council of the United States, written at London in 1860, in which he says: "Our own Council is now in a flourishing condition, nearly all of the elite of Masonry in England being ranged under our banners; although we are distinct from Grand Lodge, who acknowledge only the first three degrees, and the Royal Arch, and Grand Conclave, governing the Knights Templars. These two last degrees are in this country, perfectly different and distinct from any of the Ancient and Accepted Degrees, and of very modern origin, neither having existed previous to the middle of the last century. The Knight Templar Degree was concocted in France AND I POSSESS THE ACTUAL MINUTES AND OTHER RECORDS OF THE FRENCH CONVENT. The Royal Arch (Dermott's) was concocted by Ramsay, and modernized by a Chaplain (G. Brown) of the late Duke of Sussex." (Grand Master.)

This spurious French Knight Templar Degree differed from the Webb Templar Degree; it was carried to England and established there; it was also brought to the United States by Joseph Cerneau, who made Templars of New Orleans Masons[117] as well as he did those in New York,

---

[117] See chapter liii., pp. 1390, 1391, of this work; also chapter lviii., p. 1624

where he and his coadjutors also established bodies of Templars, and of the Rite of Perfection with twenty-five degrees, in New Orleans and New York, changed the names of his bodies as suited his pleasure, and declared himself and his coadjutors Sovereign Grand Inspectors-General of the 33d Degree.

There is no evidence that Cerneau ever had received the 33d Degree. We give below a copy of the only document he ever had to show his status as a Mason.

[Translation.] TO THE GLORY OF THE [Gr.'. ARCH.'. OF THE UNIV:]

Lux en Tenebris.

From the Orient of the Very Great and Very Puissant Council of the Sublime Princes [of the Royal Secret], Chiefs of Masonry, under the C: C: of the Zenith [which responds] to the 20d 25' N: Lat.:

To our Ill: and Very Valiant Knights and Princes, Masons of all the Degrees, over the surface of the two Hemispheres:

HEALTH!

We, ANTOINE MATHIEU DUPOTET, Grand Master of all the Lodges, Colleges, Chapters, Councils, Chapters and Consistories, of the higher degrees of Masonry, Deputy Grand Master of the Grand Orient of Pennsylvania, in the United States of America; and of the Grand Lodge and Sovereign Provincial Grand Chapter of Heredom of Kilwinning, of Edinburgh, for America, under the distinctive title of the Holy Ghost, Grand Provincial of San Domingo in the Ancient Rite, Grand Commander or Sovereign President of the Th: Puissant Grand Council of the Sublime Princes of the Royal Secret, established at Port au Prince, Island of San Domingo, by constitutive patent of 16 January and 19 April, 1801, under the distinctive title of The Triple Unity; transferred to Baracoa, Island of Cuba, on account of the events of war, Do declare, in the name of the Sublime and Th: Puissant Grand Council, do certify and attest, that the Very Resp: Gr: Elect Knight of the White and Black Eagle, Joseph Cerneau, Ancient Dignitary of the Lodge No. 47, Orient of Port au Prince, Grand Warden of the Provincial Lodge, same Orient, Venerable founder of the Lodge of the Ancient Constitution of York, No. 103, under the distinctive title of The Theological Virtues, Orient of the Habana, Island of Cuba, has been regularly initiated in all the Degrees of the Sublime Masonry, from that of Secret Master to and including that of Grand Elect Knight of the White and Black Eagle; and wishing to give the strongest proofs of our sincere friendship for our said Very Dear Bro: Joseph Cerneau, in recognition of the services which he has rendered to the Royal Art, and which he is rendering daily, we have initiated him in the highest, in the most eminent and final Degree of Masonry; we create him our Deputy Grand Inspector, for the Northern part of the Island of Cuba, with all the powers that are attached thereto, giving him full and entire power to initiate the Bros: Masons, whom he may judge [worthy ?], to promote them to the Sublime Degrees, from the 4th up to and including the 24th; provided, however, that these Masons shall have been officers of a Lodge regularly constituted and recognized, and in places only where there may not be found Sacred and Sublime and regularly constituted Asyla; from which Bros: he will receive the obligation required and the authentic submission to the Decrees of the Sublime Princes; consulting, however, and calling to his aid the BB: whom he shall know to be decorated with the Sublime Degrees; we give him full and entire power to confer in the name of our aforesaid Grand Council the highest Degrees of Masonry on a Kt: Prince Mason, one only each year, whose virtues he shall recognize, and the qualities required to deserve this favor; and to the end that our dear Bro: Joseph Cerneau, so decorated, may enjoy, in this quality, the honours, rights, and prerogatives which he has justly deserved, by his arduous labors in the Royal Art, we have delivered to him these presents, in the margin whereof he has placed his signature, that it may avail him everywhere, and␣␣useful to him alone.

We pray our Resp: BB: regularly constituted, spread over the two Hemispheres, with whatever Degree they may be decorated, whether in Lodge, Ch:, Col:, Sovereign Council . . . Sublime, to recognize and receive our dear Bro:, the Very Illustrious Sov: and Subl: Prince, Joseph Cerneau, in all the Degrees above mentioned; promising to pay the same attention to those who in our Orients shall present themselves at the doors of our Sacred Asyla furnished with like authentic titles.

Given by us, S: Sublime Princes, G: C: G: I: G'al: of our aforesaid Grand and Perfect Council, under our Mysterious Seal, and the Grand Seal of the Princes of Masonry, in a place where are deposited the greatest treasures, the sight whereof fills us with consolation, joy, and gratitude for all that is great and good.

At Baracoa, Island of Cuba, anno 5806, under the sign of the Lion, the 15th day of the 5th month called Ab, 7806, of the Creation 5566, and according to the Common Style the 15th July, 1806.

Signed, MATHIEU DUPOTET, President, Sov: ...... G'al:

A true copy: Signed, MATHIEU DUPOTET, President, S:G:I: G'al:

I certify that what is transmitted above and the other portions are conformable to my Register.

TIPHAINE,

S:P:R:S:D:I:G'al:G: Comm:

The foregoing translation of the ancient copy in French has been correctly and faithfully made by me.

March 20, 1882.

ALBERT PIKE

The Northern Supreme Council for a few years was divided into two factions and one of them compromised with and affiliated some of these irregular Masons and took them in, which resulted in a very unfavorable condition of the Northern Supreme Council, which for a time was infected with an unhealthy absorption of bad material, by this unwise compromise, which was made, as was supposed, for the good of Freemasonry.

Some of these irregular Masons had caused a division even in the Grand Lodge of New York, and the original chief of them, Joseph Cerneau, had previously represented the irregular Knights Templars of New Orleans and the irregular council of the Rite of Perfection of Louisiana in the Grand Encampment of Knights Templar of New York, as is found in the records, viz.: " on the 4th day of May, 1816, a meeting of the Grand Encampment of Knights Templar of New York was called to act upon an application by a collected body of Sir Knights Templar, Royal Arch Masons and members of the Sov. Grand Council of Sublime Princes of the Royal Secret for the State of Louisiana, sitting at New Orleans, praying that a constitutional charter be granted them, etc. They had previous to this application elected and installed their officers. The charter, by resolution, was granted them. and it was also "Resolved, That the Ill. Bro. Joseph Cerneau, having been designated by the Louisiana Encampment to be their representative and proxy near this Grand Encampment, be and is hereby acknowledged and accredited as such."

In this manner the irregular French Templar Degree that was carried from France to England got into the United States at New Orleans, and allied with an irregular rite and body, became amalgamated with the American Webb Templar Degree at New York.

These evils which have beset the Ancient and Accepted Scottish Rite of Freemasonry, have not prevented its great advancement and prosperity; and during the past decade, in the Northern Jurisdiction alone, it has increased over fifty per cent in numbers.

The Southern Supreme Council did not meet from February, 1862, until November 17, 1865, which was in Charleston, S. C. Six members only were present, and all of them are now dead.

There were no bodies of the Rite working anywhere except in New Orleans.

With indomitable energy and zeal the Illustrious Sovereign Grand Commander, Albert Pike, 33d Degree, who during the last two years and a half of the war had been engaged in rewriting and restoring the rituals of the degrees, and whose scholarship and knowledge of the Ancient Mysteries and their philosophy, assisted by Albert Gallatin Mackay, 33d Degree, the late Secretary General of the Southern Supreme Council, reconstructed the Rite at Charleston, S.C.

The Supreme Council of the Southern Jurisdiction has now its headquarters in Washington, D.C. Its library of nearly fifty thousand volumes is not surpassed by any other in the country in rare and valuable works.

The constituency is constantly increasing, with five hundred and twenty-five organized bodies of the Rite over its extended territory, and nearly approaching in numbers that of its more prosperous sister council of the Northern Jurisdiction, which was exempt from the calamities of war, as a reference to the tabular statements following this chapter will show.

The legitimate Supreme Councils duly recognized by each other around the globe are the following:

Southern Jurisdiction, U.S.A
Constituted
May 31, 1801 France (Supreme Council)
Sept. 22, 1804 Northern Jurisdiction, U.S.A
Aug. 5, 1813 Belgium
Mar. 11, 1817 Ireland
June 11, 1825 Brazil
Nov. 2, 1830 New Granada
1833 England, Wales and Dependencies
Mar. 1846 Scotland
1846 Uruguay
1856 Argentine Republic
Sept. 13, 1858 Turin, of Italy
1848 Colon (Cuba)
1855 Venezuela
1864 Mexico
April 28, 1868 Portugal
1842 Chili
May 24, 1862 Central America
May 27, 1870 Hungary

Nov. 25, 1871 Greece
June 24, 1872 Switzerland
Mar. 30, 1873 Canada
Oct. 1874 Rome, of Italy
Jan. 14, 1877 Egypt

1878 Spain

1879 Tunis
May 11, 1880 Canada

"The following Supreme Councils have been formed, but have not received formal recognition and the courtesy of an exchange of representation: Naples, of Italy, Dominican Republic, Turkey, Palermo, of Italy, Florence, of Italy, and Luxemburg."

The rituals of the degrees differ very much in their dramatic representations. In the Northern Jurisdiction they apply more directly to the history and scenes of the Crusades; in the Southern Jurisdiction they are very much more intellectual, philosophical, and historic.

Councils of Deliberation are held in each State in the Northern Jurisdiction of all the bodies from the 14th to the 32d degrees inclusive, which are presided over by the deputies for the States. In these are presented all matters of local legislation, action upon which must subsequently be approved, or otherwise, by the Supreme Council.

The Supreme Council of the Rite is the governing body over all, and as such it makes and promulgates laws and statutes for the various divisions of the organized body. This Supreme Council confers the Governing Degree, namely, 33d Degree, Grand Master of the Kadosh or Sovereign Grand Inspector-General. The active members, according to the Statutes of the Southern Supreme Council, are limited to thirty-three active members of the 33d Degree and no more, but in the Northern Supreme Council this number is doubled, so that the active members of the 33d Degree are sixty-six. These active members are for their respective States relatively the Grand Masters of the Rite.

The title of Honorary Inspectors-General is given to those who are elevated to the degree with specifically delegated powers and no others, or they are sent as special delegates to establish new bodies or propagate the Rite by communicating the degrees. These special delegates have a voice in council but no vote.

In the Southern Supreme Council, with its number of active members of the 33d Degree limited to thirty-three, there is a "Court of

Honor," which may be called the vestibule to the 33d Degree. This Court of Honor comprises two grades or ranks, both of which are carefully reserved and can only be conferred as a free NOTE. - In the Southern Supreme Council, the council or preceptory of the Knights Kadosh or 30th degree is separate from the consistory of 31st and 32d degrees, but in the Northern Supreme Council it is within the consistory gift, and a mark of appreciation for services rendered. Each active member and each Emeritus member of the Southern Supreme Council is ex-officio a member of both grades. These grades are, first, that of Knight Commander. This is conferred upon Brethren of the 32d Degree for general meritorious service rendered to the Rite, and only upon the recommendation of the Grand Consistories or by the Active Inspectors-General of the respective States. The second grade, which is higher than the grade of Knight Commander, is that of Knight Grand Cross. It is conferred with the jewel upon Brethren of the 32d Degree for extraordinary services to the Rite. Neither of these grades can be given to anyone who solicits for them; it must be repeated that they are special marks of honor, gratuitously conferred. According to the Statutes of the Southern Jurisdiction the possession of at least the first of these grades is a condition precedent of eligibility for the reception of the 33d Degree.

The difference in the working of the degrees in the rituals of the Rite, between the ritual of the Southern and that of the Northern Jurisdiction, may require some explanation, which likewise will explain why the changes were necessarily made in working the degrees. The late Ill. Brother Azariah T. Pearson, 33d Degree, Active Inspector- General for the State of Minnesota in the Southern Jurisdiction, a little while before his death, made the following statement: " That the late Masonic firm of Macoy and Sickles of New York City, both of whom are 33d degree, and belong to the Northern Supreme Council, printed in the rituals for the supreme Council of the Southern Jurisdiction as well, but who unfortunately failed in business, and that the stereotype plates which belonged to either or both regular Supreme Councils, were surreptitiously seized upon and taken by persons connected with the Cerneau fraud, who had claimed that they had bought them with the rest of the property of Macoy and Sickles, which was sold for the benefit of their creditors; and that it was with these stereotype plates of the rituals thus surreptitiously obtained that the fraudulent Cerneau Supreme Council was thus enabled to improve its own meagre skeleton, and give its subordinate bodies a semblance of the true work conferred under the authority of the regular Supreme Councils, which for self-protection against impostors and clandestine Scottish Rite Masons, had to call in all the rituals then out, and to issue new ones in lieu thereof."

It must be again repeated, with a degree of reiteration which may be tiresome but is necessary, that the Scottish Rite confers no degrees but those of its own Rite, and also that while many of its members belong to legitimate bodies of other rites of Masonry, it has no conflict with any such. The Scottish Rite has doubled its members in the last few years, and year by year gains new accessions.

Antoine Bideaud, who had been created a Deputy Grand Inspector-General and a Sovereign Grand Inspector-General, September 10, 1802, by De Grasse Tilley, at Cape Francois, in San Domingo, so soon as he had opened his Supreme Council, after the return of the French to that island, was in New York and on August 4th conferred upon J. J. Gourgas, John B. Tardy, Lewis de Soulles, John B. Desdoity, and Pierre Du Peyrot all the degrees of the A: A: S: Rite to the 32d. Two days thereafter a consistory was opened, which although exceeding his patent, was afterward confirmed by proper authority. John B. Tardy was subsequently appointed Deputy Inspector-General by Du Plessis, of Philadelphia, who had received his appointment in 1790 from Augustine Prevost, who derived his authority directly from Francken in 1774, at Jamaica.

Abraham Jacobs, who claimed to be a Grand Inspector-General, made such by Moses Cohen in 1790, came to New York in 1804, and began his work of conferring degrees.

He states, in his register, that by the wishes of J. B. Tardy there was opened a council of Princes of Jerusalem November 6, 1808, there being present J. J. Gourgas, John B. Desdoity, Maduro Peixotto, Moses Levy, John B. Tardy, and Abraham Jacobs. At this time Richard Riker received the degrees. It appears from a statement by Gourgas that Jacobs had exceeded his authority by interlining words in his patent, for which he was afterward expelled. Gourgas also says that on November 8, 1808, Daniel D. Tompkins, Richard Riker, and Sampson Simpson received the degrees, including the 32d Degree, in the consistory which was formed August 6, 1806, and that he was made a Deputy Inspector-General on November 12, 1808, Desdoityon the 8th, and Peixotto on the 16th.

In consequence of a rumor of the irregularities which had occurred in the bodies in New York having reached the Supreme Council in Charleston, De la Motta, who was an officer in that body, was sent to New York with authority from the Supreme Council to investigate the whole matter, in 1813. August 5th he conferred the 33d Degree upon J.J. Gourgas and Sampson Simpson; these three then opened a Supreme Council and conferred the degree on Richard Riker, John B. Tardy, Daniel D. Tompkins, and Maduro Peixotto. On the same day, De la Motta, by authority of the Mother Supreme Council at Charleston, regularly and constitutionally organized what was then called the "Second Grand and Supreme Council" for the United States. Daniel D. Tompkins was installed Grand Commander; the other Officers were appointed and installed. At the next meeting of the "Mother Supreme Council," at Charleston, the following December, these proceedings were duly confirmed.

As heretofore stated, a treaty was entered into by and between the two Supreme Councils, and the jurisdiction over the various States and Territories of the United States was determined for each of these.

Like all human voluntary institutions, the histories of both the Northern and Southern Supreme Councils are records of bitter controversies growing out of rival bodies which were irregularly started in opposition to each of these duly constituted Supreme Councils, and which greatly retarded the advancement of this valuable Rite.

In the Southern Jurisdiction these controversies continued to keep the Scottish Rite entirely in the shade, as it were, until General Albert Pike received the several degrees and was elected the Grand Commander. Since the close of the war in 1865 the progress has been onward and upward, as has been shown in the preceding pages of this chapter.

In the Northern Supreme Council the Rite encountered a more bitter and relentless opposition in the bodies organized by Joseph Cerneau, originally in 1807, and although that body repeatedly declined, until it would appear to be utterly extinguished, yet it would quite unexpectedly arise again, deceive the unwary, and so soon as the sunlight of Truth was poured upon it would again decline, wither, and disappear.

The opposition to which the Northern Supreme Council was subjected was of such a character that it is incumbent on us to take some notice thereof to demonstrate what the Scottish Rite of the Northern Supreme Council had to contend against in defense of the truth.

Giles Fonda Yates, of Albany, became, at an early date (1822), interested in the study of Masonry. He discovered the Warrant of the Lodge of Perfection granted by Francken at Albany and a copy of the Constitutions of 1762; he then succeeded in resuscitating the old lodge. After this a Grand Council of Princes of Jerusalem was organized at Albany, and several lodges of Perfection were constituted in other places. A consistory was instituted in 1824 at Albany, and several bodies were established in Boston. These were under patents of the Supreme

Council at Charleston. Yates received the 33d Degree from McCosh, who was the special Deputy of this council. Afterward, in 1828, Yates became a member of the Northern Supreme Council. Just at this period, from 1826, the Morgan affair having occurred, nearly all the Masonic bodies at the North became extinct, as recited in the chapter devoted to that subject. In 1832 Gourgas suspended all efforts in the affairs of the Scottish Rite. In 1842, however, the great excitement had mostly died out and the fire of persecution, bigotry, and fanaticism having had no fuel for many years, waned, and all efforts against the Institution ceased.

Yates having conferred with Gourgas and other Brethren who had not succumbed under their severe ordeal, they determined to resume their labors. June 15, 1844, a meeting was held; Gourgas was then Grand Commander, and Yates Lieutenant Grand Commander. These two, by a law of the Rite, that if only one member of a Supreme Council survives, that council does not cease to exist, opened the Supreme Council.

At this meeting, November 13, 1844, applications were received from Edward A. Raymond, Ruel Baker, and Charles W. Moore (all of Massachusetts), who, having received the 32d Degree, were crowned Sovereign Grand Inspectors-General.

At the meeting held April 3-5, 1845, Gourgas declared that the recent publication by Clavel, relating to the Ancient and Accepted Rite, was utterly incorrect, and stated that Cerneau's name was struck from the Tableau of the Grand Orient of France in 1830, the Grand Orient having written to him that it was a matter quite inexplicable to them that it should have remained there so long.

At this meeting Gourgas reorganized the Supreme Council, the officers being appointed by the constitutional provisions. From this time the Supreme Council became very industrious in establishing bodies in many cities; harmony prevailed over this jurisdiction, and the Rite, although slowly, was steadily extended.

At an important meeting held September 4, 1851, Gourgas's resignation as Grand Commander and his appointment of Yates as his successor were received. Yates presided at this meeting, the Sovereign Grand Consistory was organized, and the degrees in the various bodies were conferred. At the close of the meeting Yates resigned as Grand Commander and appointed Raymond to that position. In his address Yates gave a forcible exposition of the laws, the objects, and the history of the Rite, and it contains so much information, of interest and value to its members, that we give it in full:

ADDRESS OF M.P. BRO. GILES FONDA YATES

Respected and Beloved Associates: You have been listening to the valedictory address of our honored friend, long trieds true, and trusty. His sentiments, I am well assured, are reciprocated. He has been called by our transatlantic Brethren " the patriarch of our 'Illustrious Order,'" and not without appropriateness. John James J. Gourgas - clarum et venerabile nomen!

He has been pleased to allude to my own participation in some of the works and administrative duties of our order, but such participation, as you are well aware, has been at a later day and for a shorter period. Under the circumstances in which I now appear before you, it can hardly be deemed egotistic in me if I advert briefly to a few of the humble contributions to the cause of "Sublime Freemasonry" previous to 1840, which it fell to my lot to render. These, with the "sublime works" performed by other Brethren of our order before and since, in Massachusetts, New York, New Hampshire, Connecticut, and Rhode Island, furnish altogether evidence supplemental to that given by my predecessor, in complete confutation of the preposterous charge that "Sublime Freemasonry" has been dormant in our jurisdiction since its establishment among us. A charge of this kind has been the stereotype apology of surreptitious Masons for their occasional attempts to foist their spurious creations upon our "Sublime System" within our Masonic territory. The abundant parole testimony which can be adduced to show how untrue is this charge, can be corroborated by our archives, and will be found iterated in manifestoes issued by our own and our sister council for the Southern Jurisdiction of the United States.

I turned my attention to the history of the "Sublime Degrees" very soon after my initiation as a Mason. My intercourse in 1822 with several old Masons in the city of Albany, led to the discovery that an "Ineffable Lodge of Perfection" had been established in that ancient city on December 20, 1767. I also discovered that not only the Ineffable, but the Superior Degrees of our Rite, had been conferred at the same time on a chosen few, by the founder of the lodge, Henry A. Francken, one of the Deputies of Stephen Morin[118] of illustrious memory. It was not long, moreover, before I found the original Warrant of this lodge, its book of minutes, the patents of Ill. Brother Samuel Stringer, M.D., Jeremiah Van

---

[118] Stephen Morin was on the 27th day of August, 1761, appointed "Inspector General over all Lodges, &c., &c., &c., in the new world by the Grand Consistory of Princes of the Royal Secret convened in Paris, at which presided the King of Prussia's Deputy, Chaillon De Joinville, Substitute General of the Order." See circular issued by the Supreme Council at Charleston, S. C., December 4, 1802

Rensselaer and Peter W. Yates, Esquires, Dep. Inspectors-General, under the old system; also "the regulations and contributions of the nine commissioners," etc., 1761, and other documents that had been left by Bro. Francken with the Albany Brethren when he founded their lodge. With the concurrence of the surviving members of said lodge residing in Albany, Dr. Jonathan Eights and the Hon. and R. W. Stephen Van Rensselaer, P.G.M. of the Grand Lodge of New York, I aided in effecting its revival. The necessary proceedings were thereupon instituted to place the same under the superintendence of a Grand Council of Princes of Jerusalem, as required by the old constitutions; and such Grand Council was subsequently opened in due form in said city.

Having been made aware of "the new Constitution of the Thirty-third degree," ratified on the first of play, 1786, conferring the Supreme Power over our Rite on "Councils of Nine Brethren," I hastened to place myself in correspondence with Moses Holbrook, M.D., at the time S.G. Commander of the Supreme Council at Charleston, and with my esteemed friends, Joseph M'Cosh, Ill. Gr. Sec. Gen. of the last-named council, and Bro. Gourgas, at that time Ill. Gr. Sec. Gen. of the H.E. for this Northern Jurisdiction. Lodges of Perfection in the counties of Montgomery, Onondaga, Saratoga, and Monroe in the State of New York, were successively organized, and placed agreeably to the constitutions under the superintendence of the Grand Council before named. The establishment of this last- named body was confirmed, and all our proceedings in "Sublime Freemasonry" were legalized and sanctioned by the only lawful authorities in the United States, the aforesaid Supreme Councils.

On the 16th day of November, 1824, I received a patent, appointing me S. of S. of a consistory of S.P.R.S., established in the city of Albany. I would here also state that on the 13th day of February, 1825, a Charter was granted to Ill. Bro. Edward A. Raymond, of Boston, Mass., and eight associates, constituting them a Grand Council of Princes of Jerusalem; a Charter was also granted them for a consistory of S.P.R.S., both bodies to be holden in the city of Boston. All these several bodies named, as well as the Albany Grand Council and Consistory, have since their establishment paid due faith and allegiance to our Northern Supreme Council.

In the organization of the New York State Grand Council, and of the different lodges of Perfection under its superintendence, I received the most effective aid and co- operation of several dear companions whom "it delights me to remember." These lodges numbered on their lists of initiates some of the brightest and worthiest

Masons that State produced, and enjoyed for a series of years a good share of prosperity, until the persecuting fires of anti-Masonry swept over the land. Their labors were then intermitted for awhile, in common with those of other departments of the Masonic Institution, from the same cause. But the consequences were not in the main inauspicious. The legitimate effect was to purify and cement more closely the materials subjected to the fiery ordeal.

In 1825 I took my vows as a "Sovereign Grand Inspector General" "between the hands" of our Brother Joseph M'Cosh, he having been specially deputized for that purpose. I was shortly after constituted and accredited the "Representative" of the Southern Supreme Grand Council near this Northern Supreme Grand Council, of which last I was made, and have ever since been a member.

I would fain have you to believe, my dear Brethren, that, as a member of the Masonic Institution, if I have had my ambition, it has been to study its science, and to discharge my duties as a faithful Mason, rather than to obtain its official honors or personal benefits of any kind. Self-aggrandizement has never formed any part of my Masonic creed, and all who know me can bear witness that it never has of my practise. I accordingly shall never shirk any just responsibility imposed upon me by my obligations as a "Sublime Freemason," but continue to prefer, as I have ever done, since it is most congenial to my own taste, those I' works " and labors of the Craft not necessarily connected with its administrative duties.

As Sovereign Grand Inspectors-General, it cannot be bootless to inquire what is the charge committed to our keeping - what the trust reposed in us? Is it true that the degrees and orders of our Rite are, as our enemies allege, only superfetation? Are they naught but excrescences on the great pyramid of Freemasonry? Have they no antiquity? Are they of an irreligious character? Allow me to deliver a few of my own views on this subject - views, as you are well assured, I have not arrived at hastily.

As Brother Gourgas has well observed, our degrees and orders constitute of themselves a perfect system and Rite, which we denominate the "Sublime system," and the 'is Ancient and Accepted Rite." They have been called "Honorary." Such they are, in the true sense of the term, but not in the sense generally used, which is construed as synonymous with "side," or "detached degrees." We, however, possess, in addition to our regular series of degrees, "detached degrees," of more or less value, subsidiary to our regular degrees. But none of our degrees are, per se, subordinate or subsidiary to any other system or Rite, much less to any system or Rite which had no existence when our Rite was reorganized at the beginning of the last century. All attempts to make them so, we, as faithful conservators and guardians of our Rites, are bound to resist. Ours are not, as many have represented them, "loose," "floating," or "side degrees," nor yet are they "waifs of Masonic stragglers."[119] If the star of "Sublime Freemasonry" is never permitted to culminate in the zenith it deserves a better fate than to become a satellite to any other orbs, albeit these may shine with more distinguished luster. If it ever becomes depressed to the nadir of the Masonic horizon, it will not be because of its want of value or merit.

Our "Sublime Brother" Dalcho remarks in one of his orations[120] that our degrees imparted to him knowledge, which he had vainly sought for in the lower degrees - that they elucidated the origin and principles of the Masonic Institution and its connection with science and religion more intimately than the symbolic degrees. I have myself noticed that in the latter general ideas only are communicated and these obscurely, while in the "Sublime Degrees" these ideas become clear as particular truths; though still, like all truths regarding the mind and heart, which are invisible, they can be expressed only by figurative terms and external symbols.

By imagery, and through a veil[121] of metaphor, the light of truth and the most sublime allusions are disclosed. We may be well versed in the ceremonials of our order and yet not understand their true import; we may correctly read "the letter" of our traditions and legends, and yet remain blind to their "spirit," and ignorant of the principles and inferences they involve. By study alone can we solve the enigma, "de duo fabula narratur?" Many of the characteristic allegories, legends, symbols, and ceremonies of "Sublime Freemasonry" are counted as insignificant and valueless, because they are not palpable to the senses, and fully comprehended at the first blush. Some of our most sacred mysteries are lightly esteemed, because they furnish no disclosures that strike dumb

---

[119] We are indebted to our Worthy Brother Philip C. Tucker, of Vermont, for this appropriate designation of Masonic pretenders of a certain description. We refer to those who occasionally spring up in this country and elsewhere, and engage in "peddling" Masonic Degrees ("Marchands de Maconnere"), and who assume prerogatives which they do not possess; and over degrees which most probably they never received.

[120] See his oration delivered before the Sublime Grand Lodge, at Charleston, S. C., March 21, 1803.

[121] This idea is beautifully symbolized in one of the "high degrees" by a figure of truth covered with a semi-transparent veil

with amazement our "hidden treasures," and spiritual "riches of secret places" are unappreciated; and no "Royal Secret" which humbly professes to have a relation only to the life of the heart seems to be cared for; nor yet any "precious stone" in our mystic edifice, if the "philosopher's lawful manner. These men, perchance too, may have surreptitiously obtained some partial information from garbled MSS.; or if they have obtained any degrees lawfully, are guilty of a violation of a fundamental Masonic law in regard to" allegiance "by using and transmitting to others Masonic knowledge under assumed authority, in a manner different from that in which they received it, stone" be wanting! For men of this stamp, our degrees, or indeed any Masonic degrees, will ever fail to present attractions.

"Upon the arts of building and architecture the Order of Free and Accepted Masonry rises like a fair stupendous pyramid from a broad, square basis, tending regularly up to a summit of attainments, ever concealed by intervening clouds from the promiscuous multitude of common observers below."[122] The first fourteen degrees of our Rite are in a part an amplification of "Ancient Craft" Masonry; while the "superior degrees" are founded on those Christian and "religious and military Orders" which are declared by the oldest book of York Constitutions to be cognate to the Craft degrees of Freemasonry.

The proofs are undeniable that the learning contained in the "Sublime Degrees" was taught long previous to the last century; our M. P. Brother Dalcho thinks shortly after the first crusade. In Prussia, France, and Scotland the principal degrees of our Rite appeared in an organized form in 1713. The unfortunate Lord Der Wentwater and his associate English Brethren were working in lodges of Harodim, in 1725, at Paris, when the Grand Lodge of England transmitted to France the Ancient York Constitutions.

Many Scotch Brethren (adherents of Charles Edward Stuart) being in France about this time, also cultivated some of the high degrees of our Rite. Some of the important mysteries celebrated in the superior degrees were instituted by the successors of Jacques de Molay, and others derive their origin from the renowned Robert Bruce. The former gave the military, the latter the Christian, character to the degrees and orders of our Rite; and from what has been alluded to relative to the connection of our Scotch Brethren with our degrees and orders, I think we may readily account for the terms Ecossazs, or Scotch as applied to them.

---

[122] Quoted from an old edition of the York Constitution

No person can pretend that any one department or system of Freemasonry or any particular Masonic Rite, however unexceptionable, has from time immemorial existed in the same form in which it appears at the present day. But we contend that the (historical epoch) traditions and grades of knowledge embodied in the degrees and orders of the Rite we profess, have descended to us from remote antiquity. This fact can be proved to the reasonable satisfaction of the most skeptical, by the writings of learned Brethren who have spent years in investigating the subject. To the same effect, too, we have the incidental testimony of writers who never belonged to the Fraternity, as well as the unwilling admission of those opposed to us. Even a brief recapitulation of such proofs is not demanded by present occasion. My referring to this topic at this time is merely to remind my Brethren that our "Ancient and Accepted Rite" is incorrectly designated as a "modern Rite."[123] Then we use the term "modern" as applicable to any of our orders or degrees, it is to be taken in a comparative sense, and not in its vulgar acceptation. It refers to ours "religious and military orders" instituted since the commencement of the Christian era, and after that of "the holy wars!" of a verity, our Rite is not born of yesterday.

Many of our degrees imply prerequisites in candidates peculiarly stringent, and unknown in other departments of Freemasonry; and not a few partake of the character of official degrees. Even the lowest degrees of our Rite, the eleven "Ineffable," are designed for the "Select few" only. This is especially the case with our principal superior degrees, Prince of Jerusalem, Sov.'. Prince of Rose Cross, elected Knight K. H. Grand Inquisitor Commander, and Sublime Prince of the Royal Secret, which are virtually orders of Harodim. Some of our superior degrees confer the titles of "Commander," "Patriarch," "Grand Master," if "Prince," and "Sovereign." But it behoves me to observe that the Masonic titles in our "Inner Easts," like the jewels on our breasts, are not cherished and worn by us for show or aggrandizement; they are suggestive of holy truths and self-perfecting duties, which every conscientious "Sublime Freemason" will strive to learn and perform.

Some persons who have written and discoursed about our degrees, have obtained what little knowledge they possess of them from

---

[123] It is doubtless the case that some persons confound our Rite with "the French or Modern Rite," which is confessedly modern and was invented within the last half century. It embraces the three symbolic degrees and forms the basis, and is part, of the spurious "Scotch Rite," which aims at supplanting us. It is the same cultivated in some French lodges in this country, and by the Louisiana and other spurious Supreme Councils

spurious and corrupted sources. I do not speak unadvisedly on this subject; for I have critically examined rituals identical with those in use among the clandestine and "soi-disant" Supreme Councils, and usurping propagandists of "Sublime Freemasonry." Now and then an orthodox hieroglyphic symbol or allegory is surreptitiously obtained, but its true solution is not attained to, by the vulgar interpretations of superficialness, or it is purposely perverted by the infidel, or bigot, or sectarian, to suit his narrow purposes or by intriguers, who

"Like scurvy politicians, seem to see The things they do not."

Such rituals, too, often penned by blundering copyists, may not inaptly be likened to human skeletons, stripped of all the arteries, nerves, and muscles of the living man, deprived of soul, life-blood, and spirit.

There are some writers, who, while they may not deny antiquity to the doctrines and traditions on which some of the "high degrees" are founded, yet with a Barruel and Robison purposely confound our "Ineffable" and "philosophical degrees" with those of the political society of the Illuminati and certain infidel systems of philosophy. A learned philosophers has well observed that philosophy is not possible, unless it be founded on, and guarded by, Christianity. Christianity is the basis, and philosophy the superstructure of the edifice." It is with philosophy such as this that true Freemasonry has to do. It is worthy of note in this connection that speculative science as well as practical wisdom once ranked among the virtues. The knowledge of the Eternal Being, as understood by philosophy, reason, and religious revelation, is the basis and apex, as well of the Masonic as the scientific pyramid.[124]

"No art or learning serveth useful ends, But as the heart it guides, and life amends."

However great the acquisitions of the most successful cultivator of "the Royal art" and science, all will be vain without a practical application of the knowledge acquired. The understanding should be strengthened that the conduct may be directed and truth discovered, that it may be used "for the better endowment and help of man's life." One of the cardinal ends designed to be answered by Freemasonry, in any of its departments, is to make men better as well as wiser. The eulogy pronounced by Bro. T. S. Webb[125] on "the eleven ineffable degrees," is applicable to the whole system of "Sublime Freemasonry," that it is "intended for the glory of the Deity, and the good of mankind."

---

[124] Geoberti
[125] Bro. Webb did not pretend to be a professor of those degrees, or of any other in "Sublime Freemasonry." See his preface to his illustrations of those degrees.

Those who bring the charge of irreligion against our Rite would do well to bear in mind that learned authors[126] unfriendly to our Institution have expressed their conviction that the pure doctrines of the Zabians, which are incorrectly stigmatized as astrological and idolatrous,[127] and the doctrines of St. John the Baptist, were essentially identical; while Brethren learned in the secrets of "Ineffable Masonry," delivered only "behind the veil," and versed in the doctrines of "Sublime Freemasonry," have become penetrated with the conviction that these secrets and doctrines are in essence the same with those which were taught by the Pythagorean and Essenean rituals.

After the French revolution of 1793, Christianity in France was ridiculed into obsoleteness. Among the mass of the people who became atheists were the mass of the Masons. Numerous copies of that holy book, which we esteem as the first great light in Masonry, were committed to the flames. Under this state of things, "Sublime Freemasonry" fell into desuetude; and it was not until after the establishment of the Supreme Council at Charleston, S. C., on the 31st day of May, 1801, that the "Sublime System" was revived in France by the establishment of a Supreme Council at Paris, to wit, in 1804, by Count De Grasse, Grand InspectorGeneral, under authority from the Charleston Supreme Council. The Paris Supreme Council has been in continuous operation ever since. And here truth compels me to advert to the fact that the "Grand Orient" of France, which had a legal existence only as a "Symbolic" Grand Lodge of Master Masons, now commenced her assumption of jurisdiction over all the degrees of the "Ancient and Accepted Rite." Disputes hereupon ensued between the French Supreme

---

[126] E.g., Cardinal Wiseman - Syriac version of the Vatican code used by Adler in his "Druses Montis Libani."

[127] I here quote the words of Dr. Dewey in corroboration of the idea I have advanced in the text, because he expresses this idea clearly and briefly. It is, however, far from being a singular one, or original with him. It has been the persuasion of every philosopher and divine of celebrity who has bestowed more than a superficial examination upon the subject, both before and since Lord Bacon's day; who proves its truth in detail. "The idea that images set up as gods were worshipped, is erroneous.

They were esteemed as symbols of a higher power and as 'symbols' only. A species of images (as for example the four-faced Cherubim) was recognized even in the early worship of the Hebrews when under the immediate government of God himself I would not be understood to say: that the pure doctrines alluded to were not perverted, or that there were no persons obnoxious to the charge made by St. Paul in Rom. I. 23

Council and Grand Orient, which have never been fully settled up to the present day.

Every lover of Masonic order and constitutional authority cannot but regret this unhappy occurrence; and none the less the conduct of the Parisian Brethren on sundry occasions during the last half century, in extending their jurisdiction in both the Symbolic and Sublime degrees over territory on this continent, already lawfully occupied. Their example in this last respect has been repeatedly followed and is at this present moment producing consequences deleterious to the Craft at large. The present occasion is not the most appropriate one for descending to particularities on this head.

It is unnecessary for me to make more than a passing allusion to the troubles that have been experienced from analogous causes by our sister council at Charleston and our own Supreme Council, from 1806 to the present time. In assaulting our Supreme Councils our enemies tried to shift the issue from principals to individuals, and resorted to wilful perversions of facts; and failing to find legitimate and real subjects to attack, they for the nonce fabricated them. As "the droppings of their lips" were anything but "sweet-smelling myrrh," or the "perfume of hearty counsel," as true gentlemen and Masons we could not meet them on their own ground, or do aught else than simply pronounce their allegations false and unfounded.

A word or two with regard to the charge of interference on the part of the two only lawful Supreme Councils in this country, with the prerogatives of other departments of Freemasonry. No Supreme Councils of Sovereign Grand Inspectors-General were established anywhere in the world till after 1786.[128] Previously, Inspectors General under the enlightened Frederick of Prussia were charged with the powers and duties now vested in such Supreme Councils and the Grand Bodies under them. By them the degrees and orders of our Rite were conserved and propagated in the constitutional manner. It was not the Grand Orient of France, as is by many erroneously supposed, nor any other

---

[128] "On May 1, 1786, the Grand Constitution of the Thirty-third Degree, called the Supreme Council of Sovereign Grand Inspector-General, was finally ratified by his Majesty, the King of Prussia, who, as Grand Commander of the Order of Prince of the Royal Secret, possessed the Sovereign Masonic power over the Craft. In the New Constitution this high power was conferred on a Supreme Council of nine Brethren in each nation, who possess all the Masonic prerogatives in their own district that his Majesty individually possessed, and are Sovereigns of Masonry." Extracts from the circular letter of the Charleston Supreme Council issued December 4, 1802.

Grand Body on the Continent of Europe, except the Grand Consistory, over which presided Frederick's "Substitute General" before named, that had any authority to act in the premises. For the authors of the numerous new rites and innovations committed on the old system of Freemasonry, which were erst so rife on the European Continent, we must look elsewhere than to the lawful Deputies Inspectors-General under the old system.

The original minutes and documents left by Ill. Brother Francken, who established the Albany Lodge of Perfection in 1767, evince the most scrupulous avoidance of interference with the Master's Lodge in that city or the Symbolic Degree. As there were no R. A. Chapters or Encampments of Knights Templars established in this country till thirty years afterward, to speak of interference with them would be an anachronismic absurdity, akin to those recently spawned by ignorance or design to mislead uninformed Brethren, or for other unworthy purposes.

The first Supreme Council ever established under the new Constitution of 1786 was that at Charleston,[129] whose jurisdiction extended constitutionally over the whole of the United States, until they constituted, by their Special Deputy, E. De La Motta, III. Treas.

Gen. H.E., this Northern Supreme Council in 1813.[130] Then on December 4, 1802, our Southern Supreme Council published a

---

[129] on May 31, 1801, the Supreme Council of the 33d Degree for the United States of America was opened with the high honors of Masonry by Bros. John Mitchell and Frederick Dalcho, Sovereign Grand Inspectors-General; and in the course of the year the whole number of Grand Inspectors-General was completed agreeably to the Grand Constitutions. The other members of this Grand Council admitted in 1801 were Emanuel De La Motta, Dr. J. Auld, Dr. James Moultrie, Abraham Alexander, M. C. Livy, Thomas B. Bowen, and J. De Lieban.
[130] The Supreme Grand Council for the Northern Jurisdiction of the United States was founded on August 5, 1813, by the M. Ill. Brothers E. De La Motta, "Special Deputy- Representative" from the said Supreme Grand Council at Charleston, Daniel D. Tompkins, S. Simson, John J. J. Gourgas, Richard Riker, J. G. Tardy, and M. L. M. Peixotto. In the words of a manifesto issued by the last-named council, dated August 2, 1845, the establishment of our Northern Supreme Council is shown " by authenticated documents in the possession of this (the Charleston) Council, in accordance with the Secret Constitutions, by Emanuel De La Motta as the Representative and under the Northern and Southern Jurisdictions were defined and regulated. A candid review of all the acts of the constitutional regulators and governors of our Rite in these United States cannot fail to establish the falsity ot this charge of interference on their part. If I am not much mistaken, they have been "more sinned against than

report from which I make the following extracts. They speak for themselves:

"Although many of the Sublime degrees are in fact a continuation of the Blue degrees, yet there is no interference[131] between the two bodies. Throughout the continent of Europe and the West Indies, where they are very generally known, they are acknowledged and encouraged. The Sublime Masons never initiate any into the Blue degrees, without a legal warrant obtained for that purpose from a Symbolic Grand Lodge; but they communicate the secrets of the chair to such applicants as have not already received them, previous to their initiation into the Sublime Lodge; yet they are at the same time informed that it does not give them rank as sanction and authority of the Council at Charleston. The Masonic Jurisdiction of the Northern Council is distributed over the Northern, North-western, and North-eastern parts of the United States. And this, with the Council at Charleston, are the only recognized Councils which exist or can exist, according to the Secret Constitutions, in the United States. Their labors have never been suspended, though withdrawn for a time from the public eye - their authority has never been, and cannot be, abrogated.

They hold in their archives certified copies of the Secret Constitutions, derived from the Grand Consistory held at Paris in 1761. Their succession of officers and members has been regularly and duly continued, and the Great Light of 'Sublime Masonry,' which has been confided to their keeping, like the sacred fire of the Vestals, has been preserved unextinguished on their altars."

---

sinning." If we have not claimed the benefit of the legal maxims, Quad prius est, verius est, et quod prius est tempore, potious est jure, it has not been because we were not entitled to this benefit.

[131] "In deference to the Constitution of the York Rite practiced in this country, it waves its rights and privileges, so far as they relate to the first three degrees of Ancient Craft Masonry, which long before the establishment of any Supreme Council in this hemisphere, were under the control of Symbolic Grand Lodges " See circular letters of both Northern and Southern Supreme Councils, 1845. "The object of the Supreme Council is not to interfere with the rights of any other bodies, but simply to preserve from decay or innovation those Sublime truths and ineffable mysteries which, while they throw a brighter light upon the pure system of Ancient Craft Masonry, can be attained only by those who have sought for light in the deepest recesses of the Masonic Temple. They ask, therefore, as the legal guardians of these invaluable treasures, the sympathy and fraternal kindness of their Brethren, to whom they take this occasion of offering the right hand of brotherly love and affection." - Charleston Circular, 1845

Past Masters in the Grand Lodge.[132]

"On January 21, 1802, a warrant of constitution passed the seal of the Grand Council of Princes of Jerusalem for the establishment of a Master Mark Mason's Lodge in the City of Charleston, S.C." "Besides those degrees, which are in regular succession, most of the Inspectors are in possession of a number of detached degrees given in different parts of the world; and which they generally communicate free of expense, to those Brethren who are high enough to understand them. Such as select Masons of 27, etc., making in the aggregate fifty-three degrees." As to the Mark and Past Master's Degrees, all authority over them was surrendered to the R.A. Chapters, at that time springing into existence. Independent lodges of Mark Master Masons having no governing head were afterward established in this country, and continued in operation for a series of years; until the Gen. Grand Chapter assumed jurisdiction over both the Mark and Past Master's Degrees as "honorary grades," and incorporated them into their system.

No! Brethren, the intermeddling complained of, lies at the door of the spurious bodies established by the impostor Joseph Cerneau, et id omne genus, progeniesque, whose illegitimate works are ever and anon exhumed and revamped for sinister purposes. It ought, methinks, to be a sufficient refutation of the charge of our intermeddling with other departments of Masonry, that the leading Brethren of both our Northern and Southern Supreme Councils, ever since their establishment, have been active leaders in Symbolic Grand Lodges, Grand Chapters of R.A. Masons, and Grand Encampments of Knights Templar, the only other departments of Freemasonry in our land which we recognize and acknowledge.

"No Masonic power professing our Rite, or any of its dependent associations, can, under any pretense whatever, amalgamate or associate by representation or otherwise, with any other power, or with any association depending on any other Rite, nor consent to become a section or dependence thereof, without renouncing the object of its institution, and losing de facto its sovereign attributes." This fundamental law applicable to any department of Freemasonry is a truism, and surely needs no argument to support it.

I a well persuaded that our Supreme Grand Council will ever continue, as it has heretofore done, to illustrate the truth of one of its own sentiments, that " Sublime Freemasonry is unobtrusive, a divine manna for the clear-sighted to gather - everyone according to his own

---

[132] This practice was never adopted by the regular "Sublime Freemasons" in this Northern Jurisdiction.

taste and ability." We claim not to keep the vineyards of others, and we challenge to the proof that we have ever trenched upon them. And while we guard, as we are bound to do, our own possessions, we hope to be permitted to sit peaceful and undisturbed if under our own vine and fig-tree"!

The institution of the official dignity of Sovereign Grand Inspector-General, in 1786, and the adoption of the constitutional provisions, by which, on the decease of the great Frederick, his authority and duties over our order in both hemispheres were transferred to a limited number of Brethren in each nation, operated practically as a distribution among many Brethren of the high Masonic powers and prerogatives, originally possessed by one Grand Master. Notwithstanding the numerous efforts made to enlighten Brethren as to the true nature of the 33d Degree "governing itself and all others" of our said Rite, and conferring rights and powers, and imposing duties "agreeably to the Grand Constitutions" of our order, of an executive character,[133] it is still

---

[133] I will fortify my statement with that of our M. Puis. Bro. Dalcho, whose authority in a matter of this kind cannot be gainsaid. I quote from page 116, appendix to his oration delivered before the Sublime Grand Lodge of Charleston, S.C., March 21, 1803. "By the Constitution of the Order, which was ratified on October 25, 1762, the King of Prussia was proclaimed as the chief of the Eminent Degrees, with the rank of Sovereign Grand Inspector-General and Grand Commander. The higher Councils and Chapters could not be opened without his presence or that of his substitute, whom he must appoint. All the transactions of the Consistory of the thirty-second degree required his sanction, or that of his substitute, to establish their legality; and many other prerogatives were attached to his Masonic rank. No provision, however, had been made in the Constitutions for the appointment of his successor; and, as it was an office of the highest importance, the utmost caution was necessary to prevent an improper person from obtaining it. The King, being conscious of this, established the thirty-third degree. Nine Brethren in each nation, from the Supreme Council of Grand Inspectors- General, after his decease possessed all his Masonic prerogatives and power over the Craft. They are the Executive Body of the Masonic Fraternity, and their approval is now necessary to the acts of the Consistory, before they can become laws; and from their decision there can be no appeal."

In 1825 I received from Moses Holbrook, M.D., at that time Sov. Grand Commander of the Charleston Supreme Council, a letter in answer to some inquiries relative to the subject in question, from which letter I make the following extracts: "All the transactions of S.P.R.S. required the sanction of Frederick William II. (who had for many years been the head and patron of the Order), or that of his substitute, to establish their but most erroneously considered as an "honorary" distinction merely, and as an ordinary degree in

generally living as legality. Many other prerogatives were attached to his Masonic rank; and not least in the consideration of the day, it was thought that in the United States, just emerged from the thraldom of the mother country, after a long and arduous struggle for their liberty, it would be highly improper to have the Masonic head and jurisdiction over the Ineffable and Sublime degrees in another country, and to pay allegiance of any kind to a foreign potentate. These difficulties, added to the importance attached to the highest office in Freemasonry, and the very great caution necessary to prevent an unsuitable person from obtaining an office so respectable, influential, and important, weighed with the King and the high Consistory over which he presided. Upon reading the respectful petitions and statements made to them during the years 1784 and 1785, the subject was referred to a highly learned and able committee, who reported this degree (thirty- third) to constitute nine S.P.R.S. in each nation, a Streme Council of Sovereign Grand Inspectors-General; and they being duly organized, accredited, and approved, should at his decease possess all his Masonic prerogatives over the concerns of the Craft within the country or territory over which their jurisdiction extended; and their appointment was ad vitam. They became the Executive Body of the Masonic Fraternity within their territory. This arrangement annulled all former powers granted to individuals (Dep. Ins.-Gen.) in different parts of the world."

Freemasonry; and one to which all Brethren having the usual qualifications required for initiation into most of the lower degrees have a right to aspire.
The tenure of office in a Supreme Grand Council being for life, a seat in such a body can be vacated only by death, resignation, or removal from its jurisdiction. This is a fundamental law, and may not be changed, though its inevitable tendency is to exclude from our little circle some good, true, and worthy Brethren, who would, no doubt, adorn our assemblies, and prove faithful conservators, regulators, and governors of our Rite.
By being tenacious of official station, I may be the means of excluding Brethren whose councils are needed; and I may also stand in the way of the just preferment of my compeers. Moved by reasons like these I have named, and desirous of setting an example, which if discreetly followed may, without violation of our organic laws, serve in a degree to modify what is, albeit without good reason, deemed too exclusive a feature in our "sublime system," I have concluded to resign the official station I now hold in this council. There are other considerations also which induce me to adopt this course.
By a constitutional regulation of our order, the office of chief custodian of our archives devolves upon the Sov. Grand Commander, who should, for this and analogous reasons well understood by us, be a resident of one of the Easts in our jurisdiction.

I do in the interior of my native State, it is not meet for me to become such custodian.

Our archives, valuable and voluminous, should have a fixed and permanent depository, under the charge of their constitutional guardian.

My association for a quarter of a century with this Supreme Grand Council, and my active participation in its works and administrative duties, I have spoken of in my antecedent remarks. I avert to the fact again, and in this connection, to remind you, that it places me before you in such a position as to render, in a measure applicable to my own case, the reason for abdication advanced by my venerable predecessor, deducible from his long term of service.

My much esteemed compeer, your "Most Illustrious Inspector Lieutenant Grand Commander," Edward A. Raymond, in the event of my abdication of the presidency of this council, is pointed out by the constitutions as my successor. It gratifies me to reflect that such is the case. If there were no constitutional provision restricting my duty in the emergency named, and the selection of my successor were left to my own free choice, I could not make a selection more congenial to my feelings, or more in accordance with my convictions of duty. I have known him for three times three years twice told as a "Brother of the mystic tie," and a possessor of "the high degrees." His Masonic age and experience, derived from long and repeated services as a ruler in other departments of Masonry,' and the satisfaction he has given to his companions in the discharge of his administerial duties, afford an earnest that he will not be found wanting as a chief administrator in our ancient and Accepted Rite." I am assured that he has the requirements demanded by our Book of Constitutions, that he "can be entirely depended on, that his discretion is proof against all trials, his capacity acknowledged, and his probity untouched."

In 1859 the ambition of one man caused some trouble in this Supreme Council. Grand Commander Raymond[134] contended that "the powers of Frederick were vested in him as Grand Commander and not in the Council as a body." He had conferred the 33d Degree upon Paul Dean, and the Supreme Council had tacitly recognized him as a member. In 1860 an extra session was held, and the controversy with the Grand Commander reached the climax.

---

[134] Bro. Raymond is the present Grand Master of the Grand Lodge of Massachusetts, and has been at the head of the Grand Chapter Encampment of Massachusetts (1851)

The Grand Commander refused to put certain motions. A motion was made to close the council, to be opened at four o'clock; this he refused to put, and declared the council closed until ten o'clock on the following morning.

At that hour the council was opened and the minutes read, whereupon the Grand Commander declared the council closed sine die.

Some of the members (five) conferred together, and being advised by Gourgas, reopened the council and proceeded with the business.

Upon the report of a committee on rules, etc., previously appointed, the council adopted the Constitutions of 1860.

The record of this session was signed by Van Rensselaer, who was elected Lieutenant Grand Commander, Starkweather, Moore, Christie, Case, and Young. A preamble and resolution were adopted, deposing the Grand Commander in effect. Gourgas, Turner, Bull, and Hubbard formally approved the proceedings; Carson also did so with some qualifications.

The Grand Commander, Raymond, disregarded the action of these members after he had left the council. Both parties published the proceedings of 1860, those for the regular session being alike Raymond's being a record of his action in conferring the 33d Degree upon Lawson, Starkweather, and Field, who, it is alleged, by him were elected in 1857. It is said, however, that the records of 1857 show only the election of Starkweather.

Both of these factions continued to operate; we shall not, however, dwell upon the minutiae, but state that the Van Rensselaer body grew in numbers and importance.

There was a large accession in 1862 of very distinguished and prominent Masons; among these were Josiah H. Drummond, of Maine, and Benjamin Dean, of Massachusetts, both of whom subsequently became Grand Commanders; Hubbard, who had been elected Grand Commander, having positively declined to serve, Van Rensselaer was chosen. Raymond and Robinson having been summoned to attend, and failing to appear, were tried and expelled.

Notwithstanding the controversies between these two bodies, the Van Rensselaer body continued to prosper until 1867. With

Fac-simile of Agreement of Union
of A\A\S\R\ Bodies in U. S. A.

UNIVERSI TERRARUM ORBIS ARCHITECTONIS PER GLORIAM INGENTIS.

Dues Meumque Jus. Ordo ab Chao.

From the Orient of the Supreme Grand Council of Sovereign Grand Inspectors General of the 33d and last Degree of the Ancient and Accepted Rite, for the United States of America, their Territories and Dependencies, whose Sacred Asylum is beneath the C.'. C.'., at the V.'. P.'. of the Z.'., near the B.'. B.'., corresponding with 40d 42' 40" N. Lat., and 2d 0' 57" E. Lon.

TO ALL TO WHOM THESE PRESENTS SHALL COME, GREETING:

Be it Known, That on the 17th day of the Hebrew month Shebat, Anno Mundi 5623, answering to the 7th day of February, 1863 (E.V.), by solemn articles, the Supreme Council of Sovereign Grand Inspectors General of the 33d and last Degree of the Ancient and Accepted Rite for the Northern Jurisdiction of the United States of America, sitting at Boston, was duly consolidated with the Supreme Grand Council of Sovereign Grand Inspectors General of the 33d and last Degree of the A. and A. Rite for the United States of America, their Territories and Dependencies, sitting at New York, upon terms honorable and just alike to all parties interested therein.

Be it further Known, That the following Sovereign Grand Inspectors General, in pursuance of such consolidation, comprise the Officers of the Supreme Grand Council for the United States of America, their Territories and Dependencies. They will be recognized and respected accordingly.

Ill.'. EDMUND B. HAYS - M.'.P.'. Sov.'. Gr.'. Commander.
"
EDWARD A. RAYMOND - Asst.'.Sov.'.Gr.'.Com.'.
"
SIMON W. ROBINSON - 1st Lieut.'.Gr.'. Com.'.
"
HOPKINS THOMPSON - 2d Lieut.'.Gr.'. Com.'.
"
BENJAMIN C. LEVERIDGE - Gr.'. Orater.
"
GEORGE M. RANDALL - Gr.'. Minister of State.
"
LUCUS R. PAIGE - Gr.'. Chancellor.
"
DANIEL SICKELS - Gr.'. Sec.'. General H.'.E.'.
"
ROBERT E. ROBERTS - Gr.'. Treas.'. Gen.'. H.'.E.'.

" HENRY C. BANKS - Gr.'. Marshal General.

" AARON P. HUGHES - Gr.'. Sword Bearer.

" H. J. SEYMOUR - 1st Gr.'. Mas.'. of Cer.'.

" CHARLES T. McCLENACHAN - 2d Gr.'. Mas.'. of Cer.'.

" PETER LAWSON - Gr.'. Ex.'. Introductor.

" JOHN INNES - Gr.'. Standard Bearer.

" WM. FIELD - 1st Gr.'. Capt.'. of the Guard.

" WILLIAM H. JARVIS - 2d Gr.'. Capt.'. of the Guard.

All which is promulgated, and ordered to be transmitted to whom it may concern.

Done at the Grand East, New York city, this 8th day of the Hebrew month Adar, A.'. M.'. 5623, answering to March 1st, 1863 (E.'. V.'.)

In Testimony of all which I have hereunto set my hand, and caused the Seal of the Supreme Grand Council to be affixed.

[SEAL.] EDMUND B. HAYS 33.'.

Attest, M.'. P.'. Sov.'. G.'. Commander.

DANIEL SICKELS 33.'.

Gr.'.Sec.'.Gen.'. H.'. E.'. [SEAL.] the exception of four bodies in the city of New York, which had been organized prior to the schism, all others continued in their allegiance to this body. In 1867 there were twenty-eight active members on the roll.

In 1862 three Supreme Councils claimed jurisdiction over the Northern section of the United States. In April, 1862, by the records of Raymond Council, the Cerneau body, presided over by Hays, had made overtures to the Raymond faction for a union of the two, and committees were appointed to meet for the purpose of organizing for such union. January 23, 1863, it was reported to the Raymond body that there was a reasonable prospect of effecting the union, and the committee was granted full power to act. January 19, 1863, in the Hays body similar action ensued.

Under date of February 7, 1863, Articles of Union were agreed upon by which the two councils were consolidated. The number of members was increased to seventeen, and each member, and body, was required to take the oath of allegiance to the new body when they had the same status as they respectively had under the original bodies.

Raymond, Randall, Paige, Hughes, Robinson, Lawson, Field, and McClenachan of the Raymond body; and Hays, Thompson, Sickles, Roberts, Leveridge, Seymour, Banks, Jarvis, and Innis of the Hays body, constituted the membership of the united body. On the preceding page is shown the copy of the "Article of Consolidation."

April 15, 1863, Hays, having been agreed upon as Grand Commander, installed the Officers. All the members of both the former bodies were required to take the oath of fealty to the newly united body, hence the claim, set up a few years subsequently, that the Raymond body was merged in the Hays Council is entirely without foundation; moreover, when a few of the old Hays Council withdrew from the united body, the large majority, and the most eminent Brethren, remained true in their allegiance to that body.

A change was made in the constitution by which the active membership was increased to twenty-four, besides the nine officers.

The members of this united body became very active; a very large number received the 33d Degree; many new bodies were instituted, particularly in States where the Scottish Rite had not heretofore been worked, all in the Northern Jurisdiction.

Until 1864 the tenure of office had always been ad vitas but at the meeting this year, amendments were passed for the triennial election of the officers and for a reduction to nine.

September 11, 1865, a session was held. Communication had been resumed with the officials of the Southern Supreme Council, but the Hays Council having declared itself as having jurisdiction over the United States, this body was not in a condition to ask the recognition of the Southern Supreme Council, as it had denounced as spurious all the various bodies which had originated in New York.

At this meeting charges were presented against Harry J. Seymour, who was Asst. Grand Master of Ceremonies. A committee of his friends of the old Hays body was appointed to try these charges. At a subsequent date the committee reported. Seymour had been duly notified to appear, but he refused to do so, and he was expelled, as will be seen by the following:

SUPREME COUNCIL, 33d NORTHERN MASONIC JURISDICTION U.S.A.

Gr.'. Orient, Boston. Massachusetts, OFFICE OF THE SECRETARY GEN.'.H.'.B.'.

New York, 27 A.'.M.'., 5631

At a session of the Supreme Council 33d. for the Northern Jurisdiction U. S., held on the 10th day of the Hebrew month Elul, Anno Heb. 5625, answering to the 11th day of September, 1865, V.E., the following action was had:

Ill.'. Bro.'.C.T. McClenachan, Rose +.'. 33.'. preferred a charge with three specifications of the violation of sundry obligations by Henry or Harry J. Seymour Rose+.'. 33d, said obligations being those of the 14d. - 16d - 17d - 18d. - 32d and 33d. degrees of the A.'.A.'. Scottish Rite, as set forth in the Ritual of the degrees.

The charge and specifications were read in the presence of the Gr.'. Commander, and the Inspectors General present.

Ill.'. Bro.'. Henry C. Banks, Rose+.'. 33d., moved that the charge and specifications be referred to a Commission, which was carried, and the Gr.'. Commander announced

Ill.'. Bros.'. Henry C. Banks, 33.d, John Innes, 33d., Hopkins Thompson, 33d. said commission for the trial.

At an adjourned session of the Sup.'. Council for the Northern Jurisdiction of the U. S., held December 14, 1865, the Commission rendered the following report:

Ill.'. Bro.'. Banks, chairman of the commission appointed to investigate certain charges and specifications presented to this Supreme Council against Harry J. Seymour, a past officer of this Supreme Council, reported that they had carefully examined the said charges and specifications, and the proofs thereof; that the aforesaid Harry J. Seymour had been duly notified to attend the meetings of the commission; had been served with a copy of the charges and specifications; that in all cases he had refused or neglected to pay any attention to such notices; and that your commission have arrived at the conclusion that the charges and specifications have been fully sustained, and offer the following resolution:

Resolved, " That the said Harry J. Seymour be, and he is hereby, expelled from all the rights and privileges of Masonry in every branch of the A.'.A.'. Scottish Rite."

Signed, HENRY C. BANKS, 33d, JOHN INNES, 33d, HOPKINS THOMPSON, 33d,

On motion the report was received, and the resolution unanimously adopted, the members voting "viva voce" by roll-call, beginning with the Junior Member.

A true copy from the records,
Attest: DANIEL SICKELS, 33d [GREAT SEAL] Gr.'.Sec.'.Gen.'.H. E.

A committee was appointed to take into consideration the propriety of resuming the old name, viz.: the Supreme Council of the Northern Jurisdiction of the United States of America "in lieu of the one at present adopted." Also it was resolved "that the Grand Commander appoint one or more delegates to repair to Charleston, South Carolina, at the meeting of the Southern Supreme Council." The report of the committee was unanimously adopted in favor of resuming the old name of the "Supreme Council of the Northern Jurisdiction of the United States." Thus it appears that this Supreme Council, composed of the most distinguished Masons among the old members of the two councils, fully recognized the Supreme Council of the Southern Jurisdiction.

Brothers Paige and McClenachan had visited the council at Charleston and an oral report was made to the Supreme Council, December 14, 1865, but it does not appear on record. Hays resigned his office of Grand Commander, and Robinson was elected. It is generally inferred that the Southern Supreme Council did not agree that they would enter into recognition with a council whose chief officer was not considered a regular member of the Scottish Rite, and had denied the regularity of the union, and Raymond being dead, Robinson was his successor. As above shown, the election of Robinson followed, so that both by election and succession his title would be perfect. The record says: "A majority of all the officers and active members of the Supreme Council were present." Lucius R. Paige was appointed to visit the Southern Supreme Council at their meeting held April 16, 1866.

At the meeting of the council held in New York June 5, 1866, in the address of Robinson, Grand Commander, he stated that the Raymond Council was forced into the union with the Hays Council for self-preservation, and referred to the Brethren the question of securing friendly relations with the Southern Supreme Council.

At the Southern Supreme Council meeting held April 6, 1866, the Grand Commander entered at some length upon the occurrences in the Northern Jurisdiction, which was placed in the hands of a committee, whose report was in consonance with the views of the Grand Commander.

The report of the committee was to the following effect, namely, that Robinson had been duly appointed Lieutenant Grand Commander by Raymond before the deposition of the latter; and hence if Raymond had been legally deposed, Robinson, on his depositions would naturally succeed him as Grand Commander, and if Raymond had not been legally deposed, still Robinson, now that Raymond was dead, would be his legitimate successor. The report added that the only legitimate members of the council at the time, after the death of Hubbard, were Moore, Case, Young, and Starkweather, that both of the factions had acted in a manner that was illegal and neither of them could be recognized. This decision did not find general acceptance and was challenged on the allegation that the assumption that the Northern Supreme Council could have only nine members was erroneous in point of law. Whether this assumption by the committee was or was not erroneous is a matter of no moment at this time, as it is generally admitted that the Northern Supreme Council had the right to increase at pleasure the number of its active members.

The Northern Supreme Council, upon a summons from the Grand Commander, Robinson, met in Boston December 11, 1866. Moore, Case, Starkweather, and Young, although included in the summons, did not appear, and Robinson declared their seats vacant; thereupon, being himself as the only member, he then proceeded to fill the vacancies according to the provisions of the Constitution of 1786. There were then present twelve of the active and ten of the honorary members of the united council. The Grand Commander said that he was acting "with the unanimous consent of every member of that council."

The legal effect of these proceedings was a reorganization of the United Council, just as if the officers and members had elected themselves again. In form, no doubt, there was a dissolution of the United Council, and the organization of a new council, but the substance was as stated above. All members had the same status, no new oath was required, everyone was recognized as Grand Inspector-General, all the acts of the United Council were confirmed, and its actions of every kind recognized as still in full force. In every way the proceedings were nothing more or less than a formal reorganization of an existing body in deference to the requirements of the Southern Supreme Council. But although the action of the committee was intended to meet the wishes of the Southern Supreme Council, it did not satisfy the latter body, which desired to effect a perfect union, and had hoped to see the five members whom it had decided to be active members uniting in the action to be taken. The position of the New York Council was therefore still in doubt. In December, 1866, it published a full report of its proceedings; and it had already adopted a resolution, with a view to securing a union with the Boston Council, which was a copy of the one previously adopted with the same view to union, by the Boston body.

The committees appointed were as follows: Boston Council, Evans, of New York, Woodbury, of Massachusetts, Drummond, of Maine, Ely, of Ohio, Foss, of Illinois, Harmon G. Reynolds, of Illinois, an Honorary Member, and later Gardner, of Massachusetts. New York Council, Lewis Paige, McClenachan, and Sickles, of New York, Paige, of Massachusetts, Palmer, of Wisconsin, and Barrett, of New Hampshire.

These two committees met in May, 1867, a short time before the annual session of the Boston Council. There was considerable discussion as to the details of the union, although the general terms were soon settled. Local interests as well as personal considerations created such difficulties that at one moment it seemed as if the negotiations would have to be broken off; indeed so hopeless was the outlook that several members left their seats, prepared to quit the room. Then, to quote Drummond's account, "a brother invited all to 'break bread together,' and insisted that all should accept the invitation." Before they returned to the committee-room everything had been satisfactorily arranged. The report was signed by all the members of the two committees, and adopted by the unanimous vote of each body, and the approval of the honorary members. The two councils met as equals, and all their previous actions were held to be valid, "except expulsions on account of former differences," which were rescinded. Each council consisted of twenty eight active members, the New York Council consenting to the admission of Charles Levi Woodbury, of Massachusetts, "in recognition of his services in bringing about the union."

The two bodies by a concurrent vote met as one council. The two great commanders, Killian H. van Rensselaer, of the New York, and John L. Lewis, of the Boston Council, then conducted the Grand Commander elect of the united body to the altar, and administered to him the oath of fealty in the presence of the members of the Supreme Council. In his turn the Grand Commander administered the oath to all the members present. Other officers were then elected and installed, and a constitution was adopted, and the Northern Supreme Council was fully organized.

Until 1872 harmony prevailed in the Northern Jurisdiction. In that year H. J. Seymour, who had been expelled in 186_, put forward a claim that Hays, when Grand Commander of the "rump Council" of the Cerneanites, had given him a patent empowering him to create 33d Degree Masons and to institute a Supreme Council. He had previously, however, authorized an application to Grand Commander Drummond to be reinstated in all his rights as a member of the Supreme Council, on condition of his surrendering all his papers to the Supreme Council. It was after the rejection of this application that Seymour began his active work, and the success of his efforts, limited as it was, encouraged others who had been members of the old Hays Council, before the union with the Northern Council, to start an annexation, styled "Cernean Supreme Council revived." These men, Hopkins Thompson, Robert Folger and others, had been members of the United Council reorganized in 1867 and had remained therein till 1881, and now set the claim that in December, 1866, the Union Council was, and that all the members were, released from their allegiance to it. They did not deny that they had taken the oath of fealty to the reorganized United Council, and had been loyal members for fourteen years, but they pleaded that their conduct arose from their ignorance of the proceedings of the council in 1866, and therefore they claimed to be a revival of the old Hays Council. As such they claimed also jurisdiction over the Southern territory, a claim which Thompson and Folger and others had unanimously surrendered in 1867. They deny also the loyalty of the Southern Supreme Council, which is everywhere accepted as the "Mother Council of the World," and the source from which came the 33d and last degree.

No regular Supreme Council has ever been acknowledged as either the Cernean Supreme Council revived or the Seymour association.

GREEN DRAGON TAVERN
Boston, Mass

CHAPTER IV

ROYAL ORDER OF SCOTLAND

SCOTLAND is a country which possesses a romantic history, and is rich in legendary lore, and both romance and legend are found in the story of the ROYAL ORDER OF SCOTLAND, the most popular of the added degrees worked by the Craft. It was difficult to obtain any reliable information as to its true history till D. Murray Lyon, Grand Secretary of Scotland, in his History of the Lodge of Edinburgh, gave, in 1873, a sketch of the order. It embraces two degrees, one the "Heredom of Kilwinning," which, according to one fable, was founded in the time of David I. of Scotland; the other, "The Rosy Cross," which, according to another fable, was instituted by King Robert Bruce as a reward for the aid given to him by some Templars who fought on his side at Bannockburn. As the Order of the Templars had been suppressed by Papal Bulls in 1312, some late members may have been present in Bruce's army in 1314, but we must always remember that, to quote Lyon's remark, "the fabulous stories about the early origin and royal patronage of the Royal Order must be taken for what they are worth, which, to those who value accuracy, means notating." The fable that the Hautes Grades had their source in the "Mother Lodge, Kilwinning, is totally erroneous and based on ignorance or fraud, for that ancient lodge, as is shown by its records, never warranted or worked any degrees beyond the well-known " three degrees." It is true that the "Mother Kilwinning" did, in 1779, grant to some Masons in Dublin authority to form a regular lodge or society, and that the lodge so formed assumed the title of "High Knights Templars of Ireland, Kilwinning Lodge;" but all the evidence collected by Lyon and the Masonic historian, W.J. Hughan, proves that the Mother Kilwinning never claimed any authority beyond the three degrees, and is neither more nor less than a regular

Masonic lodge, and that the ceremony was unknown prior to the last century. In fact, when the Dublin Brethren, after conferring, in 1782, Royal Arch, Knight Templar, and Rose Croix degrees, petitioned the Mother Lodge for documents to establish beyond doubt the "authority and regularity of their warrant as High Knights Templars," the request was never granted, because impossible. Moreover, the Grand Lodge of Scotland, instituted in 1736, never officially countenanced any degrees beyond that of Master Mason, and has repeatedly objected to lending any support to ceremonies worked by authority of the Supreme Grand Royal Arch Chapter of Scotland. The Grand Lodge, although toleration has succeeded to opposition, still recognizes only three degrees, the only change being the adoption of the Mark as a portion of the Fellow-Craft degree. As regards the claim that the "Mother Kilwinning" possessed other degrees of Masonry, careful examination shows that it is utterly baseless, and devoid of any corroborative evidence.

There is no authority for the statement of Dr. Arnot that the Royal Order is so called because it is "the highest and most sublime degree in Masonry." He likewise stated that the "Rose Croix was got up by the adherents of Prince Charles Edward Stuart, and only received the name of Rose Croix (a translation of the R.S.Y.C.S. Of the Royal Order) in 1746 or 1747. It was intended to be a Roman Catholic version, or rather perversion, of the Royal Order, this last being deemed for the French too bigoted; in other words, it was too purely religious and Protestant, although it is Christianity which it really promulgates." The Royal Order in France is said to have been established by the Pretender Charles Edward Stuart, and to be sanctioned by the Grand Orient under the title of Rose Croix de Heredom de Kilwinning, and Dr. Arnot states that the Lodge of Constance at Arras preserves the original Charter signed by the Prince in 1747. Bro.

Hughan, in his valuable history, informs us that he possesses a catalogue of books advertised for sale in Paris in 1860, in which the following extract occurs.

"9. Charles Edward Stuart, roy d'Angleterre, de France, d'Ecosse et d'Irlande . . .

voulant temoigner aux macons artesiens combien nous sommes reconnaissant envers eux des preuves de bienfaisance qu'ils nous ont prodigues, etc., creons et erigeons par la presente bulle en la dite ville d'Arras un souv. chap. primatial de R.C.X., sous le titre distinctif d' Ecosse Jacobite, qui serra regi par les chevaliers Lagneau, de Robespierre, avocats. An de l'incarnation 5745."

A note is appended that "Le document authentique, sur VELIN, est revetu du grand sceau, de sept timbres et d'un grand nombre de signatures. C'est l'expedition originale pour le chapitre metropolitan de Paris."

The date, 5745, on this authentic document must be wrong, as that year, the era of the Incarnation, is still some four thousand years away, and if it is an error for Anno Mundi, it may be remarked that Charles Edward Stuart did not succeed to the empty titles enumerated above till the death of his father in 1766. All trace, however, of these documents escaped the research of such a diligent inquirer as Bro. Hughan, who comes to the conclusion that it is an error to connect the Royal Order with the Rose Croix, as the ceremonies differ essentially, the former possessing a very peculiar and quaintly rhythmic ritual.

With regard to the name Heredom of Kilwinning, many derivations of the word have been given. Some give it a Greek origin and interpret it as Holy House, others go to the Hebrew, and, as it is plural in form, translate it by "Rulers," others derive it from "Heroden, a mountain in Scotland," without assigning any reason; Bro. Hughan takes the safe course of concluding that as the rituals of both degrees do not reveal the secret, the subject can not be definitely decided one way or another. The word occurs under the form Harodim as well as Heredom, the latter seeming to be a Saxon term of the same form as Kingdom, which might be represented in modern German by Herrthum or Heerthum.

The earliest records, strangely enough, relate to England, not to Scotland, as may be seen from the following list of regular chapoters, according to seniority:

Decree of Seniority.
List, etc.
Date.

1. Grand Lodge at the Thistle and Crown, Chandos Street. . Time Immemorial.
2. Grand Chapter at the Thistle and Crown, Chandos Street.
" 3. Coach and Horses, Welbeck Street
" 4. White Boar's Head, Exeter Road
" 5. Golden Horse Shoe, in Cannon Street, Southwark
December 11, 1743.
6. The Griffin, in Deptford, in Kent
December 20, 1774;

7. Grand Chapter at The Hague, empowered to act as Grand Lodge July 22, 1750.

8. October 12, 1752

9. (1) Grand Chapter at Rouen in Normandy, empowered to act as a Grand Lodge May 1, 1782.

10. (2) Choix A Paris October 4, 1786.

11. (3) Strasburg January 4, 1787.

12. (4) L'Union Lavall January 4, 1787.

13. (5) October 4, 1787.

14. (6) Grand Lodge, Chambery April 4, 1788.

15. (7) Grand Chapter at Chambery in Saxony, empowered to act as a Grand Lodge in the Dominion of King of Sardinia April 4, 1788.

16. (8) At Martinique (?) July 4, __

17. (9) At St. Domingo July 4, __

18. (10) At Brest July 4, __

Here we find in London a Grand Lodge and a Grand Chapter, evidently the governing body of the order; two other subordinate bodies also described as "immemorial." and two, Nos. 5 and 6, of an earlier date than the Scottish Grand Ledge of Edinburgh which was originally No. 7 on the above list, the Grand Chapter at The Hague. The record-book gotten up for "The Brethren of H.R.D.M., belonging to the Hague," is stated to belong to the Grand Chapter termed the "Grand Lodge of the Royal Order at Edinburgh constituted July 22, 1750." Other records show that the Royal Order of Scotland (in England) existed much earlier than any of the other degrees in the United Kingdom except the "first three." The Royal Arch is alluded to in print in 1744, but is not again mentioned till 1752, and the minutes do not begin till ten years later. In both, the evidence of the existence and activity of the Royal Order during the early part of the last century gives it a position superior to ail additional degrees, and thus it can claim a very respectable antiquity. The notion that it was fabricated by the Chevalier Ramsey has been perfectly refuted by Bro. Gould in his history, and may be dismissed from consideration. Bro. Lyon seems to incline to the opinion that it is not of Scotch origin, alleging the fact that certain privileges were allowed to No. 7 in the list of chapters "on an acknowledgment once a year to the Grand Lodge from whom it derived its title at a quarterly Grand Lodge meeting which is always held at London on the fifth Sunday in the months having so many," and arguing therefrom that a body of Scotch origin would not so far desert its religious principles as to hold constitutional meetings on the Sunday. There is evidence, however, that in England "Masters' " lodges did meet on Sunday. To sum up the whole matter in the words of Brother Hughan, "we cannot get farther back than the Grand Lodge and Grand Chapter in London with three subordinates of 'time immemorial antiquity (so called), and the first dated constitution of December 11, 1743."

With regard to the first offshoot of the London Grand Lodge (No. 7 in the list of chapters given above), doubts arose respecting the meaning of the contraction is Prov." in the signature of the Charter constituting the new lodge. Scotland had for a long series of years been in very close relation with the United Provinces of the Netherlands. In 1444 a contract was made between the royal burghers of Scotland and the latter power by which Scotch traders were freed from several duties and governed by the law of Scotland. Among the Scots residing in Holland at the beginning of the 18th century was William Mitchell, a teacher of languages. It is stated that he had been admitted to the Royal Order in France in 1749, and in London in 1750. In this latter year Mitchell and a Brother, Jonas Kluck, of the Netherlands, presented a petition to the Pro. G. M. in South Britain, asking the London Grand Lodge for authority to enable them and other residents at The Hague to found a Prov. Grand Lodge there. The petition was duly granted, and Brother William Mitchell was appointed Prov. G. M., and the Prov. Grand Lodge was duly constituted at London, July 22, 1750. The official register is as follows:

"I did this day attend at the house of Brother Louis, S.N.C.R.T.Y., the sign of the Golden Horse Shoe, in Cannon Street, in Southwark, and did then and there constitute the following brethren residing at The Hague into a regular Chapter in full form, and did constitute and appoint our Right Worshipful and highly honored Brother William M itchell, known and distinguished among the Brethren of the Order by the sublime title and characteristic F.D.L.T.Y., and Knight of the R.Y.C.S., etc., T.R.S.T.A., by delivering the patent, etc., in due form, as usual, for the constitution of Chapters in foreign parts, and did, by virtue of my authority, exchange his characteristic, etc., for that of R.L.F."

The place mentioned, the Golden Horse Shoe, was the house where the No. 5 chapters and lodges were accustomed to assemble. The seal on the diploma appointing Brother Mitchell Prov. G. M. has been destroyed, but that on the Charter of the Prov. Grand Lodge and Chapter exists. The design represents a bridge of five arches, and above it is displayed the letter Z. and recalls to mind the bridge with the letters L.O.P., well known to members of the 16th Degree of the Ancient and Accepted Rite." The difficulty, as we have said, is connected with the signature. The presiding officer signed by his characteristic, and as may be seen in the fac-simile in Lyon's history the words " Provl. Grad. Masr." stand above, and the words "In. So. B." below, the seal. Does the contraction Provl. mean "Provincial" or "Provisional?" If the former meaning is assigned to it, it is difficult to see how it could be applied to the President of the original Grand Lodge and Grand Chapter, and therefore it is safer to assume that it means "Provisional" and that the President for the time being was Grand Master pro tempore.

The Royal Order, it may here be added, has always been and still is Christian in character, and the following prayer resembles, in its opening lines, the Old Charges of the Freemasons of the 16th century before they were changed and adopted as the Universal Freemasonry.

"The might of the Blessed Father of Heaven, the wisdom of His Glorious Son, and the fellowship of the Holy Ghost, being the glorious and undivided Trinity, three persons in one God, be with us at this our beginning, and so guide and govern our actions in this life, that at the final conflagration, when the world, and all things therein, shall be destroyed, we may be received with joy and gladness into eternal happiness, in that Glorious, Everlasting, Heavenly Kingdom, which shall never have an end."

The regular minutes of the Royal Order at Edinburgh date from October 31, 1766.

Down to 1763 the register contains only fifteen names, including Brother Mitchell, but between that date and the commencement of the regular minutes fifty were admitted, and it is recorded in the minutes of July 28, 1769, that "after much trouble and a great deal of expense they had been able to revive and establish the Ancient Order of Scots Masonry in the metropolis of their native country, which would be attested by several members of the Honorable Council." In the same year by permission of the Provost and Baillies of the city, a room was fitted up at the expense of the Grand Lodge, in a "centrical" situation. From the commencement of those regular minutes the sequence of the high officials can be traced. Down to July 4, 1776, Brother William Mitchell was the Grand Master or Governor of the "Royal Order." He was succeeded by Brother Jas. "Secresy" Kerr. He resigned in 1776, and was succeeded by Brother William "Honor"

Baillie, Advocate (afterward Lord Polkemmet). When he resigned in 1778, Brother William Charles "Eloquence" Little, Advocate, succeeded him. The chair of Deputy Grand Master was filled in 1786 by Brother William "Worship" Mason, who was admitted to the degree at Edinburgh A.D. 1754. When he resigned in 1789 there was elected Dr. Thomas "Activity" Hay, who died in 1816. In 1805 he was Grand Master, but there does not appear to have been any minutes recorded from that date to 1813.

During the period from 1770 to 1780 the office of Deputy Grand Master was filled by General Oughton, Brother Little, the Earl of Leven, and Lord Westhall. Of the four of these high officials, three were Grand Masters of Scotland, showing that at this period the Craft showed great favor to the Royal Order. But as may be seen from the fact that no minutes were made between 1805 and 1813, the order was becoming dormant, and it continued so in Scotland till the revival in 1839.

Abroad, the Royal Order spread and flourished. In Brother Hughan's catalogue of books mentioned in the preceding page, there is the entry: "No. 945, of the year 1808, is entitled

"Tableau general des officiers et membres, composant le R. chapitre du grand et sublime ordre de H-d-m de Kilwinning, sous le titre distinctif du Chozx, constitute par la grande loge de l'ordre seante a Edinbourg, le 4 Octobre, 1786. Sous les auspices de Mgr. le Prince de Cambaceres, grand maltre d'honneur en France."

Nos. 946 and 953 contain "tableaux" of the officers of the foregoing, of November 30, 1808, and A.D. 1810, the latter having another list "du meme ordre seant a Rouen," 1810, in the same volume.

Prince Cambaceres, Arch Chancellor of the French Empire, was succeeded in his office of Provincial Grand Master by the head of the Ducal house of Choiseul.

The above-mentioned Charter, for the Chapter de Choix, from the Grand Lodge of Edinburgh in 1786, was addressed to Nicholas Chadouille, Avocat en Parlament, and other Brethren. A few months previously a Charter dated Edinburgh, May 1, 1786, had established a Provincial Grand Lodge of Heredom of Kilwinning, constituting John Matthews, a merchant of Rouen, Provincial Chief, with powers to disseminate the order.

Both these documents are signed by William Charles Little, Deputy Grand Master, William Mason, and William Gibb. To commemorate the event the Chapter du Choix struck a medal which is engraved in the Tresor Numismatique Napoldon. It represents between a draw-bridge open, sinister and a ladder dexter, a tower enbattled supporting a pillar on which is an open book. On the front of the tower are two square stones, one exhibiting the square and compasses, the other the letter R. The medal is inscribed with the following legend:

Obverse, L ORDRE DE H-D-M. INTRODUIT EN FR. PAR J. MATHEUS, G. M. P., 1786.

"Reverse, in eleven lines, (1) T-R-S-T-A. N. CHADOUILLE, 1786. (2) T-R-S-T-A. L.T.

DORBAN, 1789. (3) T-R-S-T-A.

A.C. DURIN, 1806. (4) T-R-S-T-A. C. A. THORY, 1807. DEPUTE T-R-S-T-A. J. P. ROUYER.

In exergue, in three lines, the last curving, CHAP.'. DE H-D-M. Du CHOIX A PARIS, 1809, JALEY FECIT L.'. A-P-HT-N."

Jaley being the artist's name. The Medal is of copper.

A short time after the establishment of the order in France, a Provincial Grand Master was appointed for Spain, Mr. James Gordon, a merchant of Xeres de la Frontera, whose commission was signed by Deputy Grand Master Dr. Thomas Hay, and Messrs.

Charles Moor and John Brown. The Provincial Grand Lodge in France had jurisdiction over twenty-six Chapters of Heredom, including some in Belgium and Italy, but as fourteen of these chapters were not ratified by the Grand Lodge of Edinburgh from January 10, 1809, to October 4, 1811, they may have been irregular.

Coming down to our own times, we find that the following Provincial Grand Lodges and Chapters have been authorized during the last half century. Those in italics are dormant.

The Netherlands, at Amsterdam
July 4, 1843.
Eastern Provinces, at Calcutta, India
July 4,
1845.
North of France
1847.
Sweden and Norway
Jan. 5,
1852.
Sardinia
? New Brunswick, at St. John
? Province of Quebec
? Glasgow and Neighboring Counties or Isles
Jan. 4, 1859.
London (and "Royal Bruce" Chapter)

1872.
Western India, at Bombay
? China, at Shanghai
? United States, at Washington, D. C.
Oct. 4, 1877.
Lancashire and Cheshire, at Manchester
? Aberdeen
? County of Yorkshire, at York
1886.
South-east Africa, at Durban ?

ROYAL ORDER IN THE UNITED STATES.

As early as 1752 a chapter was formed in Virginia, but seems soon to have ceased all activity. We must come down to the year 1877 for the foundation of the Provincial Grand Lodge in the United States. The Warrant signed at Edinburgh October 4, 1877, is as follows:

CHARTER FOR ROYAL ORDER IN THE UNITED STATES. IN THE NAME OF THE HOLY AND UNDIVIDED TRINITY.

We, Sir John Whyte, W. D. M., President of the Judges and Council of the Great S.N.D.R.M.: Warder of the T.W.R. of R.F.R.S.M.N.T.: Deputy Grand Master and Governor of the High and Honourable Orders of H.R.M. of K.L.W.N.G. and the R.S.Y.C.S.: Sir Alexander, S.T.N.T.H., Senior Grand Warden, Sir William, B.T.Y., Junior Grand Warden, and the Remanent Knights Companions of the Royal Order of R.S.Y.C.S. in Grand Lodge assembled - {SEAL} {R.S.Y.C.S.} TO Sir Albert V.G.R. (Pike), Knight of the Order of the R.S.Y.C.S., send greeting in God Everlasting.

By virtue of the authority vested in US from time immemorial WE do hereby grant unto you and the rest of the Right Worthy and Worshipful Brethren of the Royal Order of H.R.M. and of the R.S.Y.C.S. in the United States of America, full power, warrant and authority to hold a Chapter of the order of H.R.M. in WASHINTON, or elsewhere within the United States of America, so long as you and they shall behave becometh as Worthy Brethren of the said Order, or until the powers hereby conferred shall be withdrawn, which the Grand Lodge of our Order reserves full power and authority to do when they consider proper, with full power to you to remove the same from place to place, but always within the United States of America, as occasion shall offer for the good and glory of the Order, you and they conforming to the laws and regulations of the Grand Lodge transmitted to you now or afterwards, and we do hereby appoint you T.R.S.T.A. of the said Chapter and grant you full power, warrant and authority to appoint proper officers to assist you therein, viz.: a Deputy T.R.S.T.A., a Senior Guardian, a Junior Guardian, a Secretary, a Treasurer, a Marischal, a Deputy Marischal, and a Guarder, who shall act as Examiner and Introducer.

AND FURTHER, know you that for the good and promotion of the Order of H.R.M. in general we do hereby empower you to form a PROVINCIAL GRAND LODGE of the said Order, and to nominate, constitute and appoint you, the said Sir Albert V.G.R., to preside and rule over and govern the same and the Brethren thereunto belonging, so long as you shall act conformably to the Laws and Rules of our Grand Lodge, and so long as this Charter and the powers therein conferred shall continue unrecalled, and we do hereby authorize, empower and charge you to take upon yourself, the title of PROVINCIAL GRAND MASTER of the Order of H.R.M. for the United States of America, being the Province hereby placed under your superintendence; and we do hereby grant you full power, warrant and authority to appoint proper officers to assist you in the high office hereby on you conferred, to consist of the following number and denominations: one Deputy Provincial Grand Master, a Senior Provincial Grand Warden, a Junior Provincial Grand Warden, a Provincial Grand Sword-bearer, a Provincial Grand Secretary, a Provincial Grand Treasurer, two Provincial Grand Marischals, a Senior Provincial Grand Steward, and three other Provincial Grand Stewards, and a Provincial Grand Guarder.

AND FURTHER BE IT KNOWN to all and every one of the Brethren that we hereby invest you with full power, warrant and authority to appoint such persons to be your officers as you shall think are most proper and fit for each respective post either in your Chapter or Provincial Grand Lodge, without consulting or asking the consent or approbation of any Brother of the Order whatsoever, unless of your own free will you shall think proper to pay such compliment, which we deem expedient and therefore recommend.

AND FURTHER, we hereby invest you with full power, warrant and authority to depose or displace from his or their offices any officer or officers, who have been guilty of improper conduct or dignity to your Worship, or to fine, mulct or amerce them, or any of them, for the same, without being obliged to bring them to a formal trial, or asking the consent or approbation of the Brethren for so doing, unless you shall of your own free will think proper so to do. But be it also known that if it shall appear to your Provincial Grand Lodge to be for the good of the

Order in your Province that you should relinquish, or restrict your privilege of appointing or displacing your office-bearers, either in your Chapter or Provincial Grand Lodge, or in both, and if you see proper to consent to the same, it shall be in your power so to do, notwithstanding any existing general law of our Grand Lodge appearing to the contrary, and to cause a resolution or law to that effect specifying how and Where the elections are to be in future conducted, to be endorsed upon or annexed to this Charter, and which when signed by you and registered in the Minute Book of your Provincial Grand Lodge, and a copy thereof, certified by your Provincial Grand Secretary, transmitted to and approved by our Grand Lodge, shall thereafter be as good and valid a law, so far as regards your Chapter and Provincial Grand Lodge, as if it had been made by our Grand Lodge of the R.S.Y.C.S.; and being entered in our Record Book shall be irrevocable by you and your successors in office unless by application to and with the approval of our Grand Lodge; it being, however, declared that nothing shall affect your right as Provincial Grand Master or the rights of your successors in office to appoint your or their Deputy.

AND WE FURTHER strictly require of the Brethren in general, your Provincial Grand Officers as well as others, to respect, acknowledge and obey you, the said Sir Albert V.G.R., and pay you due respect as HEAD RULER and GOVERNOR over them and their Chapter or Chapters in your said Province: And we do hereby appoint you to hold quarterly meetings of your Provincial Grand Lodge for regulating the affairs of the Order of H.R.M. in your Province.

AND FURTHER, we hereby empower you and your Chapter to advance to the Royal Order of H.R.M. (on paying a fee not less than two guineas, of which ten shillings and sixpence shall be transmitted to our Grand Lodge), such Master Masons as are companions of the Royal Arch Chapter and as are well-known to you and your Brethren to be worthy of that High Honor, but with this proviso, that you shall not have it in your power within your Provincial Grand Lodge or elsewhere to promote any Brethren of H.R.M. to the Sublime Order of the R.S.Y.C.S., without special authority obtained from our Grand Lodge for that purpose, nor even then, unless on payment of a fee of at least one guinea (of which ten shillings and sixpence shall be transmitted to our Grand Lodge).

AND FURTHER, be it known to you that we prohibit and discharge you and your Provincial Grand Lodge or Chapter from granting any PATENTS or LETTERS OF CONSTITUTION to Chapters, or Diplomas to the Brethren or Knights, under any pretence whatever, all such things being issued by us alone, and diplomas being so issued free of charge, on payment of the fees above mentioned, payable to us on advancement to the Order of H.R.M. and promotion to the Sublime Order of R.S.Y.C.S.

AND FURTHER, be it known to the Brethren in general that it is not, nor can it be, in their power to depose or displace you or your successors in office from the high office hereby on you conferred, except for high or enormous crimes tending to the scandal and detriment of the Order, and not then without bringing you to a regular trial, and an account of the proceedings therein, with the crime and sentence of the Council, being first sent to and approved by our Grand Lodge at Edinburgh.

AND FURTHER, we empower you to relinquish, give up, or resign your said office with the powers and privileges attached thereto as aforesaid, in case you shall think proper or be desirous so to do, to any worthy qualified Knight of the Order of the R.S.Y.C.S., and to no person whatsoever, under that degree, but your successor or successors, in office, before he or they shall exercise any of the powers connected with said office must be approved by our Grand Lodge.

AND FURTHER, be it known to you, that if you or your successors in office are guilty of acting contrary to our will and pleasure or any of the Laws, Rules and Regulations now appointed by us, or which may hereafter be appointed for your observance by authority of our Grand Lodge, from which you hold this Constitution or Charter, These Presents and all power there under shall forthwith cease and determine without any formal revocation on our part, and you and they shall be rendered incapable of holding any Grand Office or authority in the Royal Order, and also be liable to be extruded for contempt and disobedience.

That all companions of the Royal Order admitted in your Provincial Grand Lodge or Chapter may be duly enrolled in our Record Book, we do particularly direct your attention to the Twenty-sixth Article of our Constitution and Laws as revised and approved on Sixth January, one thousand eight hundred and sixty-two.

And for every Authority, Power and Privilege herein above mentioned, this shall be your sufficient Warrant, Patent and Charter.

In testimony whereof, this, our Charter, written by Alexander Blues Wyllie, clerk to our Grand Secretary, is subscribed by JOHN WHYTE-MELVILLE, of Bennochie and Strathkinnes, our Deputy Grand Master and Governor; ALEXANDER HAY, our Senior Grand Warden; WILLIAM MANN, our Junior Grand Warden; GEORGE

MURRAY, our Grand Treasurer, and JOHN BROWN DOUGLAS, our Grand Secretary; all Knights of the R.S.Y.C.S., duly sealed and thereupon approved and issued by our Grand Lodge of the Royal Order, at Edinburgh, this fourth day of October, in the year of our Lord one thousand eight hundred and seventy-seven, and of the Restoration of the Order 564.

J. WHYTE-MELVILLE, W.D.M.
ALEX. HAY, S.T.N.T.H.
W. MANN, B.T.Y.
GEORGE MURRAY, G.T.
J. B. DOUGLAS, G.S.

The "charter members" were thirteen in number, including several well-known and eminent Brethren (whose labors for the Craft and deep interest in its welfare are as familiar to English Masonic students as to those in America), all of whom became members of the Grand Lodge at Edinburgh.

FOUNDERS NAMES, A.D. 1877.
Brother Albert Pike, Washington, D. C
"
John Robin McDaniel, Lynchburg, Va
"
Henry L. Palmer, Milwaukee, Wis
"
Brother Jas. C. Bachelor, New Orleans, La
"
Vincent L. Hurlbut, Chicago, Ill
"
Josiah H. Drummond, Portland, Maine
"
William M. Ireland, Washington, D. C
"
Robert McC. Graham, New York, N. Y
"
Albert G. Mackey, Washington, D. C
"
Enoch Terry Carson, Cincinnati, Ohio
"
Charles Roome, New York, N. Y
"
Charles Eugene Meyer, Philadelphia, Pa
"

Samuel C. Lawrence, Boston, Mass.

The number of members in the order was divided equally between the Southern and Northern Masonic Jurisdictions of the United States; the total number was fixed at one hundred and fifty, with a margin of twenty-five.[135] Election is by ballot, which must be unanimous. At present, September, 1900, there are two hundred and fifty-seven members. There are no by-laws for the regulation of proceedings in the United States except the rules of the order, and the series of standing resolutions.

The Provincial Grand Lodge meets alternately at Washington, in the District of Columbia, and in New York, holding their annual meetings "on the Monday nearest the day fixed for the meetings of the Supreme Council." The only special regalia worn on these occasions are the "star and garter," the aprons and cordons not being obligatory.

The archives of the Provincial Grand Lodge preserve sketches and portraits of each member. Since 1883 the ladies of the Knights Companions have been admitted to their annual gatherings and banquets.

The proceedings on these occasions include an "allocution" delivered by the Provincial Grand Master. The addresses of the first Provincial Grand Master, the late General Albert Pike, have been printed in published proceedings, and from them the following extracts are taken:

Antiquity of the Royal Order. - "I value the Ancient Order, for it is eminently Masonic. It has close kinship with the three degrees of Ancient Craft Masonry. Its quaint old Ritual has throughout the old-fashioned simplicity of the Masonry of the seventeenth century, when it and those degrees were all the Freemasonry that existed in the world. We read it and breathe the air of the old days. After having been long conversant with the elaborate ones of the present day, it is like going from the pomp and show of cities into the forest and prairie, to live among the frank hunters and sturdy husbandmen who have been the builders of the States, to enjoy the long days of October in the woods, and sleep at night under the protecting stars." (October 16, 1882.)

Primary Aim of the Rite. - "We represent, not altogether unworthily, I hope, the intellect and the scholarship of the Freemasonry of the United States: Our Father who is in Heaven has given us the opportunity to serve Masonry worthily, and make it the debtor of the Royal Order, by leading the Masons of the 'Blue' Lodges to the living

---

[135] Several years ago the Constitution was changed and the number is no longer limited

springs of truth, making known to them the true meaning and profound significance of their most ancient symbols, and teaching them to set a higher value upon their Freemasonry, and to elevate it, in the estimation of the world." (September 24, 1883.)

"To see united into a Provincial Grand Lodge of our old and venerable Order a certain limited number of good men and Masons, residing in all our States and Territories, between whom the new ties of a more perfect Brotherhood might be created, and year by year grow stronger and more enduring." (October 20, 1884.)

Historical Bases of the Order. - "It was established, our Ritual declares, 'to correct the errors and reform the abuses which had crept in among the three degrees of St. John's Masonry.' It is ' for the preservation in its purity of St. John's Masonry.' One who comes to seek admission here declares that he is 'a Mason from a Lodge dedicated to St. John;' and he comes to seek a word which was lost, and which by our assistance he hopes to find.

"The Royal Order has also the early symbolism of the 'Blue' degrees, and not that borrowed from the Alchemical and Hermetic books. The column of the Tower of Refreshment has a square base of pedestal, intended to be a cube or perfect ashlar.

The shaft of the column has nine windows looking East, one for each flight of seven (7) steps. On the column is a triangular entablature; on this a book and under the letters upon its face a square, a level, and a plumb rule; over these a pair of compasses extended to a right angle. The stairway has three landing-places and the lowest flight of stairs is of seven steps, the second of five, and the 'apex' of three."

"It was an innovation to make the possession of the Degree of the Royal Arch a necessary qualification for admission into the Order; for it was at first open to Master Masons." (October 15, 1888.)

The present Provincial Grand Master is Brother Josiah H. Drummond, of Maine; nominated to succeed General Albert Pike. The Deputy Provincial Grand Master is Thomas H. Caswell of California.

The remaining officers duly appointed forming the tableau to date are:

Prov. Senior Grand Warden - George M. Moulton, of Illinois.
Prov. Junior Grand Warden - Charles H. Fisk, of Kentucky.
Prov. Grand Secretary - W. Oscar Roome, of District of Columbia.
Prov. Grand Treasurer - Thomas J. Shyrock, of Maryland.
Prov. Grand Sword Bearer - F. M. Highley, of Pennsylvania.
Prov. Grand Banner Bearer - Nicholas Coulson, of Michigan.

Prov. Grand Chaplain - Rev. M. Carmichael, of Virginia.

Prov. First Grand Marischal - G. E. Corson, of District of Columbia.

Prov. Second Grand Marischal - J. H. Olcott, of District of Columbia.

Prov. Grand Guarder - James Hays Trimble, of District of Columbia.

Prov. Grand Stewards - Allison Nailor, Jr., of District of Columbia; William Bromwell Melish, of Ohio; Harrison Dingman; H. H. Williams, of Hawaii.

The constitutions and laws of the Royal Order, as drawn up in London at the foundation of the order in 1742, remained unchanged till January 5, 1767. By one of these laws, Rule 19, fees are to be paid to the Grand Lodge of Edinburgh by members in England, and the Constitution declares that the King of Scotland is Perpetual Grand Master, and therefor not an elective officer.

By the statutes, the Grand Lodge of R.S.Y.C.S. and Grand Chapter of H.R.M. can only be held in Scotland, and the former reserves to itself the right to promote to the honor of Knighthood of the R.S.Y.C.S., but usually delegates the power to that effect to the Provincial Grand Masters, by personal patents.

The Grand Lodge officers are similar to those already noted for the Provincial Grand Lodge, only the Brother who rules that body, until a king of Scotland (called of Great Britain and Ireland) is able to become Grand Master, is termed "Deputy Grand Master and Governor," a Deputy Governor being also appointed, all having corresponding rank in the Grand Chapter of H.D.M. The D.G.M. (and Governor) and Deputy Governor of the Grand Lodge are ex-officiis Warder and Deputy Grand Warder of the T.W.R. of R.F.R.S.M.N.T., and the Provincial Grand Master enjoys a similar status in his Province; as also T.R.S.T.A. of his own chapter.

The 4th of July is election-day for the Grand Officers and also for subordinate chapters out of Scotland, or first following lawful day, if the 4th shall be a Saturday or Sunday.

The other stated meetings of Grand Lodge and Provincial Grand Lodges are October 4th, January 4th, and April 4th, with the same exceptions.

Members acting as Grand Officers pro fem. have power to sign diplomas, charters, patents, etc. A copy of a certificate issued to William James Hughan, the historian, under the seal of the Royal Order at Edinburgh, dated March 6, 1867, is annexed:

COPY OF THE ROYAL ORDER CERTIFICATE, A.O. 553.
IN THE NAME OF THE HOLY AND UNDIVIDED TRINITY.

We, Sir John Whyte, W.D.M., President of the Judges and Council of the Great S.N.D.R.M., and Warder of the T.W.R. of R.F.R.S.M.N.T., Deputy Grand Master and Governor of the High and Honourable Order of H.R.M. of K.L.W.N.G. and the R.S.Y.C.S.; Sir Alexander, S.T.N.T.H., Senior Grand Warden, and Sir William, B.T.Y., Junior Grand Warden, and the remanent Knights Companions of the ROYAL ORDER of the R.S.Y.C.S. in Grand Lodge assembled.

We do hereby certify and declare that our Trusty and well Beloved Brother William James Hughan, {L.S.} GREENnMaster Mason of the Lodge Number 594, holding of the Grand Lodge of England, and Companion Royal Arch Chapter, Number 50 in Scotland, whose signature is on the margin, having been advanced to the Order of H.R.M. of K.L.W.N.G. at Glasgow, in the Chapter of the Provincial Grand Master for the County of Lanark, and others, on the twenty-eighth day of February, one thousand and eight hundred and sixty-seven, by the characteristic of Geometry, and promoted on the said twenty-fifth day of February, one thousand eight hundred and sixty-seven, to the Honourable Order of the R.S.Y.C.S. in the Provincial Grand Lodge for the County of Lanark, and others, has been recorded in the Books of our Grand Lodge here, and therefore we recommend him as a lawful member of the ROYAL ORDER, Brother of H.R.M. and Knight of the R.S.Y.C.S., to all Knights and Brethren of the Order wherever found and established.

Given under our hands and seals of the Royal Order at Edinbzgrgh, this sixth day of March, A.D. One thousand eight hundred and sixty-seven, and of the Restoration of the Order 553.

Gustavus K. Flindt, P.T.W.D.M. T.D. Porteous, Prov. Grand Sy. David Sutherland, P.T., S.T.N.F.H. J. B. Douglas, Grand Sec'y, G. L. Brodie, P.T., B.T.Y.

The minimum fee for the H.D.M. and Knighthood is three guineas; subject in all cases to the approval of the presiding officer as respects promotion to the " R.S.Y.C.S." Conviction of crime by any court of justice involves permanent extrusion.

On the 4th of April, 1855, the Supreme Council 33d Degree of Scotland, and on the 11th of May following, the Grand Lodge of the Royal Order agreed to a reciprocal treaty, by which only members of the Royal Order can be admitted to the 18th Degree, and all Knights of the Royal Order, provided they are Royal Arch Masons, have special privileges as to fees in joining the A.'.A.'.S.'. Rite.

M. W. Brother John Whyte-Melville was the Deputy Grand Master and Governor for many years, and on his decease was succeeded by the Right Honorable, the Earl of Rosslyn, in 1885, who died September 6, 1890, and was succeeded by _____ The Grand Secretary is the Scottish Masonic historian, Brother D. Murray Lyon.

The Year of the Restoration of the Order" dates from 1314, so that A.D. 1900 or A.L.

4900 would be "Anno Ordinis 576 to St. John the Baptist Day; but after that festival it would be 577. A similar mode had long been followed by the Knights Templars (which, doubtless, refers to De Molay's martyrdom), in relation to the same year, only termed "Anno Caedis," thus suggesting an intimate connection between the two bodies.

TRANSCRIPTION VLTIMO JULY 1599.

The qlk day George Patoun maissoun grenttit & confessit that he had offendit agane the dekin & mrs for placeing of ane cox ane to wirk at ane chymnay heid for tua dayis and ane half day, for the qlk offenss he submittit him self in the dekin & mrs guds willis for qt vnlaw they pless to lay to his charge, and thay having respect to the said Georges humill submissioun & of his estait, they remittit him the said offenss, Providing alwayis that gif ather he [or] ony vther brother comitt the Iyke offenss heirefter that the law sall stryke vpoun thame indiscreta wtout exceptioun of personis. This wes done in prcs of Paull Maissoun dekin, Thoas Weir warden, Thoas Watt, Johne Broun, Henrie Tailzefeir, the said George Patoun, & Adanz Walkar

Ita est Adamus Gibsone norius Paull Maissottn dekin

PART SIX

FREEMASONRY IN OTHER COUNTRIES
FREEMASONRY IN CANADA
BY WILL H. WHYTE, P.G.M\: K.T. OF CANADA

THE history of Freemasonry in British North America, or that part of the continent now better known as the "Dominion of Canada," is a most interesting one. Upon the advent of Confederation, July 1, 1867, local control in each Province for the government of the Masonic Fraternity of the Dominion took a strong hold as a predominant idea, and prevailed. Each Province has now a Grand Lodge, and in order of their organization are as follows: Canada, having jurisdiction only in Ontario, 1855; Nova Scotia, 1866; New Brunswick, 1867; Quebec, 1869; British Columbia, 1871; Manitoba, 1875; Prince Edward Island, 1875; Alberta, 1905; Saskatchewan, 1906. The first marks of the Ancient Craftsman have been found in Nova Scotia. A mineralogical survey in 1827 found on the shore of Goat Island in the Annapolis Basin, partly covered with sand, a slab of rock 2 1/2 X 2 feet, bearing on it those well-known Masonic emblems, "the Square and Compasses," and the date 1606. Who were the Craftsmen, and how the stone came there, must be left to conjecture.

Nova Scotia.

The records of the Craft in Boston, Mass., state that Bro. Henry Price was appointed Provincial Grand Master of New England by Viscount Montague, Grand Master of the Premier Grand Lodge of England (Moderns), and that his authority was subsequently extended to all North America.

On the 13th of November, 1737, Erasmus James Phillips, an officer of the Fortieth Regiment, then stationed at Annapolis Royal, visited Boston and was made a Mason in the "First Lodge in Boston."

This Bro. Phillips was a nephew of Col. Richard Phillips, the first governor of Nova Scotia and the secretary of the governor's council, and evidently obtained an appointment as Deputy from Bro. Price, the Provincial Grand Master at Boston.

The first lodge established in Nova Scotia was at Annapolis and under authority from Boston by the St. Johns Grand Lodge of Massachusetts. Under date 1740 the minutes read:

'The Rt. Worshl Grand Master granted a Deputation at the Petition of sundry Brethren for holding a lodge at Annapolis in Nova Scotia, and appointed the Right Worshipful Erasmus James Phillips, D.G.M., there, who afterward erected a Lodge at Halifax and appointed His Excellency Edward Cornwallis their first Master."

Bro. Phillips, having organized this lodge at Annapolis as stated, later on - on the petition of the Brethren at Halifax in 1750 - granted a Warrant for a lodge and appointed Bro. Edward Cornwallis, the founder of Halifax, 1749, and first governor of Nova Scotia (and an uncle of the Lord Cornwallis who figured in Revolutionary times in the United States), as its first Master. This lodge was instituted at Halifax July 19, 1750.

Bro. Phillips held the position of Provincial Grand Master until 1758, and in the minutes of the First Lodge at Boston in 1739 is entered as Grand Master of Nova Scotia.

In 1756 lodge meetings were held in Halifax, by the Lodge of "Social and Military Virtues," No. 227, Irish Registry, then attached to the Forty-sixth Regiment of Light Infantry. This lodge is now "Antiquity Lodge," No. 1, Montreal, on the Registry of the Grand Lodge of Quebec.

The Grand Lodge of Nova Scotia is in possession of a large amount of valuable and interesting Masonic documents, among them a Charter to form a Provincial Grand Lodge, dated December 27, 1757, from the Grand Lodge of the "Ancients," signed Blesington, Grand Master, and Laurence Dermott, Grand Secretary.

On the 2d day of June, 1784, a Warrant (apparently a renewal of the 1757) was granted by authority of Grand Master Antrim, Deputy Grand Master Laurence Dermott, and Robert Leslie, Grand Secretary. Under this Warrant, a Provincial Grand Lodge was formed on September 24, 1784 - Bro. John George Pyke, Provincial Grand Master. By this Warrant, the officers "together with their lawful assistants, that is to say the regular Masters, Wardens and Past Masters only," were authorized to "nominate, choose, and install their successors upon or near every St. John the Evangelist day forever."

From 1786-1791, His Excellency, John Parr, Governor-in-Chief of Nova Scotia, was Provincial Grand Master, followed by the Hon. Richard Bulkeley, 1791-1800; Duncan Clark, 1800-1; Hon. John Wentworth, LL.D., 1801-10; and John Geo. Pyke, 1810-20. At this time, after thirty-six years, there were thirty-one lodges on the Provincial Registry.

Trouble then arose over a successor to Bro. Pyke and he continued in office another year, followed by John Albro from 1821 to 1829. At this period the number of lodges had been reduced to sixteen. For another forty years this Provincial Grand Lodge continued its work until, after an existence of eighty-five years, its lodges united with the new Grand Lodge of Nova Scotia in 1869.

The subject of an independent Grand Lodge had been agitated for five years, for the Grand Lodges of England, Ireland, and Scotland had lodges chartered under their authority in this Province.

In 1861 a committee was appointed from the Provincial Grand Lodge of Scotland to act in conjunction with a similar committee from the Provincial Grand Lodge of England regarding the practicability of forming a Grand Lodge of Nova Scotia. Upon reference to the parent Grand Lodges, England refused permission. Scotland never answered.

On the 16th January, 1866, a meeting of delegates from all the Scottish lodges was held, twelve out of thirteen being represented. It was decided to call a convention of all the lodges in the Province at Halifax on the 20th February, and at this meeting the Grand Lodge was duly formed and M.W. Bro. W. H. Davies elected Grand Master.

From 1866 to 1869 the Grand Lodge increased to twenty-five lodges. In this latter year, the District Grand Lodge under the English Registry decided to affiliate, as did also the remaining lodge under Scotland. On the 23d June, 1869, the amalgamation took place, the twenty-five English and one Scotch Lodge uniting with the twenty-five Nova Scotia lodges under the designation of "The Grand Lodge of Ancient Free and Accepted Masons of Nova Scotia." The three oldest lodges now working under this jurisdiction are in Halifax and are "St. Andrew's," chartered March 28, 1768, London, Laurence Dermott, Grand Secretary; "St. John's," chartered June 30, 1780, London, and "Virgin" Lodge, February 18, 1782.

1906. Nova Scotia has sixty-six lodges on the roll and a membership of 4,500.

New Brunswick.

The Province of New Brunswick previous to the year 1786 formed a part of Nova Scotia. On March 6, 1784, application was made to John George Pyke, Esq., Provincial Grand Master elect, at Halifax, by Elias Hardy, Master of Lodge 169, for a dispensation to establish a lodge of "Ancient York Masons" at Parr Town. Parr Town, now the City of St. John, was named after His Excellency John Parr, Captain General and Governor-in- Chief, and who had been elected Provincial Grand Master of the "Ancient" Masons of Nova Scotia 1786-91.

On August 22, 1792, a Warrant was granted by the Provincial Grand Lodge at Halifax for Solomons Lodge, No. 22 (now No. 6 on the Registry of New Brunswick), to be located at "St. Anns," now Fredericton, the capital of New Brunswick. On June 7, 1826, J. Albro, Provincial Grand Master at Halifax, appointed Benjamin L. Peters Deputy Grand Master for the city of St. John and the town of St. Andrews in New Brunswick.

On March 10, 1829, a Warrant, No. 52, was made out by the Provincial Grand Lodge at Halifax for Albion, No. 841, St. John. This lodge, formerly also under the English Registry as No. 400, is now No. 1 on the Registry of New Brunswick.

The Act confederating the Provinces into the "Dominion of Canada" came into force July 1, 1867. This new state of political existence brought prominently to the front the Masonic status in each Province, and the formation of an Independent Grand Lodge for the Province of New Brunswick was agitated. On the 16th of August, 1867, a meeting of the Masters and Past Masters in the city of St. John was held and it was resolved to address a circular to every lodge in the Province. On the 10th day of October, 1867, the Grand Lodge of Ancient Free and Accepted Masons of New Brunswick was formed by representatives of fourteen lodges. There were nineteen lodges represented, but the delegates from St. Andrews Lodge, 364 R.S. retired from the convention, while those from Howard, 668 and Zetland, 886 E.R., though favoring the movement, stated they had no authority to vote for a new Grand Lodge. The representatives of two others were not present when the vote was taken. V.W. Bro. Robert T. Clinch, District Grand Master, E.R., was elected Grand Master but declined, as he had not resigned his office under the English Registry. Bro. B. Lester Peters was then unanimously elected Grand Master, the installation taking place on the 22d of January, 1868. During the year 1867- 68 ten lodges holding under the English Registry became of allegiance to the Grand Lodge of New Brunswick, and in September, 1872, St. Andrews Lodge, at Fredericton, also affiliated, rendering the jurisdiction of this Grand

Lodge complete. 1906. There are thirty-five lodges on the roll, with a membership of 2,200.

Quebec.
Although it has been affirmed by French and other writers that a lodge of Freemasons existed in the city of Quebec in the year 1755, no records or other evidences are known to be in existence, and Masonry in the Province only dates its existence from the time of "Wolfe," when the "Lily" flag of the Bourbon was replaced by the "Union Jack" over the citadel of Quebec.

Quebec capitulated in September, 1759, and among the regiments taking part in the capture the following seven held travelling warrants for lodges, as follows: No. 245, I.R., warranted 1754, in the Fifteenth Regiment; No. 35, I.R., warranted 1734, in the Twenty-eighth Regiment; a lodge in the Twenty-eighth, "Louisburg," Boston warranted 1758; No. 205, I.R., warranted 1749, in the Thirty-fifth Regiment; No. 42, E.R.

"Ancient," warranted 1755, in the Fortieth Regiment; No. 192, I.R., warranted 1748, in the Forty-seventh Regiment, and No. 218, I. R., warranted 1750, in the Forty-eighth Regiment. There were likewise lodges in seven or more regiments taking part in the capitulation of Montreal, September 9, 1760, holding under English, Irish, Scotch, and Colonial charters.

The following extracts from a document in possession of the Grand Librarian of England succinctly tell the story of the formation of the first "Lower Canada" Grand Lodge on December 27, 1759, in the city of Quebec.

"In the winter of 1759 the Masters and Wardens of all the Warranted Lodges held in the Regiments garrisoned there, assembled together and unanimously agreed to choose an acting Grand Master to preside over them. Agreeable thereto they made choice of Bro. Guinnett, Lieutenant in the Forty-seventh Regiment, and drew out, signed and sealed, a Warrant empowering him and his successors elected, to congregate them together as a Grand Lodge for the intent before mentioned, they having the Constitution as their chief guide."

"The 24th June, 1760, Brother Simon Fraser, Colonel of the Highland Regiment, was elected to preside over the Lodges, and Brother T. Dunckerley of His Majesty's Ship the 'Vanguard,' who was possessed with a power from the Grand Lodge of England to inspect into the state of the Craft wheresoever he might go, installed Brother Fraser in his high office."

This Provincial Grand Lodge for the "Province of Quebec," annually elected a Grand Master and officers, and was in existence for thirty-two years, 1759-91. Among the Grand Masters following the Hon. Simon Fraser were, Capt. Milborne West, 1761; Lieutenant Turner, 1763; Hon. John Collins, 1765; Sir Guy Carleton (Lord Dorchester), 1786, and Sir John Johnson, Bart., who resided at Montreal, 1788.

According to M.W. Bro. John Hamilton Graham, LL.D., who compiled that valuable work The History of Freemasonry in Quebec, there has been traced some forty lodges holding under or emanating from this Grand Lodge. The first lodges it chartered were in the city of Quebec: "Merchants," No. 1, "St. Andrews," No. 2, "St. Patrick's," No. 3, and Select, No. 0 1759-61. The next warranted was No. 4, St. Peter's, Montreal, instituted 1761, and lapsed about 1792. The next Montreal charter was St. Paul's, No. 10, and of date November 8, 1770, which had an existence up to 1796. Among other lodges warranted was one at Vergennes, Vt., U.S.A., named "Dorchester," and of date May 5, 1791, granted by Sir John Johnson, Bart., Prov. G.M., and still in existence as No. 1, Vermont.

In 1752 the schism occurred in the Grand Lodge of England which caused the formation of a rival Grand Lodge under the cognomen of the "Ancients." The rivalry between these two Grand Lodges was at its height in 1791, when "Prince Edward," grand-father of His Majesty King Edward VII, arrived in Quebec as Colonel of the Seventh Royal Fusiliers, and with the advent of the "Prince" came a new era in Masonry in the Province.

On March 7, 1792, the Grand Lodge of the "Ancients" in England issued a patent deputing Prince Edward "Provincial Grand Master" of "Lower Canada," and on June 22, 1792, His Royal Highness was installed with great eclat, a religious service and procession to the "Recollect Church" (R.C.) Quebec, forming part of the ceremony. In 1799 H.R.H. was created "Duke of Kent," and remained Grand Master until 1813, when he resigned to accept the Grand Mastership of the "Ancients" in England, being succeeded in Quebec by the Hon. Claude Denechau, M.P.P., who filled that important post until 1822. This new Provincial Grand Lodge in a period of over thirty years, 1791- 1823, warranted some twenty-six lodges, five of them still in existence, under the present Grand Lodge of Quebec, viz.: "Dorchester" at St. Johns; "Select Surveyors" now "Prevost," at Dunham; "Nelson," now at St. Armand Station; "Golden Rule," at Stanstead; and "Sussex" now St. Andrews," at Quebec. It also warranted among others "Zion," No. 10, now No. 1 at Detroit, of date September 7, 1794, and St. Paul's, No. 12,

May 1, 1797, which was apparently formed from among some of the late members of St. Paul's, No. 10, under the former Provincial Grand Lodge, and again lapsed as a provincial Lodge about 1824.

April 2, 1823, marked another era in the history of the Craft in the Province of Quebec.

The lodges in Montreal as well as others in the Province forwarded their provincial or Canadian Charters to the "United Grand Lodge of England," and exchanged them for Warrants under that body. They then petitioned said Grand Lodge to establish a Provincial Grand Lodge for Montreal and the Borough of William Henry, now Sorel; and the Grand Lodge across the ocean saw fit to grant the request, and the Hon. William McGillivray was appointed Provincial Grand Master. The lodges in the cities of Quebec and Three Rivers being also formed into another Provincial Grand Lodge under the Hon. Claude Denechau.

On the 5th September, 1826, John Molson, Esq., was installed as Provincial Grand Master at Montreal. In 1836 the Hon. John Molson died, and the Provincial Grand Lodge did not meet again for over ten years.

On May 20, 1846, the Provincial Grand Lodge at Montreal was revived to install the Hon. Peter McGill as Grand Master. In 1849 the Hon. Peter McGill resigned his office and was succeeded by the Hon. William Badgley until his decease in 1888.

In "Quebec," the Hon. Ciaude Denechau, deceased, was succeeded by Thomas Harington, Esq., 1852, and he in turn by James Dean, 1857.

The Provincial Grand Lodge at Quebec finally dissolving in 1870, the members joined the then new "Grand Lodge of Quebec." That of "Montreal and William Henry" with three lodges had no active existence after the formation of the Grand Lodge of Canada, and in the later years of the late Judge Badgley, never met.

A third period of thirty years had thus elapsed when in October, 1855, the representatives of forty-one lodges in Canada West (now Ontario) and thirteen in Canada East (now Quebec) met in Hamilton and formed the "Grand Lodge of Canada," holding jurisdiction over the two Provinces.

From 1855 to 1869 the Grand Lodge of Canada was the controlling Masonic power in the Province of Quebec, but with the birth of the Dominion came also the agitation for separate Grand Lodges. Several meetings were held, and finally, on the 20th October, 1869, the Grand Lodge of Quebec was formed by twenty-eight of the Warranted

Lodges then in the Province, with M.W. Bro. John Hamilton Graham, LL.D., as Grand Master.

A number of the lodges did not at once join in this movement, but gradually were absorbed. Those remaining under the Grand Lodge of Canada (which Grand Lodge vigorously and strenuously opposed the formation of the new Grand Lodge) continued until September 23, 1874, when "Canada" withdrew, and its lodges affiliated with Quebec.

On the 27th of January, 1881, three lodges holding under warrants from Scotland also affiliated, leaving three claiming allegiance to the Grand Lodge of England.

1906. The Grand Lodge of Quebec has now on the roll fifty-eight lodges and a membership of 5,000.

Canada (in Ontario).

The history of the Craft in the Province of Ontario has been exhaustively compiled by Most Wor. Bro. John Ross Robertson in his admirable work, The History of Masonry in Canada. Lodge No. 156 in the Eighth Regiment of Foot appears to have been the first lodge to hold meetings in this Province, at Fort Niagara, about 1755-80. From 1780 to 1792 some ten lodges appear to have worked in what was called "Upper Canada." Some chartered by England, others by the Provincial Grand Lodge at Quebec, among them St. James in the King's Rangers, No. 14, at Cataraqui (Rintrston), 1781; St. John's, No. 15, at Michilimakinac (Michigan), then part of Canada; St. John's, No. 19, at Niagara, and Oswegatchie Lodge, 1786, at Elizabethtown (Brockville).

On March 7, 1792, Bro. William Jarvis was appointed Provincial Grand Master of Upper Canada by the "Ancient" or "Athol" Grand Lodge of England. Bro. Jarvis resided at Newark (Niagara), the then capital of the Province. During his Grand Mastership, 1792 to 1804, twenty warrants for lodges were issued for various parts of the Province.

In 1797 Bro. Jarvis removed from Newark to York (now Toronto), when the capital was transferred to the latter place.

The Brethren at Niagara continued to be active and enthusiastic, and urged Bro. Jarvis to assemble Grand Lodge there, but he refused. This refusal caused much dissatisfaction, and the Brethren of Niagara District met in 1803 and elected Bro. Geo. Forsyth as Provincial Grand Master, and trouble and friction ensued.

In 1817, at Kingston, a Grand Convention was called by the Lodges in the Midland District under R.W. Bro. Ziba M. Phillips. All the lodges attended excepting those in the Niagara District. This convention was held annually during the years 1817, 1818, 1820, 1821, 1822.

After repeated entreaty to England during these years, R. W. Bro. Simon McGillivray came to Canada in September, 1822, with authority from the Duke of Sussex to reorganize the Craft in Upper Canada. The Second Provincial Grand Lodge was thus formed at York in 1822, with R. W. Bro. Simon McGillivray as Provincial Grand Master, and met regularly up to 1830; but the Morgan excitement in the United States also told somewhat on the Fraternity in Canada, and while a number of the lodges remained active, the Provincial Grand Lodge became dormant and remained so until 1845.

In 1845 Masonic enthusiasm once more gained the ascendency, an urgent appeal was sent out, and a Third Provincial Grand Lodge organized in Hamilton with Bro. Sir Allan MacNab Provincial Grand Master of "Canada West," appointed by the Earl of Zetland.

This body was an energetic one, and continued work until 1858.

In 1853 a number of the lodges holding Irish Warrants organized a Grand Lodge, but it was not very successful. They then endeavored to secure the cooperation of the Provincial Grand Lodge in forming a Grand Lodge for Canada, but the Provincial Grand Body declined. But Home Rule and a self-governing body for Canada was the idea uppermost and would not down, and finally on October 10, 1855, a convention of all the lodges in the two Provinces was called at Hamilton and the Grand Lodge of Canada was formed. Forty-one lodges were represented, twenty-eight in Canada West (Ontario) and thirteen in Canada East (Quebec), and M. W. Bro. William Mercer Wilson was elected Grand Master.

In September, 1857, the Provincial Grand Lodge under England met and resolved itself into an independent Grand Lodge under the name of "Ancient Grand Lodge of Canada," but the next year in July, 1858, they united with the Grand Lodge of Canada.

In October, 1869, the majority of the lodges in the Province of Quebec held a convention and decided to form a Grand Lodge for that Province. The Grand Lodge of Canada strenuously opposed this new body, and an edict of suspension covering all the lodges and Brethren taking part was issued. The Grand Lodge of Quebec, however, becoming duly recognized by all the leading Grand Lodges of the world, the Grand Lodge of Canada, in 1874, likewise decided to do the same and withdrew from the Province; all the lodges of her obedience joining the Quebec Grand Body. In 1875 a schism occurred and a number of

Brethren organized a "Grand Lodge of Ontario." This breach was finally healed and the Brethren and lodges became of allegiance to the Grand Lodge of Canada in 1896.

In 1886 the words "in the Province of Ontario" were added to the title of the "Grand Lodge of Canada," owing to the representations of other Grand Lodges that the title did not represent the jurisdiction of that Grand Body.

1906. The Grand Lodge of Canada has now 395 lodges and a membership of 37,628.

British Columbia.

The first lodge established in this Province was Victoria, No. 783, by the Grand Lodge of England, March 19, 1859, and the first chartered by the Grand Lodge of Scotland was Vancouver Lodge in 1862.

In 1871 the Grand Lodge of England had three lodges in the Province, and the Grand Lodge of Scotland six lodges. A convention was held on the 21st day of October, 1871, and the Grand Lodge of British Columbia duly organized. Eight out of the nine lodges in the Province were represented. The Provincial Grand Master of Scotland and the District Grand Master of England both took an active interest in the formation of the new Grand Body, and M.W. Bro. Israel Wood Powell, M. D., was unanimously elected Grand Master.

In 1872 the only lodge not represented at the formation of the Grand Lodge, viz., "Union Lodge" of New Westminster, late 899 E.R., affiliated with twenty-three members.

In 1875 two of the lodges in Nanaimo, "Caledonia" and "Nanaimo," amalgamated under the name of "Ashlar."

In 1878 Victoria, No. 1, and British Columbia, No. 5, of Victoria, united as Victoria Columbia Lodge, and Vancouver and Quadra Lodges, also at Victoria, united as Vancouver Quadra Lodge.

1906. Grand Lodge has now thirty-nine lodges and a membership of 2,859.

CHARLES T. McCLENACHAN

Manitoba.

In 1864 a dispensation was issued over the signature of M.W. Bro. A.T. Pierson, then Grand Master of Masons in Minnesota, and "Northern Light" Lodge was organized at Fort Garry (Winnipeg), with

Bro. Dr. John Schultz, Worshipful Master, A.G.B. Bannatyne, S.W., and Wm. Inkster, J.W.

In 1867 Bro. Bannatyne was elected W.M. and the lodge went out of existence, shortly before the Red River insurrection. At this time, the country was claimed by the "Hon. Hudson Bay Co."; but when the transfer was made to Canada in 1870 and the Red River Settlement, as it was then known, became the Province of Manitoba, the Grand Lodge of Canada assumed jurisdiction and shortly afterward issued Charters to "Prince Rupert's" Lodge, Winnipeg, December, 1870, and Lisgar Lodge, Selkirk.

On May 12, 1875, the three lodges then existing, viz., "is Prince Rupert," "Lisgar" and "Ancient Landmark," held a convention and formed the "Grand Lodge of Manitoba," electing M.W. Bro. the Rev. Dr. W. C. Clarke as Grand Master. Unfortunately he removed from the Province before his year of office expired.

In 1878 the question of Ritual created considerable trouble, and a number of the Brethren endeavored to form another Grand Lodge, but happily peace was restored the following year.

On the 28th July, 1881, a Warrant was ordered issued to "Al Moghreb Al Asku," No. 28, to be opened at Gibraltar, but protests from the Grand Lodges of Scotland and England following, it was shortly afterward transferred to Tangiers in Morocco.

This Grand Lodge held jurisdiction over the Northwest Territories and the Yukon Territory as well as Manitoba until 1905, when the Provinces of Alberta and Saskatchewan were formed, followed by the organization of Grand Lodges for these two new divisions, upon which the Grand Lodge of Manitoba withdrew.

1906. Grand Lodge of Manitoba has now eighty chartered lodges and six U.D., with a membership of 4,410.

Prince Edward Island.

Previous to November, 1798, Prince Edward Island was called St. Johns Island, the name being changed by Imperial Act on that date.

On the 9th October, 1797, St. John's Lodge, now No. 1 on the Registry of that Province, was established by Warrant at Charlottetown by the Grand Lodge of England. The then Lieutenant-Governor, General Edward Fanning, was one of the Charter members. In 1857 Victoria Lodge at Charlottetown was chartered by Scotland.

In 1875 there were seven lodges in this Province working under English Warrants, viz., St. John's, King Hiram, St. George, Alexandra,

Mount Lebanon, and True Brothers, and one under the Scottish Register, "Victoria."

On the 23d day of June, 1875, these eight lodges met and formed the Grand Lodge of Prince Edward Island. The Hon. John Yeo was elected Grand Master and was installed, together with his officers, the following day by M. Wor. Bro. John V. Ellis, Grand Master of New Brunswick.

1906. There are fourteen lodges, with a membership of 635 on the roll.

Alberta.

Previous to October, 1905, the lodges in the "Northwest Territories" of Canada were under the jurisdiction of the Grand Lodge of Manitoba.

The political changes which culminated in the division of these Territories into the Provinces of "Alberta" and "Saskatchewan" on the 1st of September, 1905, brought forward the question of Provincial Autonomy for the Craft; accordingly "Medicine Hat" Lodge, No. 31, took the initiative and requested the Senior Lodge in the Province, "Bow River Lodge," No. 28, to call a convention at Calgary. This convention was held on the 25th day of May, 1905, and arrangements were made for a formal meeting on the 12th day of October, 1905. Seventeen lodges out of eighteen in the jurisdiction were represented by seventy-nine delegates, and the "Grand Lodge of Alberta" was duly formed, with M. W. Bro. Dr. George MacDonald elected as Grand Master. The Most Wor. the Grand Master of Manitoba, M.W. Bro. W.G. Scott, was present at this convention and installed the officers.

1906 Twenty lodges, with a membership of 1,206

Saskatchewan.

The Brethren of the Province of Saskatchewan assembled at Regina on the 10th day of August, 1906, and formally resolved themselves into the "Grand Lodge of Saskatchewan." Twentyfive lodges out of twenty-eight located in the Province were represented. M. W. Bro. H. H. Campkin was elected Grand Master and was installed by M. W. Bro. McKenzie, Grand Master of Manitoba.

Newfoundland.

The Ancient Colony of Newfoundland still remains without the Confederation of the Canadian Provinces.

Masonry in this island dates back to 1746, the first Warrant being granted by the Provincial Grand Lodge at Boston. Bro. J. Lane's list gives six lodges warranted in the eighteenth century The Grand Lodge of the Ancients (England) is credited with four - one in 1774 and three in 1788 - and the Grand Lodge of England (Moderns) with two - one each in 1784 and 1785. Nine others were chartered by the present Grand Lodge of England up to 1881, a number still remaining active.

MEXICO.

WE learn from several writers that about the year 1810 Civil and Military officers of the Monarchy introduced the "Scottish Rite" into Mexico - then the principal colony of Spain. The Grand Lodge of Louisiana after this erected lodges in 1816 and 1817, respectively at Vera Cruz and Campeachy. The Grand Lodge of Pennsylvania also established a lodge in 1824 at Alvarado; subsequently confusion ensued, Masonry and politics being so closely interwoven that any attempt at separate treatment is quite hopeless.

The Escoceses and the Yorkinos divided the country into two factions, moderate measures being in favor with the former under a constitutional monarchy, and republican institutions being advocated by the latter with the expulsion of the "old" or native Spaniards.

Among the Escoceses, or "Scots Masons," were persons having titles of nobility; all the Catholic clergy; many military officers; and all classes of native Spaniards.

The republicans appreciating the progress of their opponents, resolved "to fight the devil with his own fire," and thereupon a revival faction was organized with the title of Yorkinos, whose members were thought to be of the York Rite. Mackey is authority for the statement that the Grand Lodge of New York established three lodges in the city of Mexico in 1825.

These lodges were formed into a Grand Lodge of the York Rite by Mr. Joel R. Poinsett (American Minister), a former G.M. of South Carolina. There is no record that since the year 1815 any foreign lodges have been warranted by the Grand Lodge of New York.

But however established, the so-called York Rite, or, in other words, pure English Masonry, flourished, and toward the end of 1826 there were twenty-five lodges, with a membership of about seven hundred." The Escoceses, or 'Scots Masons,' finding their lodges deserted, regarded the Yorkinos as renegades and traitors, and with a view to counterbalance the fast increasing power of the latter, they formed the Novenarios, a kind of militia, which derived its name from a regulation requiring each member to enlist nine additional adherents. These ingratiated themselves with the clergy, who, after having been the most embittered enemies of the Craft in past years, now joined the Escoceses almost in a body.

"The Yorkinos, becoming aware of these proceedings, tried to outdo their rivals by recruiting their own lodges upon the plan of receiving all applicants without distinction, provided they belong to the federal, zip., the patriotic party. Thus, the system of Masonry very soon degenerated into a mere party question, and at last all the adherents of one side styled themselves Escoceses, and of the other side, Yorkinos. In 1828 the two parties resorted to open warfare, with a view to deciding the question at issue by the sword, and the civil war then commenced lasted for more than a generation.

"Somewhere about this time, while Dr. Vincente Guerrero - G. M. under the York Rite - was President of the Republic, a law was enacted by which all Masonic lodges were closed. The Yorkinos obeyed their Grand Master, and discontinued their meetings. The Escoceses went on working, but some of their most influential lodges were suppressed, and the members vanished. Subsequently, all native Spaniards were expelled from Mexican territory.

"This internecine strife seriously affected the Fraternity in general, and gave birth, during the darkest hours of the struggle for supremacy, to an organization called the National Mexican Rites formed by Masons, and composed of distinguished men, but containing innovations and principles so antagonistic to Masonic usage and doctrine, that it was never accorded recognition, even in Mexico, by any Masonic body of acknowledged legality.

"This new school of Masonry was established by nine Brethren of both rites, and who had belonged to the highest grade of either system, in 1830. To guard against the intrusion of unworthy members and the revival of political antagonism, they resolved to create a rite which should be national, in the sense of not depending upon any foreign Grand Lodge for its Constitution, and to obviate by safeguards and precautions of an elaborate character, the dangers to be apprehended from the reception of either Escoceses or Yorkinos.

"The National Mexican Rite consisted of nine degrees, which, omitting the first three, were 4d, Approved Master (equal to the 15d, 'Scots'); 5d, Knight of the Secret (equal to the 18d, 'Scots'); 6d, Knight of the Mexican Eagle; 7d, Perfect Architect or Templar; 8d, Grand Judge, and 9d, Grand Inspector General. All of these degrees had their equivalents in the grades of the A. and A. S. R. 33. With the 'St. John's' (or purely Craft) degrees certain special signs were associated, which, however, were not required from foreigners unless they had acted as auxiliaries in any of the party contests.

"A Grand Orient, composed of members of the 9d, was supreme in matters of dogma or ritual. There was also an administrative body or National Grand Lodge, whose members were elective and met in the metropolis. The Provincial Grand Lodges had their seats in the State capitals, and were formed by the 'three lights' of at least five St. John's lodges.

"But although still preserving a nominal existence, the several Grand Bodies, owing to political convulsions, were virtually dormant for many years after 1833. A lodge - St. Jean d'Ulloa - was constituted at Vera Cruz, by the Supreme Council of France, in 1843; and another - Les Ecossais des Deux Mondes - at the City of Mexico, by the Grand Orient of the same country, in 1845.

"The National Mexican Rite appears to have somewhat recovered from its torpor in 1863. At that date we find in the Metropolis a National Grand Lodge with six working lodges, though of these one - belonging to the A. and A. S. R. - was constituted by the Grand Lodge of New Granada, and consisted chiefly of foreigners; in Toluca a Prov. Grand Lodge with five lodges; in Vera Cruz and Guadalajara two lodges each; and in five other cities single lodges.[136]

"In the year 1858 or 1859," according to the official report," Bro. Lafon de Ladebat went to Mexico, with authority from Bro. Albert Pike (of Washington, D. C.) to organize and establish Masonry on a sound basis in that country.[137] However, Bro. Ladebat did not organize a Grand Lodge of Symbolic Masonry first, as instructed, but constituted the Supreme Council with jurisdiction over the three degrees of E.A., F.C., and M.M."[138]

The Grand Lodge of Yorkinos ceased to exist, and the "Scots- a Supreme Council 33d, this being done after the overthrow of the Maximilian Empire. This Supreme Council and the Supreme Council of 1858-59 were joined in 1868 and both were fused with the National Grand Lodge, the President of the Republic, Benito Juarez, being one of the highest officials. However, this union was more of a friendly pact than of a thorough nature, as each rite was independent of the other with regard to its own ritual and internal government. The National Rite

---

[136] Gould, vol. vi.

[137] Proceedings of the Grand Lodge of Louisiana, 1884.

[138] This was entirely in opposition to Brother Pike's wishes
Rite," divested of all political coloring, erected - December 27, 1865

numbered thirty-two, and the A. and A. S. R. twenty-four, lodges in 1870.

"It would seem as if the authority of Juarez alone held these rites together, since at his death in 1872 - although he was succeeded as President by his chief follower, Sebastian Lerdo de Tejeda, also a prominent Freemason - dissensions arose, and they fell asunder, Alfredo Chavero becoming G. M. of the Grand Orient, and Jose Maria Mateos of the National Grand Lodge. In 1876 a Lodge of Germans left the G.O. and joined the National Grand Lodge, but in the following year, with the consent of the latter, affiliated with the Grand Lodge of Hamburg - under which body there is also (1886) another lodge at work in Vera Cruz."[139]

About 182 the two rites probably seem to have been again united, though information is so meager that this is not definite, however, it is quite possible that the National Mexican Rite continued to exist though its proceedings are not recorded. As far as there is any evidence, it appears that Grand Lodges were organized by the lodges which were under the jurisdiction of the Supreme Council[140] the capital a Central Grand Lodge was formed, having jurisdiction over the subordinate lodges, and there was very little interference upon the subject of Symbolism except by the Central Grand Lodge, though the Supreme Council did not formally waive its authority thereover.

"In 1883 there were the following State Grand Lodges: Vera Crux and Jalisco, each with seven lodges; Puebla, Yucatan, and Guanajuato, with six; and Morelos and Tlaxcala, with five; thus making a total of seven Grand and forty-two subordinate lodges, exclusive of the Central Grand Lodge and the metropolitan lodges.

"It will be seen that at this period there existed at Vera Cruz a State Grand Lodge, but from the fact that it was subordinate to the Central Grand Lodge, it was not deemed by the Grand Lodge of Colon to exercise legitimate authority over Symbolism in that State. Indeed, the whole of Mexico was regarded by the lastnamed body as 'unoccupied territory,' and it therefore proceeded to charter three lodges, which in January, 1883, formed themselves, at the City of Vera Cruz, into the 'Mexican Independent Symbolic Grand Lodge.'"

"Two of the lodges taking part in this movement had originally held Mexican warrants, but having quarreled with their superiors, solicited and obtained charters from the G. L. of Colon (now Colon and Cuba), shortly after which the third lodge was formed, and then, finally,

---

[139] Gould, vol. vi.
[140] Recommended by General Pike

the Grand Lodge, although the Supreme Council of Mexico had formerly protested against the invasion of its territory. Indeed the step thus taken by their former superiors appears rather to have accelerated the action of the three lodges, as in the record of their proceedings it is stated, 'that they hasten to constitute themselves into an Independent Grand Lodge, pending the protest of the Supreme Council of Mexico, to relieve their friend and mother, the Grand Lodge of Colon, from any further unpleasant complications.'

'The Supreme Council of Mexico, in a Balustre numbered XXX., and dated April 25, 1883, renounced its jurisdiction over the symbolical degrees, and promulgated a variety of relations with regard to Grand and subordinate lodges. This threw the Craft into the utmost confusion, and might have ended in the destruction of the greater number of Mexican lodges, or at least in the establishment of some half dozen Grand Bodies, all claiming supremacy, had it not been for the skill and address of Carlos Pacheco, who succeeded Alfredo Chavero as Sov. G. Com. 33d.

"The former Balustre was revoked, and by a new one (XXXII.), dated May 27, 1883, the Supreme Council renounced, in favor of the State Grand Lodges then existing or which might afterward be formed, the jurisdiction over Symbolism conferred upon it by the Constitutions of the A. and A. S. R. 33d. The transmission of powers was to take effect from June 24th them ensuing. The lodges having no Grand Lodge were to remain under the jurisdiction of the Grand Lodge nearest to them, or the oldest if two were equidistant, until they organized their own in accordance with Masonic usage and precedent. The lodges of the Federal District, however, were directed to form and inaugurate their Grand Lodge on June 15th then following. Balustre XXXII. was signed (inter alias) by Carlos Pacheco, Mariano Escobedo, Alfredo Chavero, and Porfirio Diaz.

"On June 25, 1883, twelve lodges at the capital met and established the Grand Lodge of the Federal District (or city) of Mexico, with Porfirio Diaz as the first G. M. The event was announced to the Masonic world in two circulars, the first of which is in Spanish - an immense document of one hundred and eighty pages! The second is in English, and its only noticeable feature is a declaration that the American system of State Grand Lodges, each with exclusive jurisdiction, has been adopted. Grand Lodges have since been established on the same plan - i.e., in conformity with the edict of the Supreme Council, as promulgated in Balustre XXXII. - in the States of Vera Cruz, Tlaxcala, Morelos, Puebla, Campeachy, and Lower California. The complications, however, already existing in the Republic, were still further increased in 1883, by the action of the Grand Lodge of Missouri, in granting a Charter to the Toltec Lodge, in the City of Mexico, which had been provisionally established at the close of the previous year under a dispensation from the Grand Master."[141]

"The recognition of the Grand Lodge of which Porfirio Diaz became the head, by the Grand Lodges of Louisiana and Florida, was duly protested against by Carlos Pacheco, Sov. G. Com. 33d, and Carlos K. Ruiz, the latter of whom claimed to be himself the legitimate G. M. It would appear from ' La Gran Logia,' a bulletin published by some members of the Ruiz Grand Lodge, and denominated their official organ, that on the same day, at the same hour, and in the same hall, when and where the Diaz Grand Lodge was organized and installed, the other body was organized also. There was this difference, however, that whereas the Diaz party transacted their affairs within the body of the lodge, the supporters of Ruiz were reduced to the necessity of attending to theirs in the anteroom - the latter Brethren having withdrawn from the original convention while it was being organized, but not leaving the building, in the vestibule of which they afterward conducted their own proceedings."[142]

Extract from Proceedings of Grand Lodge of Iowa.
Report on Foreign Correspondence, Theo. S. Parvin, Chairman, 1896.

"The year 1890 opens before us the new, and present era of Mexican Masonry. The functions of the Supreme Council being limited and confined to the legitimate Scottish Rite degrees 4th and 33d, inclusive, with no organized jurisdictions of Masonry of the symbolic degrees except the Grand Lodges of the State of Vera Cruz and the Federal District (city of Mexico), both of which had been recognized by the Grand Lodge of Iowa as well as many other Grand Lodges, the Lodges, to the number of one hundred and twenty-two of the one hundred and twenty-five, met in convention, and after a session of ten days, on the 20th of July, 1890, unanimously created and organized a new and governing body of Masonry, styled 'The Gran Dieta Symbolical or the Grand Diet of Symbolic Masonry for the Republic of Mexico. It elected for its Grand Master, and who has since by annual re-election been continued in office, Bro. Porfirio Diaz, the distinguished and illustrious President of the Republic; and for its Grand Secretary another

---

[141] Gould, vol. vi.
[142] Ibid

distinguished citizen and Mason, Ermilo G. Canton, the Clerk of the Supreme Court of the United States of Mexico, who also, by annual reelection, still continues in office.

"The Gran Dieta promulgated a Constitution of forty-seven pages, consisting of eleven titles and one hundred and forty-five articles. The three sections of this Constitution relating to Masonic power and authority, read as follows (we give the translation):

"'ARTICLE 30. The powers of Symbolic Masonry in this Republic are constituted in the governing Grand Lodge, which goes by the name of the "Grand Symbolic Diet of the United States of Mexico," whose duty it shall be to watch over the welfare, absolute liberty and independence of the three blue degrees, or Symbolic Lodges, under the Grand Lodges of the different States.'

"'ART. 31. The Sovereign Masonic Power resides essentially and originally in the great body of Masons, who deposit their obedience for its exercise in the Grand Diet.'

"'ART. 32. The Supreme Authority of Symbolic Masonry shall have the title, 'Grand Symbolic Diet of the United States of Mexico.'"

"All of the Grand Lodges save three that of the State of Vera Cruz, the Federal District, and one other - together with the subordinate Lodges that had not participated in its organization, transferred their allegiance to the Gran Dieta. These constituent Lodges now number about two hundred, and the membership exceeds ten thousand; the reporter for the Grand Lodge of Texas makes the former two hundred and fifty, and the latter twenty thousand - too high, I think - among whom I found, during my visit, were enrolled among its members not only the President of the Republic, but the Governors of all the principal States (some sixteen of which I visited), the Mayors of the cities, and the Judges of the Supreme Court. The Gran Dieta is, therefore, a sovereign and independent body, organized after the manner of the Grand Masonic Bodies of the United States. It, and it alone, exercises supreme authority and control over 'the three symbolic degrees of masonry' in Mexico.

"The constituent elements in the Gran Dieta of Grand and Subordinate Lodges and in the membership consists of Masons both of the York and Scottish Rite. We have learned from the general history presented, that there was at one time some twenty Lodges, with a membership of near eight hundred, that had obtained their charters from Grand Lodges in the United States, and that the old York element has existed in Mexico ever since, and, like the leaven of old, will yet under fostering care more and more each year permeate the system of Masonry now established upon a new basis.

The ritual, however, used in a majority of these Lodges and Grand Lodges is that of the three degrees of the Scottish Rite as practiced in Lodges created by the Supreme Council, the exceptions being the Lodges composed exclusively or principally of American citizens resident in the various cities of the Republic, in which the American ritual is used. There are now some half dozen so-called American Lodges - that is, Lodges composed of American citizens resident in Mexico and other cities of the Republic. These Lodges all hold their charters from the Grand Dieta, which is and must continue to be the only governing body of Symbolic Masonry in Mexico. The last effort of the Grand Lodges in the United States to establish a Lodge in Mexico, was that of the Grand Lodge of Missouri which chartered Toltec Lodge some ten or more years ago, but which, upon the organization of Gran Dieta, surrendered its charter and took out one from the Gran Dieta, under which it now works.

"There are thousands of American citizens, hundreds of them being Masons, residing in the various cities in Mexico, many of whom are affiliated with the so-called American Lodges, while others yet hold membership in the Mexican Lodges, and this number is increasing each year.

"Upon the organization of the Gran Dieta it made no special effort to secure recognition of American Grand Lodges, and it was some two or three years later that the Grand Lodges of Texas and New York recognized it, as they do still, and then the subject of its recognition was presented to other Grand Lodges, which deferred action for further information, as it had been currently reported, especially through a publication issued by an American resident of the city of Mexico, that the Gran Dieta by its constitution authorized the making of women Masons, and prohibited the use of the Great Light in their lodges. These statements I had heard and read while I was yet writing the Reports on Correspondence for this Grand Lodge, and so declined to present the subject of recognition of the Gran Dieta to the Grand Lodge of Iowa until I could satisfy myself more fully in relation to these rumors developing into published statements. I examined the Constitution of the Gran Dieta, to which I have referred, and could find nowhere within it any provision prohibiting the use of the Great Light in their Lodges, or authorizing the making of women Masons; the Constitution is entirely silent upon both subjects. During my visit to the Republic of Mexico in February and March of 1895, I had an opportunity to satisfy myself upon these subjects. I found that the Gran Dieta did not, by any law, much less constitutional provision, prohibit or exclude the Great Light from its altars - it did and does permit its use; it does, however, require by law the use of the Book of Constitutions upon its altars. I found during my visit to Lodges and Grand Lodges in some, and especially all of the American Lodges, the Great Light open upon the altar; in other Lodges the Book of Constitutions only; and notwithstanding the requirement that the Book of Constitutions should be used, I found in some Lodges that it was laid aside in open view, and the Great Light substituted, and the action was not called in question by any authority. It is not true, therefore, as has been stated, that the Bible is excluded; its use, while permitted, is not required.

"In reference to this subject, I fail to find any warrant or requirement in the 'Book of Constitutions,' the Constitution or Code of Iowa, or any other Grand Lodge I have examined, requiring the use of the Great Light in our American Lodges. The Constitution of the United States has no reference to God or a Supreme Being, and many of our Presidents, in their annual messages, have omitted all reference to a Supreme Being, so that a class of Christians are year after year clamoring for an amendment to that National Charter, as if we would become more a Christian nation by its insertion. The 'Book of Constitutions' not only does not, any more than the Constitution of the Gran Dieta, require the use of the Bible in Lodges, but, on the contrary, we learn from it that it 'charges the Masons of every country to be of the religion of that country or nation,' and so, of course, authorizes the use of the book of the religion of the people of such country and nation. It has been well said by high authority that 'he that is without sin among you, let him first cast a stone.' Until the Grand Lodge of Iowa and other Grand Lodges, by constitutional or legal enactment, shall first require the use of the Great Light in their Lodges, let them be sparing of their criticisms and censure of another supreme and independent Grand Lodge possessing all the rights and privileges they claim. Without the exercise and practice of this Christian and Masonic charity, Masonry can never become, as the Constitutions affirm it is, 'the center of union and the means of conciliating true friendship among persons that must otherwise have remained at a perpetual distance.' Our people and Masons are fast becoming important factors in the business and social relations (even marrying and being given in marriage) of the cities of the Mexican Republic; they are already in large numbers enrolled as members of their Lodges; and if given a Chance, will yet bring the Masonry of that country more in harmony with ours.

"Another of the objections urged heretofore against the recognition of the Gran Dieta is, that it made Masons of women. From a thorough examination of the Constitution, I learn that this was not authorized or warranted by any constitutional provision; it was not, indeed, until a year later, in 1891, that the Gran Dieta, by a law provided for the initiation of women, and also for the issuing to them of charters for Lodges. From what I saw and the best information I could obtain, there were some two or three only of the Grand Lodges that had sanctioned this practice, and about the same number of Lodges that had acted under the permission thus given. I found both in the city of Mexico and the city of San Luis Potosi, which is the capital of the State of the same name, and a city of about the size of our State capital, Des Moines - a woman's Lodge; that is, I saw the charters hanging upon the wall of the ante-room side by side with the charters of some four or five men's Lodges occupying the same hall; the charters were filled out upon the same blanks, in the same manner, signed by the same Grand Officers, and with the great seal of the Gran Dieta - the only difference being the insertion in one, of the names of women rather than of men. Moreover, I find from an examination of the Masonic Bulletin, the official organ of the Gran Dieta for 1891-94, edited by the Gran Dieta, and especially in the number for February, 1893, which contains the official list of a hundred and more Lodges all owing obedience to the Gran Dieta, among them one or two Lodges of women, chartered by the Gran Dieta and organized by the Grand Secretary himself, as I was informed by the brethren. In the official Bulletin for February, 1892, pages 175-201, there is a list of the officers and members, of some twenty Lodges, all of them constituent members, of the Gran Dieta, and among them I find that of Martha Washington Lodge, No. 156, with a list of the names of its officers and members, and the name of the Master is Maria C. Beall, the Secretary Josefina S.

Rivera. These ladies I know very well - have known the former from her childhood - Mrs. Beall is a native of Iowa City, was educated in our State University (where for years, I was a professor), was graduated in 1876, and went to Mexico as a missionary, where she met and married her husband, who was a member at that time and later Master of a Mexican Lodge in the same city, as his name appears in the published record to which we have referred. The father of this lady is and has been for many years a leading physician of Iowa city, and a prominent Mason for half a century. The Secretary is the niece of the Governor of the State, the Grand Master of the Grand Lodge, and the daughter of Gen. Rivera, one of the leading citizens of the Republic, and the second officer in a Lodge that has in its membership several prominent Americans, among them the Rev. Mr. Winton, who has long been a resident of the city, and thoroughly informed as to Mexican Masonry. From them I learned, as also from the Masters and other officers of Mexican Lodges I visited in the city of Mexico, that the women were accustomed to visit the men's Lodges at pleasure.

"Wherever I went and visited, either Grand or subordinate Lodges, being received with the greatest courtesy and welcomed by eloquent addresses delivered by the Grand Orator, an officer attached to every Lodge for the purpose of welcoming visitors, I took occasion in my responsive addresses, which I delivered upon every occasion and at considerable length, to cite attention to this practice, which I found had obtained in a few cases, and which was very objectionable to American Masons; and I assured them that while it continued, many of our Grand Lodges would not recognize the Gran Dieta, under whose jurisdiction they worked. I was everywhere informed, in public and in private, that an overwhelming majority of the Lodges and members were opposed to the practice, and were very anxious to be brought into closer and more intimate relations with American Masons and Masonry. This sentiment was communicated to me by President Diaz, who honored me with two very interesting interviews, as also by his Deputy, both in the Supreme Council and Gran Dieta, and other prominent Masons.

"A few months after my return home I learned that the Gran Dieta had repealed the law under which women were authorized to be made Masons, and upon receiving this information, I replied that that would not satisfy American Masons; they must go further, and provide by law for the revocation of charters issued to women, and still more, deny to them the right of visitation to men's Lodges, both of which the Gran Dieta has since done, as I am informed. Further than this I do not see what they could do. They cannot unmake the women who are made Masons any more than we can by expulsion declare that a man is no longer a Mason. We only do as they have done, deny them all the rights and privileges of Masonry.

"The making of women Masons is not a new departure in Masonry; its has only been more recent, upon a larger scale, and brought nearer home. Every well-read Mason knows full well that in the last century a Lodge in Ireland, Num. 44, at Doneraile, initiated a woman, Miss Elizabeth St. Leger, daughter of the Right Honorable St. Leger, Viscount Deneraile, whose son and successor was Master of the Lodge at the time.

She afterwards married Hon. Richard Aldworth, of the County of Cork, and has left a most honorable record as a woman and a woman Mason. Moreover, the Masonic student may learn that during the reign of Napoleon, the First Emperor, a woman was made a Mason, he being Grand Master at the time. she was a colonel, and a very brave and distinguished officer in his army; served with distinction for many years, and her sex was not discovered until she was severely wounded, when, upon her recovery, the Masons, prompted by a spirit of gallantry, conferred upon her the three symbolic degrees. Within the past decade the Grand Master of the Grand Lodge of Hungary, a Symbolic Grand Lodge, which takes a prominent part the present year with the officials and people of Hungary in the celebration of their Millenium Festival, a thousand years of honorable history, conferred, himself, the degrees of Masonry upon his own wife.

While the Masonic press commented upon this last case as Masonic historians have upon the former, I have yet to learn that any Masonic Grand Body ever withdrew, or even withheld, their recognition from those Grand Lodges of Ireland, France, and Hungary. They were all recognized by the Grand Lodge of Iowa as independent Grand Masonic Bodies; and it was only when the Grand Lodge of France eliminated from its ritual the requirement of 'a belief in a Supreme Being,' that the Grand Lodge of Iowa, following the example of the Grand Lodge of England, and later followed by American Grand Lodges other than our own, withdrew its recognition, or rather, refused to hold further Masonic intercourse with that Grand Body.

"Another, and the third, objection has been very recently urged against the recognition of the Gran Dieta as a lawfully constituted Masonic body, and the very sweeping charge has been made, not only against the Gran Dieta, but against very many of the Grand Lodges of the world, especially those of Europe, Asia, Africa and South America, nearly all of which owe their origin to Supreme Councils of Scottish Rite Freemasonry.

It has been published that 'there is no lawful Masonry anywhere that is not descended from the Free and Accepted Masonry of the British Isles, the Masonry of the Charges of a Freemason;' and it is declared by the same writer that this is 'an indisputable fact.' He further says that the Lodges in Mexico are 'clandestine;' that 'their members are impostors and dissenters from the original plan of Masonry,' and that 'whoever visits them violates his Masonic vows.' If these statements be true, then all the Grand Lodges to which we have referred are clandestine, and their members are impostors and dissenters, and all who visit them, as and thousands of other American Masons have done, are guilty, as charged, of violating our vows. The writer affirms that the statements made by him are 'indisputable facts.' They are not only disputed now, but have been through the whole history of Freemasonry in the United States. In the Reports on Correspondence of the past year, Past Grand Masters Drummond, of Maine, and Anthony, of New York, two among the ablest Masonic writers of the day, and certainly the peers in Masonic knowledge of any other two in the country, not only deny the statement, but affirm, to which an overwhelming majority of Grand Lodges and Masonic writers give their adherence quite as 'indisputably,' that 'a Lodge created by a Supreme Council in a country where, by the Masonic law then prevailing, it may be done, is just as lawful a Lodge, and its Masons as regular Masons, as any to be found outside of those which can trace their origin back to the British Grand Lodges. The bodies of the York Rite do not,' they say, 'embrace the whole of pure and accepted Masonry.' To this I give my unwavering adherence.

"One of the so-called landmarks of Masonry, and quite as essential and important in its character, and which has received the assent of quite a large number of Masonic writers, affirms and declares that 'Masonry is cosmopolitan,' and is universal, in which statement they are borne out by the Book of Constitutions itself.

"Let us refer briefly to the history of the English Grand Lodge. The first Grand Lodge of which Masonic history gives any record, is that of England, organized by the 'four old Lodges of London' in 1717. The Constitution (Charges and Regulations) for its government was presented by Dr. Anderson (and since known by his name), and adopted in 1823. This Grand Lodge, we all know, was constituted by only four Lodges, leaving a larger number out in the cold, while the Gran Dieta was constituted by one hundred and twenty-two of the one hundred and twenty-five Lodges in the Republic.

While there had never been an earlier Grand Lodge, there had been and were at that time other Lodges constituted in the same way as those four - by voluntary action and without any warrant or authority save the brothers' common consent. Now, the Constitution of the Grand Lodge of England, then and there adopted for its government and it alone - for it was not and is not binding upon any Lodge or Grand Lodge till accepted as such - is either a truth or a lie. It reads, Head. VI, Division 2, that 'we are also Masons of all nations, tongues, kindreds, and languages,' which is corroborated by all history; that there was at that time other and 'lawful Masonry' elsewhere than in England. England, while her political flag floats on every sea, has no 'monopoly' of

Masonry, outside of her own dominions. There was and is 'lawful Masonry' in other parts of the globe, and so recognized by the Grand Lodge of England itself, by Scotland, Ireland, Canada, and all English colonies, as by a majority of the Grand Lodges of the United States, including Iowa. It cannot be said, as some have asserted, that the Lodges in other nations sprung from the loins of the English Grand Lodge, because at that date, 1723, the Grand Lodge of England had not warranted a single Lodge beyond England and it was several years before she constituted one beyond the 'British Isles.'

"Not only has the Grand Lodge of Iowa, but a majority of the Grand Lodges of this country as well as those of England and Europe have recognized the Grand Lodges of Cuba, Veracruz, and the Federal District in Mexico, together with those of Chili, Peru, Brazil, Argentine Republic, and others in the Western Hemisphere, and in the Eastern, those of Spain, Portugal, Italy, Roumania, Hungary, and others, all of which, as we have stated, were created by supreme Councils. We have not had time to look into many of the proceedings of Grand Lodges, but those which we have at hand, and into which we have looked, are those of California, Canada, Louisiana, New York, as well as Iowa, all of which have recognized the aforesaid Grand Lodges as lawfully constituted Grand Lodges of Masons. It will never do for us or others to assert that all knowledge, all wisdom, and all Masonic intelligence reside either in Illinois or Iowa, or any other American Grand Lodge, or even in the Grand Lodge of England, which has always acknowledged and recognized a majority, if not all, of the several Grand Lodges we have named. Moreover, the Grand Master of the Grand Lodge of England, the Prince of Wales, who has served his Grand Lodge and Freemasonry now for twenty- one years, was made a Mason in a Lodge under the jurisdiction of the Grand Lodge of Sweden; and the Grand Lodge of Norway, which is now seeking recognition at our hands, has been recognized recently by some of the American Grand Lodges, as well as in former years by others.

"These statements and averments prove that Masonry is universal, wide spread and cosmopolitan in its character; it embraces, as the Constitutions say, 'Masons of all nations, tongues, kindreds, and languages,' Mohammedan, Hindoos, and even Pagans have Lodges and Grand Lodges, using the Koran, the Vedas, and other sacred books of their religion, instead of the Bible. I have myself sat in Lodges and Grand Lodges with native aboriginal Americans, full-blooded Indians. One of the Presidents of the United States, a former Grand Master of a Grand Lodge, ordered the degrees of Masonry conferred upon Indian chiefs visiting the Secretary of War at the National capital on business pertaining to their nation, and those men had very little knowledge of the Great Light in Masonry, or of any other sacred book, except the great volume of nature, and as little, also, of the Book of the Constitutions, or the laws of the Grand Lodge under whose jurisdiction they were made.

"Let us inquire what is a 'clandestine Lodge' and see whether Lodges I visited in Mexico were 'clandestine.' What is a 'clandestine Lodge,' and an impostor and dissenter or 'clandestine Mason?' The (Anderson) Constitutions declare, Section 8, that where a number of Masons shall take upon themselves to form a Lodge without the Grand Master's warrant, the regular Lodges are not to countenance them nor own them as fair brethren, and duly formed.' In other words, a Lodge formed without a warrant from the Grand Master (we now say Grand Lodge) is s clandestine,' and so a 'clandestine Mason' is one made in a Lodge without a warrant. The Gran Dieta Symbolica of Mexico, and the Lodges under its obedience, are as regular and legal bodies of Masons as is the Grand Lodge of Illinois, Iowa, England, or any other Grand Lodge in the world. The Gran Dieta is composed of Grand and subordinate Lodges that obtained their charters from both Supreme Councils of the Scottish Rite and Grand Lodges of the York Rite, but that does not militate, there more than here, against its lawful character.

"So, too, a lawfully-constituted (warranted) Lodge cannot make 'clandestine Masons.' There is a great difference between an 'irregularly-made' and a 'clandestinely-made' Mason. The making of a person who is not a 'good and true man;' one who is not 'freeborn;' one who is not of 'mature and discreet (legal) age;' or a 'bondman,' a 'woman,' or an 'immoral or scandalous man,' and not of 'good repute,' is declared by Anderson's Constitutions to be irregular and not permissible - but that irregularity does not make them 'clandestine.' There are few, not any among all my brethren of many years' standing in Masonry, who have not visited Lodges which had violated one or more of these six commandments, called by some 'landmarks.' The violation of a 'landmark' by a Lodge or Grand Lodge does not make it or its members clandestine.

Were this so, the Grand Lodge of England itself, the oldest of Grand Lodges, would be declared clandestine by all English-speaking Grand Lodges in the world, for there is no fact more notorious than that the Grand Lodge of England, very many years ago, upon the manumission of slaves in its colonies, changed one of the fundamental landmarks, so recognized, from 'free born' into 'free man,' and thereby authorized the making of, and did make, Masons of those who were born in slavery. Moreover, the Grand Lodges of England, of Pennsylvania, and several other Grand Lodges in the United States - even our neighboring Grand Lodge of Missouri - knowingly, and I may say willfully, made Masons of those of nonage. We have residing in the State of Iowa to-day a Mason made a Mason in his eighteenth year in a Lodge in Missouri, and the Lodge so making him was fully cognizant of the fact. These are irregularities, and no irregularity, however great, can vitiate the charter or the legal existence of the body performing the act, however offensive it may be in the eyes of the brethren.

"Any and all Masons may visit any and all Lodges in Mexico without violating, as charged by the ignorant or malicious, any O.B. of which I have any knowledge, or known to the rituals here or elsewhere from the first to the thirty-third and last degree in Masonry.

"The Grand Lodge of England was the first Grand Lodge and it was not created till 1717, nor its Constitution adopted till 1723;[143] yet within twenty years there was a schism and a secession of a number of brethren, who constituted another Grand Lodge, calling themselves the 'Ancients,' and by some strange hocus pocus their mother Grand Lodge the 'Moderns' - all this about the middle of the last century. This new schismatic, Clandestine Grand Lodge, engineered by a more intelligent, active and energetic Grand Secretary,

Laurence Dermott, grew rapidly, and soon assumed large and permanent proportions.

It, too, published a Book of Constitutions, called by its author, the Grand Secretary, the 'Ahiman Rezon,' and planted its Lodges 'at home' and abroad, especially in America, for Bro. Hughan, the great Masonic antiquarian and historian, says that it secured the 'almost unanimous support of the Grand Lodges of America.' That 'a stream cannot rise above its fountain,' 'nor can a pure stream flow from an impure fountain,' are unquestionably axioms in nature and in Masonry. Now, there are a few Grand Lodges in the United States in whose veins the blood of the 'Ancients,' the 'rebel Dermott,' and his clandestine Grand Lodge, so declared from 1750 to 1813, when the mother Grand Lodge condoned all offenses and gave her the 'kiss of peace,' better by far than that of the 'betrayal.' If there is no Dermott blood in Iowa and Illinois, the veins of the Grand Lodge of Pensylvania are full of it, and they still glory in their 'Ahiman Rezon,' and reject and 'cast over among the rubbish' the Anderson's Constitutions. Nor is the Grand Lodge of Pennsylvania alone in this, but she has illustrious associates; and yet who

---

[143] Constitution was adopted 1721, and first edition printed 1723. - EDITOR

ever heard of an Illinois or Iowa Mason, or one from any other jurisdiction, calling those Grand Lodges clandestine, or refuse, Masonically, to visit their Lodges or hold Masonic intercourse with their members, charging them with being 'impostors and dissenters from the original plan of Masonry?'

"The difference between the Masonry of Mexico and the United States is just here: Their origin and pedigree is more pure and lawful than ours, while their practices were not only objectionable to us but to others, and to even a majority of their own membership, as they have repealed and abrogated the law under which such objectionable practices had obtained by only two of the twenty or more Grand Lodges, and the same number out of more than two hundred subordinate Lodges.

"It has been publicly proclaimed that the Gran Dieta has not only repealed the law under and by which women were made Masons, but revoked and recalled the charters (only three, and that is three too many) granted to women Lodges, but gone further - further they could not go - and forbidden Lodges to admit women Masons as visitors or to recognize them (though they be as lawful Masons as the men).

"The Gran Dieta being a lawfully constituted Masonic Body, with some two hundred Lodges and (it is stated) twenty thousand members, with several American Lodges and many of our citizens affiliated therein, and having not only proved that it did not forbid or exclude, but permits, as she has always, the use of the Great Light and moreover settled the question of the past woman, she knocks at the door of the American Grand Lodges for recognition. Let it be borne in mind that recognition is not essential, or even necessary to legality. It only bears in its train a more enlarged and fraternal intercourse among and between their members.

CHAPTER III

CUBA AND PORTO RICO

Cuba.

On December 17, 1804, the Grand Lodge of Pennsylvania chartered at Havana Le Temple des Vertus Theologales, No. 103, Joseph Cerneau being the first Master.

Under the same sanction other lodges were erected - in 1818, Nos. = 157, 161; in 1819, Nos. 166, 167; in 1820, No. 175 (at Santiago de Cuba), and in 1822, No. 181.

They existed up to 1826, at which time the charters of Nos. 175 and 181 had been revoked for failure of meeting for more than a year, and the others had died out. The Grand Lodges of Louisiana and South Carolina next assumed the warranting of lodges on the island. Under the former Grand Lodge, bodies sprang up, in 1815, No. 7, in 1818, Nos. 11 and 14, and under the latter in 1818, No. 50, and in 1819, No. 52. The Grand Orient of France in 1819 established a lodge and consistory (32), and two further lodges in 1821. The Grand Lodge of South Carolina received from the G.L. of Ancient Freemasons in Havana in 1821, a communication stating that a Grand Lodge had been organized there, to which the Lodge La Amenidad, No. 52, desired permission to transfer its allegiance. A favorable answer was returned, but La Constancia, No. 50, was retained on the roll of the G. L. of South Carolina for some years, after which the Warrant was surrendered by the members "in consequence of the religious and political persecutions to which they were subjected."

For many years Masonry languished in the is Pearl of the Antilles," its votaries practicing their rites in secret, but not daring to indulge in any overt acts, which might entail not only expulsion from the country, but also confiscation of their property. At length, however, a faint revival set in, and a Warrant was granted, November 17, 1859, by the Grand Lodge of South Carolina to St. Andrew's Lodge, No. 93, "for the purpose of establishing, with the co-operation of two other Lodges[144] already existing on the island, a Grand Lodge," which was accomplished on December 5th of the same year.

An independent "Grand Lodge of Colon" was thus established at Santiago de Cuba, and - December 27, 1859 - a Supreme Council of the A. and A. S. R. 33d was founded in the same city by Andres Cassard.[145]

At this time, it must be recollected, the practice of assembling as Freemasons was forbidden by the Spanish laws, which laws, moreover, though destined to become - after the dethronement of Queen Isabella (1868) - innocuous in the Peninsula, remained for a long time in full force in Cuba.

Several, indeed, of the Captains General and other officers who ruled the islands were Masons, and therefore from time to time the Craft was tolerated, but its members being always compelled to work to a great extent in the dark, found it necessary to observe the most inviolable secrecy, and even to shield themselves under "Masonic names," lest by the discovery of their own, they might incur the most grievous penalties.

For the same reason the Supreme Council and the Grand Lodge, which soon after united in forming a Grand Orient, found a convenient title for the amalgamated body in the name of Colon - the Spanish for Columbus - it being desired above all things to conceal from the public ken the seat of the "Grand East" of the Society.

At the formation of the Grand Orient of Colon, a constitution published at Naples in 1820 was adopted as that of the new organization. By this the Supreme Council necessarily became a section of the Grand Orient. In 1865 a new constitution was promulgated. The Sov. G. Com. of the Supreme Council became - ex officio - G.M. of the Grand Orient, but the G.M. of the Grand Lodge was still required to submit himself for election. All charters for lodges were issued by the Grand Lodge, but had to be confirmed and vised by the Supreme Council.

In 1867 the Grand Lodge promulgated a constitution of its own, in which, while recognizing its continued membership of the Grand Orient, it claimed the exclusive power to enact its own by-laws,

---

[144] Brothers Albert Pike and Josiah H. Drummond agree that these were Spanish lodges, having warrants from Spain.

[145] Sanctioned by S. C. 33d Southern Jurisdiction

issue charters, constitute and regulate lodges. Their right to do this was denied by the Supreme Council. In 1868, September 30th, the Grand Lodge suspended its constitution until a meeting took place of the Grand Orient, convoked for November 30th. But before that time the revolution broke out, and Freemasons, being regarded by the Spanish Government as revolutionists, the G. O. could not meet. The Grand Lodge, so far as it was possible, resumed labor. But the times were unpropitious. In the winter of 1869, at Santiago de Cuba, by order of Gonzales Bret, an officer of the Government, eighteen persons were seized without warrant, and immediately shot, without trial, for being Freemasons - one of them the M.W.G.M. of Colon - and many others were arrested and committed to prison for the same offence.

The number of Cuban lodges, which in 1868 amounted to about thirty, had fallen in 1870 to about seven, and in the latter year the S. C. organized a Provincial Mother Lodge at Havana, against which the Grand Lodge very naturally protested. The Warrant to this if "Mother Lodge" was soon after recalled, but the dispute between the S. C. and the Grand Lodge continued. In 1873 - April 11th - the Grand Lodge resumed work openly, and in the following year entered into a compact with the Supreme Council, whereby it was agreed that the former should have exclusive jurisdiction over Symbolic Masonry, with the sole right of chartering lodges, and that it should establish a Provincial Mother Lodge in the western section of the island to govern the lodges there, but in submission to the laws of the Grand Lodge. After this compact it was intended that the Grand Lodge, though still nominally a section in the Grand Orient, should have full jurisdiction over the Symbolic Masonry. Nevertheless, it is quite clear that there was a divided authority, and apparently great Masonic confusion on the island.

The Grand Lodge of Colon held five meetings in August, 1876, at the last of which - August 26th - it declared itself free from all other authority, a sovereign body, with full and unlimited powers over its subordinates.

This action, however, was accelerated by an event which had taken place on August 1st, when the representatives of nine chartered lodges, and of four under dispensation, met at Havana, and formed the Grand Lodge of Cuba. This body from the very first kept itself free from the blighting influence of the (so-called) high degrees, which it willingly consented - December 31, 1876 - should be ruled in Cuba by the Grand Orient of Spain. In a circular of September 4, 1876, the Grand Lodge of Colon claimed to have on its register thirty-six lodges and 8,000 members; while its newly formed rival, the Grand Lodge of Cuba, in 1877, possessed an apparent following of seventeen lodges.

In the latter year - June 3d - a second Grand Lodge of Colon (or Columbus) at Havana was added to the two existing Craft Grand Bodies.

Thus we find three organizations, each claiming to be the regular Grand Lodge. From a circular of the Grand Lodge of Cuba, we learn that in 1879 the three lodges which formed the Grand Lodge of Colon, at Santiago de Cuba in 1859, and four others, adhered to that body; but that the remaining lodges, excepting those under the Grand Lodge of Cuba, were subject to the control of the Grand Lodge of Colon at Havana. To local jealousies must be attributed this multiplication of Grand Lodges. The representatives of some of the Havana lodges who seceded from the old (or original) Grand Lodge of Colon at Santiago de Cuba, met as the Grand Lodge, and decreed its removal to Havana.

Eventually, however, the Grand Lodges of Colon (at Havana) and Cuba formally united, and March 28, 1880, the G. M. of one body became Grand Master, and the G. M. of the other body Deputy Grand Master. The title assumed by the new organization was the United Grand Lodge of Colon and the Island of Cuba, and it entered upon its career with a roll of fifty-seven lodges, and between 5,000 and 6,000 Masons. The lodges under the original Grand Lodge of Colon at Santiago de Cuba remained true to their allegiance.

In 1885 the number of lodges under the "United Grand Lodge" had apparently increased to eighty-two, with Provincial Grand Lodges at Santiago de Cuba and Porto Rico; but on the official list there were only fifty-eight lodges in all upon the roll. Of these, thirty are in the capital, or in its vicinity, and twenty-eight in other parts. It is possible that further schisms may have disturbed the peace of Cuban Masonry; and it is somewhat remarkable that the Provincial Grand Lodge of Porto Rico - with the fourteen subordinate lodges on that island, shown in sundry calendars for 1886 - have wholly disappeared in the official list of current date.

It only remains to be stated, that, from the statistics before me, there would appear to have been in existence on the island thirteen lodges under the National Grand Orient, and twenty-seven under the Grand Lodge of Spain. The latter were subject to a Prov. G. M., whose jurisdiction also extends to Porto Rico.

Since the suppression of Masonry in Cuba by Spanish authority, and the murder of Masons at Santiago de Cuba, no authentic information of the status of the Institution in the island has been attainable. No official documents have been issued, but after the war of the United States with Spain ended, a notice announcing that several bodies of the Fraternity in the island had resumed their labors was issued, and under the new regime there is no doubt that Masonry will flourish there, and its prosperity spread into other parts of the Antilles.

Porto Rico.

The early Masonic history of this island is very vague and conjectural, as are all questions relating to the problem of Spanish Masonry. In 1860, at Mayaguez, there was in existence a Lodge Restauracion under the G. O. of Colon, but the changes which took place in Cuba during the struggle for existence of the Grand Lodges there, had their influence throughout all of the Spanish islands.

The lists show that the Provincial Superintendent of Cuba and Porto Rico under the Grand Lodge of Spain (of which Becera was the G. M.) was Don Manuel Romeno. The lodges are not enumerated in the list, but five are on the roll of the Grand Orient of Spain, however, without a Provincial Superintendent named. Le Phenix, No. 230, constituted in 1874, was the only lodge representing the S. C. of France. At one time the United Grand Lodge of Colon in Cuba had under its jurisdiction fourteen lodges in the island. However, these were formed into an Independent Grand Lodge, September 20, 1885. The greatest centres of Masonic activity have been San Juan, Ponce, and Mayaguez, the last-named toxvn not only having two lodges, but also a consistory of 32d, a council of 30d, and a chapter of 18d.

While the lodges of Porto Rico severed their connection with the "United Grand Lodge" of Colon in the island of Cuba, the chapters and other associations of Masons in this Spanish dependency retained their allegiance to the Supreme Council of the same title.

Upon this a little light is thrown by the action of Don Antonio Romero Ortiz (at the same time presiding over the Grand Lodge of Spain), who, in a decree, dated March 13, 1883, "denounced the Grand Lodge of Colon and Cuba, and the Masons of its obedience as traitors to the Government and to the Mother Country," simply because they declined to recognize his authority to govern or interfere in the affairs of "Symbolical Masonry" in Cuba. In the same year the United Grand Lodge of Colon and Cuba announced by circular that there being in all three Supreme Councils and three Grand Lodges in Spain, it had recognized the Grand Lodge of Seville as being "the only really independent organization of Craft Masonry" then existing in that country.

This, of course, was dealing very summarily with the pretensions of the Grand Lodge (or Orient) under Ortiz, which Mr. Albert Pike pronounced to be the only Grand Body in Spain legitimately entitled to recognition as a regular Masonic body. The name last quoted being, as many will be aware, that of the Sov. G. Com. of the S. C. 33d for the U. S. A., Southern Jurisdiction - the body of which he is the head being to other Supreme Councils what the Grand Lodge of England is to other Grand Lodges, and his own personal authority perhaps ranking higher than that of any other Mason either in the Old World or the New.

The Grand Lodge and Supreme Council of Colon and Cuba have therefore followed different roads, the latter treading in the beaten track traversed by Supreme Councils in amity with that presided over by the patriarch and law-giver of the rite, and the former boldly striking out a path of its own.

Owing to the state of political affairs in the island, and from the influential position held by Ortiz in Spain, the charges he made were calculated to subject the Cuban Masons both to surveillance and persecution on the part of the authorities. At Porto Rico the circumstances were somewhat different. Out of Cuba itself the S. C. of Colon was long regarded - and not alone by votaries of the A. and A. S. R. 33d - as a more stable institution than any other of the numerous Grand Bodies which sprang up like mushrooms in the island. When, therefore, the two governing bodies at Havana, each in its own way, attempted to solve the problem of Craft sovereignty in Spain, it is not to be wondered at that the confusion existing in the peninsula was reproduced with more or less fidelity in the Spanish Antilles. In Porto Rico there were no less than five chapters of 18d, besides a council of 30d, and a consistory of 32d. These, as already related, adhered to their allegiance; but the lodges on the island set up a Grand Lodge of Porto Rico at the city of Mayaguez in 1885, and it is satisfactory to state that the Grand Lodge of Colon and Cuba subsequently established fraternal relations with the new body.

CHAPTER IV

FREEMASONRY IN ASIA AND CAPE COLONY

We are greatly indebted to Gould's "History of Freemasonry" for the following sketches of Masonry in Asia and other countries in the Eastern Hemisphere. He says: "It has been the practice of Masonic writers to pass lightly over the history of Free Masonry in non-European countries and to exclude almost from mention the condition or progress of the Craft, in even the largest Colonies or Dependencies within the sovereignty of an Old World Power."

Information on this point must be sought amid the records of the countries discussed.

Too little emphasis has been laid by writers upon other than European countries, and slight attention given to their dependencies. Of these latter Findel says: " The lodges existing in these quarters of the globe were one and all under the Grand Lodges of England, Scotland, Holland or France, and therefore their history forms an inseparable part of that of the countries in question." This statement, to say the least, is inexact.

Owing to the varied admixture of peoples found in the Asiatic countries into which Europeans have entered, the practice of the craft emanates from many different sources.

While in the Greater Antilles arose Masonic Innovations claiming equality with or superiority over the Grand Authority of the Craft, in the Lesser Antilles, lodges connected with different European Grand Bodies existed in the same localities. This state of affairs necessarily induced a convict of jurisdiction. Rebold says:

"After Holland had become incorporated with the French Empire (July, 1810), the Grand Orient of France assumed the control of all the Dutch Lodges which then existed, with the exception of those of the Indies. which remained under the obedience which had created them, and which carried on the title of Grand Lodge of the United Provinces of the Low Countries."

Likewise the Provincial Grand Lodge of Bengal, in British India, was more than once independent in fact, if not in name, and its archives must be examined for Hindostanee Freemasonry or else nothing would be known of lodges the names of which do not appear upon the rolls of those European Grand Bodies under which Findel avers they came.

India.

George Pomfret was authorized in 1728 by the Grand Lodge of England "to open a new Lodge in Bengal." This lodge was established in 1730 by Captain Ralph Farwinter, the successor of Pomfret, as "Provincial Grand Master of India." This lodge is described as No. 72, Bengal, and is distinguished by the arms of the Company in the Engraved Lists.

James Dawson, Zech Gee, and Roger Drake, in order, succeeded Captain Farwinter.

Drake was Governor of Calcutta, but escaped the horrors of the Black Hole in 1756 by flying to the ships. He returned with Clive, but does not appear to have resumed his Masonic office.

At the period in question it was the custom in Bengal "to elect the Prov. G. M. annually by the majority of the voices of the members then present, from among those who had passed through the different offices of the (Prov.) Grand Lodge, who had served as Dep. Prov. G. M."

Under this practice Samuel Middleton was elected in 1767 and confirmed October 31, 1768. But a few years previously Earl Ferrers had granted a roving commission to "John Bluvitt, commander of the Admiral Watson Indiaman for East India, where no other Provincial is to be found." The annual election referred to was confirmed by the Grand Master of the Grand Lodge of England without its being thought an infringement upon his prerogative. But the dispensation confirming Middleton's election was regarded as abrogating annual elections. He held office until his death in 1775.

The records of the Bengal Grand Lodge only extend back to 1774. But prior to this date other lodges were formed. A second one, of whom nothing, save its existence, is known, arose and seven members of this organized a lodge April 16, 1740, and on petition the Grand Lodge of England ordered "the said Lodge to be enrolled (as requested) in the lists of regular lodges, agreeable to the date of their Constitution."

Other lodges were formed at Chandernagore, Calcutta, Patna, and Burdwan, the names of only some of which are preserved, but the numbers given them show that others must have existed.

In 1774 there were only three lodges in Calcutta. Besides these and the lodges at the other places mentioned, there were lodges at Dacca, Moorshedabad, and "at some military stations or with army brigades."

"The Grand Lodge of Solomon at Chinsura," which was under Holland, worked in harmony with the Provincial Grand Lodge under England, visits being interchanged and officials of both engaging in the same ceremonies.

"In 1775, February 15, the Prov. Grand Lodge, 'taking into consideration the propriety of preserving concord and unanimity, recommend it to the Brethren who call themselves "Scott and Elect" that they do lay aside the wearing of red ribbons, or any other marks of distinction, but such as are proper to the Three Degrees, or to the Grand Lodge as such, 'a request, we are told, which was cheerfully complied with."

Upon the death of Middleton in 1776, Charles Stafford Pleydell was elected in his stead. Under Philip Milner Dacres, the successor of Stafford, the Prov. Grand Lodge of Bengal assembled for the last time January 25, 1781.

The war in the Carnatic, which nearly swept Masonry out of India, had much to do with this dissolution.

"Industry and Perseverance" of the lodges in Calcutta, "where alone in Bengal Masonry may be said to have existed," may be said to be the only one which survived with a feeble light.

However, the Provincial Grand Lodge was re-opened July 18, 1785, under George Williamson, a former Deputy P.G.M., under a patent from England appointing him Acting P.G.M., and authorizing a meeting for election of Grand Master.

Upon an election November 14th, Edward Fenwick, former Grand Warden, was elected, receiving six votes, while Williamson received four. The former was installed March 17, 1786, though under his patent Williamson was clearly entitled to hold his acting appointment until the confirmation from London of the election of Fenwick.

This led to trouble. Williamson was sustained by the Grand Lodge of England, but the Prov. Grand Lodge maintained its position and, despite protests, Fenwick continued in the duties of his office and his election was confirmed May 5, 1788.

A letter of February 6, 1788, from the Prov. Grand Lodge to Grand Secretary White contains the following:

"An interesting account of the state of Masonry in Bengal appears in a letter of February 6, 1788, from the Prov. Grand Lodge to Grand Secretary White, from which I extract the following:

"'We earnestly wish to see the whole number of Lodges which existed in 1773 or 1774 reestablished. But the Subordinates at Patna, Burdwan, Dacca, and Moorshedabad now consist of such small societies, and these so liable to change, that we must confess it rather to be our wish than our hope to see Lodges established at any of these places.'

"At this assembly, the Wardens of Lodge 'Star in the East' said their meetings had been interrupted, because, in the absence of the Prov. Grand Lodge, no new Master could be installed. Williamson, however, ordered them to proceed with the election of a new Master, and engaged to convene a Prov. Grand Lodge for his installation.

"A letter from G. Sec. White, dated March 24, 1787 - continuing to Williamson the powers specified in his patent of 1784 - was read in the Prov. Grand Lodge on August 27 of that year. In the discussion which ensued, the Master of Lodge Star in the East observed: . . . 'Mr. Williamson, whose affairs have long been in a most anxious situation - who has been obliged, for a long time past, to live under a foreign jurisdiction - who now cannot come to Calcutta, but on a Sunday, or, if he comes on any other day, is obliged to conceal himself during the day time, and to be extremely cautious how he goes even when it is dark!'

"The patent, however, did not arrive in India until March 4, 1789.

"'With respect to the Brigades, they have been divided into six of Infantry and three of Artillery. This regulation has lessened the number of officers in each, and they will be more liable to removals than formerly. The first circumstance must be a great discouragement to the formation of Lodges in the Brigades, and the second would sometimes expose such Lodges to the risk of being annihilated. However, we shall give all encouragement to the making of applications, and all the support we possibly can to such Lodges as may be constituted.'

"A grand ball and supper was given by the Prov. Grand Lodge, January 14, 1789, to which invitations were sent, not only to residents in Calcutta, but also to 'Bro. Titsingh, Governor of Chinsurah, and other Masons of that Colony; to Bro. Bretel, and the other Masons of Chandernagore; and also to the Masons of Serampore, and to the Sisters of these Colonies, according to what has been customary on such occasions formerly.'

"In 1790 - December 27 - Fenwick resigned; and on the same day the Hon. Charles Stuart was elected and installed as his successor. The latter, however - owing to the government of the country devolving upon him in consequence of the absence of Lord Cornwallis from Calcutta - appointed Richard Comyns Birch 'Acting Prov. G. M. of Bengal.'

"The Lodges in the Presidency are thus described in the Freemasons' Calendar for 1794:

    Star in the East, Calcutta, 1st Lodge of Bengal 1740 Lodge of Industry and Perseverance, Calcutta, 2d Lodge of Bengal 1761 Lodge of Unanimity, Calcutta, 3d Lodge of Bengal 1772 Anchor and Hope, Calcutta, 6th Lodge of Bengal 1773 Lodge of Humility with Fortitude, Calcutta, 5th Lodge of Bengal 1773 Lodge of True Friendship, with the 3d Brigade, 4th Lodge of Bengal 1775 At Futty Ghur, Bengal 1786 Lodge of the North Star, Fredericksnagore, 7th Lodge of Bengal 1789 At Chunar, in the East Indies, 8th Lodge of Bengal 1793 Lodge of Mars, Cawnpore, 9th Lodge of Bengal 1793"

There was also another lodge, the Marine Lodge, Calcutta, and a Stewards' Lodge under the Grand Lodge of England.

From the first two lodges of the above list the officers of the Prov. Grand Lodge had always been selected, which induced resentment upon the part of the other lodges.

This feeling brought about a general defection from the Prov. Grand Lodge of Bengal and by consequence from the Grand Lodge of England. An ephemeral lodge - No. 146 - under the Atholl (or Ancient) Grand Lodge was established at Calcutta in 1767, but no others were founded until later.

"The Lodges 'True Friendship' and 'Humility with Fortitude' were the first who transferred their allegiance, the former becoming No. 315, or No. 1 of Bengal, Dec. 27, 1797; and the latter, No. 317, or No. 2 of Bengal, April 11, 1798. The 'Marine Lodge' followed their example, and obtained a similar warrant - No. 323 - March 4, 1801.

Meanwhile, Lodge 'Star in the East' fell into abeyance, and 'Industry and Perseverance' was on the point of closing also. One meeting only was held in each of the years 1802, 1803, and 1804, after which, for a long period, there were no more. Lodge 'Anchor and Hope' obtained an Atholl warrant as No. 325 - Oct. 11, 1801. Little is known of Lodge 'Unanimity,' which, though carried forward at the union (1813), must have died out at least several years before.

"During the ten or eleven years that intervened between the obliteration of the Prov. Grand Lodge and its re-establishment in 1813, Masonry in Calcutta was represented almost exclusively by the Lodges which had seceded from the (older) Grand Lodge of England.

"On St. John's Day (in Christmas), 1809, the Lodges, True Friendship, Humility with Fortitude, Marine, No. 338 (Ancients) in the 14th Foot, and the 'Dispensation Lodge,' working under a warrant granted by No. 338, walked in procession to St. John's Church, where a Masonic sermon was delivered by the Rev. Dr. James Ward.

"Happily, Lodges Star in the East, and Industry and Perseverance, were revived in 1812, and on December 22 of that yeas; accompanied by the 'Officers' Lodge,' No. 347 in the 14th Foot, and Humility with Fortitude, also walked in procession to the same church, and benefited by a like sermon from Dr. Ward.

"On October 4, 1813, the Earl of Moira - who had been appointed Acting Grand Master of India - arrived in Calcutta. The first Masonic act of the Governor-General was to constitute a new Lodge in that city - the Moira, Freedom and Fidelity - November 8, and his second, to re-establish the Prov. Grand Lodge of Bengal under the Hon. Archibald Seton."

Upon the union of the two Grand Lodges, the "Atholl" lodges, three in number, at Calcutta came under the jurisdiction of the Prov. Grand Lodge.

Two others of the secession are not mentioned in the records of the Province, 1814-40.

"At the period of this fusion, there were the following Lodges under the old sanction: The Stewards, Star in the East, Industry and Perseverance, and Sincere Friendship (Chunar). Of these Lodges, the first never held a London warrant, and the last was struck off the roll inadvertently at the Union. There were also then in existence the Moira Lodge, and three others, constituted since the revival of the Prov. Grand Lodge, the names of which head the following table of Lodges erected during the period 813 - 26:

Moira, Calcutta, November 13, 1813, Oriental Star, Noacollee, April 21, 1814.

Aurora, Calcutta, June 23, 1814.

Courage with Humanity, Dum Dum, July 12, 1814.

Northern Star, Barrackpore, July 18, 1816.

Sincerity, Cawnpore, January 8, 1819.

Hasting Lodge of Amity and Independence, Allahabad, April 9, 1821.

United Lodge of Friendship, Cawnpore, June 13, 1821.

Humanity with Courage, Prince of Wales' Island, July, 1822.

Amity, St. John's, Poona (Deccan), January 30, 1824.

Kilwinning in the West, Nusseerabed, October 20, 1824.

Larkins' Lodge of Union and Brotherly Love, Dinapore, October 20, 1824 Independence with Philanthropy, Allahabad, October 26, 1825.

South-Eastern Star of Light and Victory, Arracan, October 26, 1825.

Tuscan, Malacca, October 26, 1825.

Royal George, Bombay, December 9, 1825.

Union and Perseverance, Agra, October 23, 1826.

Kilwinning in the East, Calcutta, December 23, 1826.

"Out of these eighteen Lodges, however, only seven - Nos. 2, 3, 4, 6, 7, 13, and 18 above - secured a footing on the roll of the Grand Lodge of England, and it is not a little curious that of the two now alone surviving, Courage with Humanity (1814), and Independence with Philanthropy (1825), which were placed on the general list in the same year (1828) in juxtaposition, the latter bears the earlier number, and has the higher precedence!"

The Duke of Sussex empowered Earl Moira, whose sway extended over India, to appoint Provincial Grand Masters, as if appointed by himself.

Acting Prov. G. M. Seton, leaving India in 1817, the Governor General, Marquis of Hastings, selected Hon. C. Stuart to succeed him, but he does not appear to have qualified. So Hon. C. R Lindsay was appointed by Marquis of Hastings, Prov. G. M.

January 17, 1818, and by the Deputy G. M. of India January 13, 1819.

November 30, 1818, request was made to the Grand Master of India by eight persons for permission to meet as a lodge at St. Andrew, to make the Hon. Mountstuart Elphinstone a Mason and also to install him, when made, as deacon. No record of any reply has been kept.

John Pascal Larkins succeeded Lindsay as D.G.M. of India and Prov. G. M. of Bengal December 24, 1819. He returned to Europe in 1826, and until 1840 the Craft in Bengal was ruled by a Deputy in Calcutta. From this resulted the overthrow of all order and constitutional authority.

"The Lodges in Bengal made their returns regularly, and forwarded their dues punctually, to the Prov. Grand Lodge; but as no steps were taken for the transmission of these returns and dues to their destination, the Grand Lodge of England ceased to notice or regard the tributary Lodges of Bengal. On the submission of a motion for inquiry - March 22, 1828 - the Deputy Prov. G.M. 'felt himself constrained to resign his chair on the spot, and the Grand Wardens also tendered their resignations.'

"This led, at the instance of Lodge Aurora, to the formation of a representative body, styled the Lodge of Delegates, who were charged with the duty of preparing a memorial to the Grand Lodge of England, which, bearing date August 22, 1828, was sent to the Duke of Sussex, signed by the Masters and Wardens of the following Lodges: True Friendship, Humility with Fortitude, Marine, Aurora, Courage with Humanity, and Kilwinning in the East.

"To this no reply was vouchsafed. The letters of the Lodges in Bengal remained unanswered, and their requests unheeded. The usual certificates for brethren made in the country were withheld, notwithstanding that the established dues were regularly remitted; and applications for warrants were also unnoticed, though they were accompanied by the proper fees. This state of affairs continued antil 1834, when the question of separation from the Grand Lodge of England was gravely and formally mooted in the Lodges. Overtures for a reconciliation at length came in the shape of certificates for brethren who had by this time grown gray in Masonry. Answers to letters written long ago were also received; but the most important concession made by the Grand Lodge of England was the constitution of the first District Grand Lodge of Bengal - under Dr. John Grant - which held its first meeting, February 28, 1840."

"In 1834 some Masons at Delhi applied to their brethren at Meerut for an acting constitution of this kind, which might serve their purpose until the receipt of a warrant from the Grand Lodge of England. At the latter station there were two Lodges, one of which, however, was itself working under dispensation, and could not therefore dispense grace to another. The other belonged to the 26th Foot, No. 26, under the Grand Lodge of Ireland. This Lodge declined giving a dispensation, for the somewhat Irish reason that the Cameronian Lodge had already granted one to another Lodge, of the propriety of which act they had great doubt; and that until an answer had been received from Ireland they could not commit a second act of doubtful legality! The custom, however, was a very old one. In 1759, Lodge No. 74, I.R., in the 1st Foot (2d Batt.), granted an exact copy of its warrant - dated October 26, 1737 - to some brethren at Albany, to work under until they received a separate charter from Ireland. This was changed - February 21, 1765 - for a warrant from George Harrison, English Prov. G.M. of New York; and the Lodge - Mount Vernon - is now No. 3 on the roll of the Grand Lodge of that State."[146]

In the British Army the Grand Lodge of Ireland has been the favorite of Grand Bodies, and yet only one stationary lodge has been erected in India under its jurisdiction. This was in 1837 at Kurnaul, but it seems to have lived only one year. At Bombay, in 1862, an attempt was made to organize another lodge. But the attempt failed, as the Grand Lodge of Ireland refused a warrant on the ground that there were already two jurisdictions in India, the English and Scotch

"In the decennial periods 1840 - 50 and 1850 - 60 there were in each instance 12 additions to the roll. In 1860 - 70 the new Lodges amounted to 19, and in 1870 - 85 to 38. These figures are confined to the English Lodges, but extend over the area now occupied in part by the District Grand Lodges of Burmah and the Punjaub, both of which were carved out of the territory previously comprised within the Province of Bengal in 1868. The following statistics show the number of Lodges existing - January 1, 1886 - in the various states and districts which until 1868 were subject to the Masonic government of Bengal: under the Grand Lodge of England - Bengal (D.G.L.), 39; British Burmah (D.G.L.), 7; and Punjaub (D.G.L.), 24. Under the Grand Lodge of Scotland, II - the earliest of which, St. David (originally Kilwinning) in the East, No. 371, Calcutta, was constituted February 5, 1849.

"The Dutch Lodges in Hindostan have passed out of existence, but with regard to these, and also to certain other Lodges established by the Grand Lodge of Holland in various places beyond the seas, the materials for an exhaustive list are not available to the historian."

Madras.

At this place in 1752 was established the earliest lodge in Southern India. In 1765 three others were formed at the same station.

---

[146] Cf Barker. "Early Hist. of the Grand Lodge of New York," preface, p. xviii

Captain Edmund Pascal was appointed Provincial Grand Master for Madras and its Dependencies, about 1756. In the following year a fifth lodge was erected at Fort St. George. The other English settlements in India were dominated by this presidency for a short period, and the Carnatic figures largely in Indian Masonic history during the latter half of the 18th century owing to the continuous wars with the French, and afterward with Hyder Ali and his son.

"In 1768 a lodge - No. 152 - was established by the Atholl (or Ancient) Grand Lodge of England at Fort St. George; and in 1773 one by the Grand Lodge of Holland at Negapatam. The next event of importance was the initiation, in 1776, of Umdat-Umara, eldest son of the Nabob of Arcot, at Trichinopoly, who in his reply to the congratulations of the Grand Lodge of England, stated 'he considered the title of an English Mason as one of the most honorable he possessed.'"

A Provincial Grand Lodge under the Atholl sanction was established at Fort St. George in 1781, "but the dissensions in the settlements had so rent asunder every link of social life, that even the fraternal bond of Masonry has been annihilated in the general wreck."

Under Brigadier-General Horn, "Prov. G.M. for the Coast of Coromandel, the Presidency of Madras and parts adjacent," the union of the Brethren in Southern India was effected.

All the older lodges at this time seem to have been extinct; but there was established at Arcot in 1786 the C.M.L. The following year Lodge No. 152 tendered its allegiance to General Horn and joined one of the lodges under that officer.

Of these, four were added to the roll in 1787. Nos. 510 - 513 - Perfect Harmony, St. Thomas Mount; Social Friendship, Madras; Trichinopoly; and Social Friendship, St. Thomas Mount - and styled Nos. 3, 4, 5, and 6, Coast of Coromandel. Two other lodges were also established in the same year, the Stewards and Perfect Unanimity, which, according to the loose practice of those days, were given the places on the list of the two earliest Madras lodges, and became (in 1790) Nos. 102 and 233 respectively.

A lodge of happy nomenclature - La Fraternite Cosmopolite - was constituted at Pondicherry in 1786 by the Grand Orient of France, and a second - Les Navigateurs Reunis - 1790.

In the latter year - July 5th - John Chamier received a similar patent, as Prov. G.M., to that previously held by General Horn, and was succeeded by Terence Gahagan, 1806, and Herbert Compton, 1812. During this period four lodges were added to the roll - Solid Friendship,

Trichinopoly, 1790; Unity, Peace and Concord, 1798; St. Andrew's Union, 19th Foot, 1802; and Philanthropists, in the Scotch Brigade (94th Foot), 1802, at Madras. These lodges were numbered 572, 574, 590, and 591 on the general, and 7, 9, 10, and 11 (Coast of Coromandel) on the local, lists respectively.

After the union the Province was ruled by Dr. Richard Jebb, 1814; George Lys, 1820; and in 1825 by Compton once more. The name of this worthy only disappears from the Freemasons' Calendar in 1842, and with it the provincial title, "Coast of Coromandel" - exchanged for "Madras," over which Lord Elphinstone had been appointed Prov. G.M. in 1840.

Within this period - 1814 - 42 - numerous Lodges were warranted locally, as in Bengal; but thirteen only - of which seven were in Madras itself - secured places on the London Register.

Eighteen English lodges have since been established in the Presidency, and there are at present in existence twenty lodges on the register of England and two on that of Scotland - both erected in 1875 - but the introduction of Scottish lodges into India will be referred to in the ensuing section.

The French lodge of Pondicherry - La Fraternite Cosmopolite - was revived (or a new one established under the old title) in 1821. Another - L'Union Indienne - was erected at the same station in 1851. At the present date, however, there exist throughout India and its dependencies no other lodges than those under the Grand Lodges of England and Scotland respectively.

Bombay.

During the 18th century there were established in this Presidency a lodge at Bombay in 1758, and one at Surat in 1798, which were carried on in the lists until 1813, but disappear at the union. Jas. Todd was appointed in 1763 Provincial Grand Master, and his name only drops out of the Freemasons' Calendar in 1799. The 78th foot, a regiment under Sir Arthur Wellesley in Mahratta war, and which took part in the decisive victory of Assaye, received an Atholl Warrant in 1801. A lodge at Poona was established in 1818. No more were established in the Presidency until 1822, when the Benevolent Lodge, Bombay, was placed on the lists. In the Bombay Artillery in 1823 there was "installed" at Poona a military lodge as No. 15 - Orion in the West - Coast of Coromandel, November 15th. The Proceedings of this lodge show that members "were examined in the Third Degree T.D. and passed into the chair of the Fourth Degree" - paying a fee of three gold mohurs.

"Among the Masons about this time in Bombay were thirteen non-commissioned officers who were too poor to establish a lodge of their own, and too modest to seek admittance in what was considered an aristocratic lodge. They met, however, monthly in the guard-room over the Apollo Gate, for mutual instruction in Masonry. This coming to the knowledge of the Benevolent Lodge, the thirteen were elected honorary members of No. 746, for which they returned heartfelt thanks. At their first attendance, when the lodge work was over, and the Brethren adjourned to the banquet, the thirteen were informed that refreshments awaited them downstairs. Revolting at the distinction thus made among Masons, they one and all left the place. The next morning they were sent for by their commanding officer, who was also one of the officers of the lodge, and asked to explain their conduct. One of the party - Mr. W. Willis (by whom this anecdote was first related to me) - told him that as Masons they were bound to meet on the level and part on the square, but as this fundamental principle was not practiced in No. 746, of which they had been elected honorary mernbers, they could not partake of their hospitality. The astonished Colonel uttered not a word, but waived his hand for them to retire. Ever after this, the Benevolent Lodge - including the thirteen - met on the level, both in lodge and at the banquet-table."[147]

Burnes, in 1836, may be best described, in ecclesiastical phrase, as a Prov. G.M. "in partibus infidelium," for whatever lodges then existed throughout the length and breadth of India were strangers to Scottish Masonry. But the times were propitious.

There was no English Provincial Grand Lodge of Bombay; and under the Chevalier Burnes, who had been bountifully endowed by nature with the qualities requisite for Masonic administration. "Scottish Masonry presented such attractions, that the strange sight was witnessed of English Masons deserting their Mother Lodges to such an extent that these fell into abeyance, in order that they might give their support to lodges newly constituted by the Grand Lodge of Scotland. In one case, indeed, a lodge - Perseverance - under England went over bodily to the enemy, with its name, jewels, furniture, and belongings, and the charge was accepted by Scotland."

"From this period, therefore, Scottish Masonry flourished, and English Masonry declined, the latter finally becoming quite dormant

---

[147] Gould's "Hist" vol. vi p. 354, note 2.

until the year 1848, when a lodge, St. George, No. 807 on the roll of the Grand Lodge of England, was again formed at Bombay, and for some years was the solitary representative of English Masonry in the Province."[148]

Rising Star, No. 413, was established by Burnes at Bombay, for the admission of natives - a beautiful medal, cut by Wyon, was struck in consequence - No. 414, St. Andrew in the East, at Poona was formed by him.

Nos. 421, Hope, Kurrachee, and 422, Perseverance, Bombay, 1847, followed.

In 1824 there was established at Poona a second lodge which, however, has passed out of existence and left no trace thereof. The civilian element of the military lodge at Poona, No. 15, seceded in 1825 and, also at Poona, formed a lodge, 802, the Lodge of Hope. At this point Lodge 15, unrecognized at home, aided in the secession of some of its members who obtained a Warrant, on the recommendation of the parent lodge, from the Grand Lodge of England.

In 1828, Perseverance, No. 818, was erected at Bombay. No notification of the existence of Orion in the west had been received by the Grand Lodge of England, nor had any fees been paid, though regularly paid to the Provincial Grand Lodge of the Coast of Coromandel, though this was not ascertained until 1830. Also it was ascertained that the Prov. G.M. of the Coast of Coromandel had gone beyond his powers in permitting the erection of a lodge at Bombay, though ultimately there was granted from England July 19, 1833, a new Warrant, No. 598.

As yet there had been no invasion of the jurisdiction of the Grand Lodge of England; but the Grand Lodge of Scotland, in 1836, appointed Dr. Jas. Burnes Prov. G. M. of Western India and its Dependencies. But not until January 1, 1838, was a Prov. Grand Lodge formed. Subsequently there was erected in Eastern India a second Scottish Province. This was absorbed within the jurisdiction of Dr. Burnes on the retirement of the Marquis of Tweeddale, who became Prov. G.M. for all India, in 1846, with the proviso, however, that any future subdivisionof the Presidencies was not to be restrained by this appointment.

After this, in Bengal, Scottish lodges were established - Kilwinning in the East, Calcutta, 1849; and in Arabia Felix, Aden, 1850. At the beginning of 1886, from the Grand Lodge of Scotland, there had

---

[148] Ibid., vol. vi., p. 335

been received charters by nineteen lodges under Bombay, eleven under Bengal, two under Madras, and one in Afghanistan - thirtythree lodges in all.

In 1849, Burnes, leaving India, was succeeded in Western India only by a Prov. G. M.

However, Captain Henry Morland became Prov. G. M. of Hindustan in 1874, and subsequently became Grand Master of All Scottish Freemasonry in India.

Of the lodges under the Grand Lodge of England, St. George, erected in 1848, was the only representative of its class for ten years. However, "Concord" and "Union" were established at Bombay and Currachee respectively, in 1858. From its dormancy, "Orion in the West " aroused a year later. A Provincial Grand Lodge was established in 1861, and other subordinate lodges were subsequently chartered.

At first Freemasonry did not take any real root among the native population of India.

"Umdat-ul-Umara, son of the Nabob of Arcot, was admitted a member of the Society, in 1776. The princess Keyralla Khan (of the Mysore family) and Shadad Khan (ex-Ameer of Scinde) joined, or were made Masons in, the lodge of "True Friendship" in 1842 and 1850 respectively; and in 1861 the Maharajahs Duleep and Kundeer Sing were initiated in lodges "Star of the East" and "Hope and Perseverance" - the last-named personage at Lahore, and the other three in Calcutta.

A By-law of the Prov. Grand Lodge of Bengal, forbidding the entry of Asiatics without the permission of the P.G.M., was in force until May 12, 1871; and there was at least a popular belief in existence so late as 1860, that Hindus were ineligible for initiation.

The Parsees of Western India were the first of the native races who evinced any real interest in the institution, and are to be congratulated on the recent election (1886) of one of their number - Mr. Cama - to the high position of Treasurer of the Grand Lodge of England.

In 1876 a Scottish lodge, No. 587, "Islam"- presumably for the association of Mohammedans - was erected at Bombay. The extent to which Freemasonry is now practiced by the Hindus - who form 73 1/2 per cent. of the total population of India - I am unable to determine. The first of this class of religionists to fill the chair of a lodge was Mr. Dutt, whose election in 1874 may not have been without influence in the diffusion of Masonic light.

The Indian Freemasons' friend, a publication of rare merit, was set on foot at Calcutta in 1855, but was short-lived. A new or second series was commenced in May, 1861, and lasted to the end of 1867. In Bombay, the Masonic Record of Western India enjoys an extensive circulation, and is very ably conducted.

East India Islands.

Ceylon. - This, for convenience, is grouped under the heading "East India" and in these islands the Grand Lodge of Orient established Masonry. In 1771 Fidelity was erected at Colombo; in 1773 Sincerity at Point de Galle; in 1794 Union, another at Colombo.

When the British possessed themselves of the Dutch settlements on the Island, it was annexed to the Presidency of Madras, but in 1801 was formed into a separate crown colony. The Grand Lodge of Scotland granted a Charter February 9, 1801, to the 51st Regiment, stationed at Colombo, for the Orient Lodge. There were also formed on the islands two other lodges under Atholl (or Ancient). In 1810 Sir AlexanderJohnston was appointed Prov. G.M. by the Grand Lodge of England, though his name disappears from the lists before 1838. However, greater activity was displayed under other jurisdictions. At Colombo, in 1821, an Irish lodge was erected, and in 1822, a French one under the G.O. In 1832 there was revived the latter, or there was formed a new lodge of the same name.

Sumatra.

There was established at Bencoolen, in 1765, an English lodge, and in 1772 and 1796, at Fort Marlborough, two others. Until 1813 these appeared in the lists, but the "Marlboro," which ultimately became No. 242, was carried forward at the union but was erased March 5, 1862, having omitted to make any returns for several years. Under John Macdonald, in 1793, Sumatra was erected into an English Province, and he was succeeded by H.R. Lewis, as Prov. G. M., December 10, 1821, but continued to hold office until his death in 1877, there having been in existence at the date of his original appointment one lodge, and none at all for fifteen years preceding his decease.

Java.

The Grand Lodge of Holland constituted a lodge - Star in the East - into this island in 1769. There are no precise records, but it is known that others sprung up in the Capitol and larger towns. In 1771 there was erected at Batavia a second lodge, and at Sama rang in 1801, and at Sourabaya, 1809, charters were granted. In 1886 there were eight lodges in Java.

Celebes.
There was erected at Macassar, in 1883, under the Grand Lodge of Holland, one lodge - Arbeid Adelt.

Borneo.
An English lodge - Elopura - was established in North Borneo, in 1885, at the station of the same name.

The Philippines.
In 1886 there were four lodges in existence in these islands, one under the National Grand Orient, and three under the Grand Lodge of Spain. The latter form a Province, and are subject to a Provincial Superintendent.

Persia.
"Thory informs us that Askeri-Khan, ambassador of the Shah at Paris, and who was himself admitted into Masonry in that city - November 24, 1808 - took counsel with his French Brethren respecting the foundation of a lodge at Ispahan. Whether this project was ever carried into effect it is impossible to say, but two years later we find another Persian - also an ambassador - figuring in Masonic history. On June 15, 1810, " His Excellency Mirza Abul Hassan Khan" was granted the rank of Past Grand Master of the Grand Lodge of England. This personage - the Minister accredited from the Court of Persia to that of Great Britain - in addition to having been a great traveler both in Hindustan and Arabia, had also performed his devotions at Mecca. In the course of his journey from Teheran he passed through Georgia, Armenia, and Antolia. At Constantinople he embarked in a British man-of-war, and reached England in December, 1809.

"Sir Gore Ousely, Bart., whowas selected to attend upon the Mirza 'as Mehmander - an officer of distinction, whose duty it is to receive and entertain foreign princes and other illustrious personages' - in the following year (1810) received the appointment of ambassador to the Shah of Persia, and was also granted an English patent as Provincial G.M. for that country. No lodges, however, were established in Persia at any time by the Grand Lodge of England, nor - so far as the evidence extends - by any other external authority. The Mirza Abul Hassan Khan was made a Mason by Lord Moira in 1810. The extent of his services to the Craft we must leave undecided; but it was stated somewhat recently in the Masonic journals, on the authority of a Persian military officer then pursuing his studies in Berlin, that nearly all the members of the Court of Teheran are Brethren of our Society."

The Straits Settlements.

The Duke of Atholl established Neptune Lodge, No. 344, at Penang (or Prince of Wales Island) by Warrant September 6, 1809, which became extinct in 1819. Three years subsequently a military lodge - Humanity with Courage - was warranted from Bengal.

This body, however, having become irregular by the initiation of civilians, the Duke of Sussex renewed the Charter of the Atholl Lodge, which, having flourished for a time, eventually fell into decay, and was erased, together with another lodge "Neptune" also at Penang - erected in 1850 - No. 846 on the English roll, March 5, 1862. The only lodge now existing in this settlement is No. 1555, warranted by the Grand Lodge of England in 1875.

In Malacca, a lodge was formed under the Prov. Grand Lodge of Bengal in 1825, which never secured a place on the general list. In Singapore, English lodges were established in 1845, 1858, and 1867, named Zetland in the East, Fidelity, and St. George, Nos. 748, 1042, and 1152 respectively. Of these the first and last survive, and, together with the lodge at Penang, compose the province of the Eastern Archipelago, of which Mr. W. H. Read was appointed the first Prov. G. M. in 1858.

Cochin-China.

In this French dependency, a lodge - Le Reveil de Orient - was established by Warrant of the Grand Orient of France, October 22, 1868.

China.

During the last century two lodges of foreign origin were constituted in the Celestial Empire - the lodge of 'Amity," No. 407, under an English, and "Elizabeth" under a Swedish, Warrant. The former was erected in 1767, the latter in 1788; and in each case the place of assembly was Canton. The English lodge was not carried forward at the union (1813), and " Elizabeth," as we are informed by the Grand Secretary of Sweden, came to an end in 1812.

The next lodge erected on Chinese soil was the Royal Sussex, No. 735, at Canton, for which a Warrant was granted by the United G.L. of England in 1844. A second Zetland, No. 768 - was established at

Hong-Kong under the same sanction, in 1846; and a third - Northern Lodge of China - at Shanghai, in 1849. No further increase of Lodges took place until 1864, in which year two were added to the English roll, at Hong-Kong and Shanghai respectively; and one each at the latter port under the Grand Lodges of Scotland and Massachusetts. The progress of the craft in the "Middle Kingdom" has since been marked, but uneventful, though as yet Freemasonry has failed to diffuse its light beyond the British Colony of Hong-Kong, and the various ports of the mainland opened up by treaty to the merchants of foreign powers. Mr. Samuel Rawson was appointed by Lord Zetland Prov. G.M. for China in 1847; and a second Province was carved out of the old one in 1877, by the appointment of Mr. Cornelius Thorne as District G.M. for northern China.

In 1886 there were in existence at Victoria (Hong-Kong) and the Chinese treaty-ports thirteen English, one American, and four Scottish Lodges; and with a solitary exception - No. 1217, at Ningpo, formed in 1868, under the Grand Lodge of England, but now extinct - all the lodges erected in China or Hong-Kong since the revival of Masonry in the Far East (1844) were still active, and can therefore be traced in the calendars of current date by those desirous of further information respecting them.

Japan.

"English Lodges bearing the following numbers were erected at Yokohama - 1092 and 1263 - in 1866 and 1869; at Yedo (now extinct) - 1344- in 1870; at Kobe - 140I - in 1872; and at Tokio - 2015 - in 1883. These are subject to a Prov. G.M., who was appointed in 1873.

"There are also three lodges under the Grand Lodge of Scotland - Nos. 498, 640, and 710 - at Kobe, Yokohama, and Nagasaki."

Cape Colony.

Prior to the acquisition of this colony by Great Britain, two Dutch lodges had been erected at Cape Town, in 1772 and 1802, respectively. While these survived, several other lodges under the same jurisdiction passed away without leaving any trace of their existence.

Afterward the Grand Lodge of England, established at the capital lodges in 1811 and 1812 - the "British," No. 629 under the old sanction, in the former year; and the "Cape of Good Hope" Lodge under an Atholl Warrant in the Tenth Battalion of the Royal Artillery.

The first band of English settlers arrived in 1820, and in the following year a second stationary lodge, under the United Grand Lodge of England - Hope, No. 727 - was erected at Cape Town, where, also, a lodge bearing the same name, under the G.O. of France, sprang up, November 10, 1824. A third English lodge, Albany, No. 817, was established at Grahamstown in 1828. "The Dutch lodges received the English Brethren with open arms, and with great satisfaction. When English Masonry had increased, and it was considered right to form a Provincial Grand Lodge, the Brother selected for the office of Prov. G.M. was the Deputy G.M. Of the Netherlands, who continued till his death to hold the two appointments." This must have been Sir John Truter, who received an English patent in 1829; for although an earlier Prov. G.M. under England, Richard Blake, had been appointed in 1801, the words quoted above will not apply to the latter. Between 1828 and 1850 there was no augmentation of the lodges; but in the latter year a revival set in, and during the decade immediately ensuing, 1851-60, six were warranted by the Grand Lodge of England.

In 1860, to the jurisdictions already existing (those of Holland and England), was added that of Scotland, under the Grand Lodge of which country a lodge, Southern Cross, No. 398, was erected at Cape Town. Shortly afterward, in a single year (1863), two Dutch lodges were established in Cape Colony, and one at Bloemfontein, in the Orange Free State. This period coincides with the appointment, after an interregnum, of the Hon. Richard Southy as Prov. G.M. under the G.L. of England; and it will be convenient if I here proceed to describe seriatim the progress of Masonry under the three competing jurisdictions. Commencing with that of England between the date to which the statistics were last given (1860) down to the close of 1885, sixty-two lodges were added to the roll. The number at present existing in South Africa, as shown by the official calendar of current date, is fifty-four, viz.: Eastern Division, twenty-four; Western Division, eight; Natal, eleven; and eleven not subject to any provincial authority, some of which were formerly under the District Grand Lodge of Griqualand (now abolished), and two, No. 1022, at Bloemfontein (Orange Free State), and 1747, at Pretoria (Transvaal), are situate in foreign territory. Within the same period (1860-85) twelve lodges have been established under the Grand Lodge of Scotland, and now compose a Masonic District (or Province). The Dutch Masonic Calendar for 1886 shows twenty four lodges as existing in South Africa. Of these, as already related, two were erected before 1803, and three in 1863. The latest on the present list dates from 1884. These lodges are distributed throughout the British possessions, and the different Boer Republics, as follows, viz .- In British South Africa, sixteen; in the Orange Free State, four; and in the

Transvaal, four; and at the head of all is a Deputy National G.M., Mr. J.H. Hofmeisr, at Cape Town.

Between the English and Dutch Masons at the Cape, there have always been the most friendly relations. In 1863 the D.G.L. under England was re-erected, and there assisted at its re-inauguration the Deputy G.M. under the Grand Lodge of the Netherlands. And the Dutch Fraternity placed their Masonic Hall at the disposal of the English Brethren.

For a long time it was the custom on St. John's Day for the English and Dutch Masons to assemble at different hours of the day so that the Brethren might be present at both meetings. On June 5, 1867, there was stated at a communication of the Grand Lodge of England that "recently an objection has been raised by some of the younger English Masons against the establishment of some new Lodges lately formed by the Dutch, on the ground that the Convention of 1770 prohibits their doing so, the Cape now being an English possession, and having been so since the early part of the present century. In this view, the District Grand Lodge does not seem to participate. That body is anxious that the amicable relations that have so long subsisted between the English and Dutch Masons should continue. After setting the foregoing facts before the Grand Lodge, the Grand Registrar expressed an opinion that whatever might have been the intention of the Convention of 1770, it had not been acted on in the Cape Colony, but that the G.M. of England, by appointing the Deputy G.M. of the Netherlands to be his Prov. G.M. over English Lodges, virtually recognized the Dutch Lodges. It must be taken for granted that both the contracting parties have tacitly consented that it should not apply to the Cape. He was of opinion that as both parties seem to have considered that the Cape was neutral ground, and the existence of two Grand Lodges having been allowed to continue side by side, it would be for the benefit of the Brethren in that Colony, that as they have gone on working as friends and brothers, they should continue to do so." A resolution embodying the foregoing was then put and unanimously adopted.

CHAPTER V

AUSTRALASIA

New South Wales.
    The Lodge of Social and Military Virtues - No. 227 on the roll of the Grand Lodge of Ireland - attached to the 46th Foot in 1752, after undergoing many vicissitudes, was at work in the same regiment at Sydney in 1816. This paved the way for the establishment of stationary lodges, and Irish warrants were issued to Nos. 260, Australian Social, in 1820, and 266, Leinster, in 1824. The third (strictly colonial) lodge, No. 820, Australia, was erected by the Grand Lodge of England in 1828. The last named, as well as the Irish lodges, met at Sydney, the capital. The first established in any other part of the Colony was No. 668, St. John, constituted at Paramatta in 1838, and the second, No. 697, the Lodge of Australia Felix, at Melbourne - then included in the government of New South Wales - 1841. An Irish lodge - No. 275 - was erected at Windsor in 1843, and in the same year, No. 408, Australasian Kilwinning, at Melbourne, received a Charter from the Grand Lodge of Scotland.
    During the two decennial periods ensuing, there were issued in the Colony twenty-one English, eight Scottish, and two Irish lodges. Between 1864-85 there were added forty- seven English, forty-one Scottish, and four Irish lodges. Up to 1886 there were seventy- four English, one Irish, and fifty Scottish active lodges. In 1839 an English Provincial Grand Master was appointed, and one for the Grand Lodge of Scotland in 1855, and that of Ireland in 1858.
    "While the question of separation from the Mother Grand Lodges was first formerly mooted in Victoria, still for some years, at least, there had existed in Sydney a body styling itself 'the Grand Lodge of New South Wales,' formed from the great majority of a regular lodge - St.

Andrew's. It affected to make, pass, and raise Masons, grant charters, and issue certificates.'

"On December 3d, 1877, the representatives of twelve or (at most) thirteen Scottish and Irish lodges met at Sydney, and established another Grand Lodge of New South Wales, to which, however, the preexisting body of the same name eventually made submission, and accepted an ordinary Lodge Warrant at its hands. At this time (1877) there were eighty-six regular Lodges in the Colony; English, forty-seven; Scottish, thirty; and Irish, nine. The thirteen lodges which thus assumed to control the dissenting majority of seventy-three, sheltered themselves under a perverted principle of Masonic law - applied to a wholly illusory state of facts. This was, that any three lodges in a territory 'Masonically unoccupied' - the three jurisdictions already existing being thus coolly and quietly ignored - could form themselves into a Grand Lodge, and that when so formed, the remaining lodges - averse to the movement - were they one hundred or one thousand in number, would be irregular!"

Mr. Jas. F. Farnell, appointed Prov. G.M. under the Grand Lodge of Ireland, 1869, was a leader in this movement. The flag of independence was first raised by the Irish lodges. While there were great disadvantages in having the Australian lodges working under warrants from distant Grand Lodges, still there were reasons not entirely sentimental, which raised an opposition to separation from the earlier existing Grand Lodges. Whenever matters are in proper condition for the erection of an Independent Grand Lodge, the matter will happily culminate, and a large majority of the lodges and brethren interested will unite therewith. Should, however, the movement be premature, the outcome of the agitation will largely depend upon the character and influence of the leaders, or what is the same thing, upon the extent of the following.

Mr. Farnell for twenty years was a member of the parliament of New South Wales, and was also Prime Minister, but does not seem to have had great influence as a Mason.

The Irish Province of New South Wales had its affairs in great confusion when he was elected Grand Master. And not the smallest of the motives which weighed with his supporters - Scotch as well as Irish - seems to have been the disinclination to be taxed by (or remit fees to) the mother countries.

The new organization, at the close of 1885, had been recognized as the only regular governing Masonic body in the Colony of thirty-eight Grand Lodges, chiefly, however, American. There seems, indeed, in the United States a decided inclination to regard each uprising of the lodges in a British colony as a tribute to the efficacy of a certain doctrine which has been laid down by Dr. Mackey with regard to the formation of Grand Lodges. But those American jurisdictions which have lent a willing ear to the specious representations of the Grand Lodge of New South Wales are now running the gauntlet of intelligent criticism, and the several committees by whom they have been hoodwinked or misled, may read with profit some of the reports on correspondence in the larger States, notably, Illinois, Pennsylvania, and New York, where the unaccountable delusion into which so many Grand Lodges have fallen is discussed with equal candor and ability. It is almost needless to say that a Grand Lodge thus constituted by a small minority of the lodges in New South Wales, has been refused recognition by the Grand Lodges of the British Islands.

Victoria.

The lodges of Australia Felix and of Australasia (now Nos. 474 and 530) were established at Melbourne by the Grand Lodge of England in 1841 and 1846 respectively. Scottish Masonry obtained a footing in the same city - with "Australasian Kilwinning"--in 1843; and an Irish lodge - Hiram, No. 349 - was also chartered there in 1847. In the same year a third English, apparently the fifth Victorian, lodge - Unity and Prudence, No. 801 - was constituted at Geelong. After this the Craft advanced in prosperity by leaps and bounds. Thirty-six English lodges were added to the list between 1847 and the close of 1862; twenty-eight during the ensuing thirteen years, and twenty within the decennial period commencing January 1, 1876. During corresponding intervals of time, the Irish warrants granted in the colony were respectively twelve, seven, and three; and the Scottish, three each in the first two periods, and two in the last.

The first Provincial G. M. of Victoria (or Australia Felix) was the Hon. J. E. Murray. The date of his appointment by the Grand Lodge of Scotland has not been recorded, but he was succeeded by Mr. J. H. Ross, August 3, 1846. The present District G.M. is Sir W.J. Clarke, who received his Scottish patent in 1883 English and Irish Provinces were established in 1855 and 1856 respectively, and the following has been the succession of English Provincial (now District) Grand Masters: Captain (now Major General Sir Andrew) Clarke, 1855; Captain F.C. Standish, 1861; and Sir W.J. Clarke, 1883. The rulers of the Irish Province have been Mr. J.T. Smith, 1856-79; and from 1880, Sir W.J. Clarke.

The lodges now at work under the three jurisdictions, all of which, however, are in a manner united under a single Provincial G.M., are: English, ninety-one; Irish, seventeen; and Scottish, twelve (including one in Levuka, Fiji).

The idea of forming an independent Grand Lodge of Victoria seems to have been first launched in 1863, and after encountering the opposition of the Earl of Zetland, was debated - March 2, 1864 - in the Grand Lodge of England, by which body a resolution was passed declaring its "strong disapprobation" of the contemplated secession. It was observed in priecient terms by the late John Havers, that "every new Grand Lodge was the forerunner of new and conflicting degrees. It was a stone pulled away from the foundations of Masonry, and opened another door for inroads and innovations; "and he exhorted the Brethren in Victoria to "remember that union was strength, and universality one of the watchwords of Masonry."

In 1876 the agitation for a local Grand Lodge was renewed, but again slumbered until 1883, when the scheme was fairly carried into effect by an insignificant minority of the lodges.

In the latter year a meeting was held, and a Masonic Union of Victoria formed, April 27.

At this time there were seventy English, fifteen Irish, and ten Scottish lodges in the colony - total, ninety-five. On June 19th certain delegates met, and the adhesion of eighteen lodges - twelve Irish, five Scottish, and one English, to the cause was announced. But the number has since been reduced by the subtraction of the English lodge and one other, which were erroneously named in the proceedings. By this invention it was resolved "that the date of founding the Grand Lodge of Victoria should be July 2, 1883." Thus we find sixteen lodges, with an estimated membership of about eight hundred and forty, calmly transforming themselves into the governing body of a territory containing ninety-five lodges, and a membership of five thousand!

This organization has a following of about twenty subordinate lodges; and as the proceedings of some Grand Lodges baffle all reasonable conjecture, it will occasion no surprise to learn that by seventeen of these bodies the titular "Grand Lodge of Victoria" had been duly recognized at the close of 1885, as the supreme Masonic authority in this Australian colony. At the same date Mr. Coppin entered upon the second year of his Grand Mastership, having been installed - November 4th - in the presence of the Grand Masters of New South Wales and South Australia.

Meanwhile, however, the English, Irish, and Scottish lodges, which have remained true to their former allegiance, are united in a solid phalanx under a single Provincial (or District) G.M. - Sir W. J. Clarke; and should the day arrive when independence is constitutionally asserted by the century and more of lodges which obey this common chief, those bodies by whom the soi-disant Grand Lodge has been accorded recognition, will find themselves confronted by an interesting problem, not unlike that propounded with so much dramatic effect by the late Mr. Sothern in the role of Lord Dundreary, viz., "Whether it is the dog that wags its tail, or the tail that wags the dog?"

Sough Australia.

The South Australian Lodge of Friendship, Adelaide, No. 613 (and later, No. 423), on the roll of the Grand Lodge of England, was constituted at the British metropolis in 1834. The founders were all in London at the time, and two persons - afterward Sir John Morphett, President of the Legislative Council, and Sir D. R. Hansen, Chief Justice of the colony, were initiated. A second English lodge was established at Adelaide in 1844, and in the same year, also at the capital, a Scottish one.

In 1855 the first Irish Charter was received in the colony, and in 1883 the total number of lodges formed in South Australia was as follows: English, twenty active, one extinct; Irish, seven active, three extinct; and Scottish, six, all active.

The initiative in forming a Province was taken by Scotland in 1846, a step followed by England in 1848, and Ireland in 1860.

In 1883 there were premonitory symptoms that the lamentable examples set by a minority of the lodges in the adjacent colonies of New South Wales and Victoria, in usurping the authority and honor which should belong to the majority, would be followed in South Australia. The imminence of this danger induced Mr. H. M. Addison to form a Masonic Union, whose labors resulted - April 16, 1884 - in a convention of eighty-five delegates, representing twenty-eight lodges, by whom the Grand Lodge of South Australia was established. The proceedings of the executive committee of the Masonic Union, which were characterized throughout by the most scrupulous regularity, were crowned by an unprecedented unanimity of feeling on the part of the lodges. A resolution in favor of independence was carried nem. con. in eighteen English, four Irish, and six Scottish lodges, and with a single dissentient in one English, and with two dissentients in one Irish, lodge; while in the sole remaining lodge under England, and in the "Mostyn" under

Ireland, a majority of the members joined the Union. Thus, in effect, out of a grand total of thirty-three lodges under the three British jurisdictions, only a single lodge - No. 363 - Duke of Leinster (I.), has adhered to its former allegiance. The new Grand Lodge (besides the usual indiscriminate recognition of American Grand Bodies) has been admitted to fraternal relations with the Grand Lodges of England, Ireland, and Scotland. The privilege, however, accorded by the last named in August, 1885, was cancelled in the November following; a proceeding, there is every reason to believe, arising out of the inconsistent action of the colonial Grand Lodge in recognizing the authority of the Grand Lodge of New South Wales the irregular establishment of which, it was declared by Mr. Addison, at the formation of the Masonic Union in Adelaide, July 30, 1883, would, if initiated, " bring Masonry in South Australia into disrepute throughout the world."

The Hon. S. J. Way, Chief Justice of the Colony, and Mr. J. H. Cunningham, formerly District Grand Secretary (E.), have been Grand Master and Grand Secretary respectively, since the foundation of the Grand Lodge. The subordinate lodges are thirty-six in number, with a total membership of two thousand two hundred and seventy- seven.

Queensland.

The North Australian Lodge was established at Brisbane by the Grand Lodge of England in 1859, and two others under Irish and Scottish warrants respectively, were constituted at the same town in 1864.

Each jurisdiction is represented by a Provincial (or District) G. M., and the number of lodges is as follows: English, twenty-six active, two extinct; Irish, eleven active, three extinct; and Scottish, twelve, all active.

West Australia.

Eight lodges in all have been formed in this colony, the first of which - St. John, No. 712 - was erected at Perth in 1842. Seven of these survive, and being included in no Province, report direct to the Grand Lodge of England, which in this solitary instance has not suffered from the exercise of concurrent jurisdiction by other Grand Bodies.

Tasmania.

Lodges under the Grand Lodge of Ireland were established at Hobart Town in 1823, 1829, 1833, and 1834, but the three earliest of the series are now extinct. A fourth lodge under the same sanction was constituted at Launceston in 1843, and it was not until 1846 that English Masonry obtained a footing on the island. In that year Tasmanian Union, No. 781, was formed at Hobart Town, and a second English lodge - Hope - sprang up (in the first instance under a dispensation from Sydney) in 1852. In the following year the Rev. R. K. Ewing became the Master of the latter, and in 1856 the lodges of Faith and Charity were carved out of it - Mr. Ewing then becoming, on their joint petition, Prov. G.M. The other English lodge - Tasmanian Union - objecting to these proceedings, as having been carried on clandestinely, was suspended by the Prov. G.M., and remained closed for nine months. The strife thus engendered nearly put an end to English Masonry in Launceston. Lodge faith became dormant, Charity was voluntarily wound up, and even in Hope the light almost went out. Soon, however, there was a revival, and in 1876 the Grand Lodge of Scotland also began to charter lodges on the island, where there are now four in existence under its jurisdiction. These are included in the Province of New South Wales. The Grand Lodges of England and Ireland have each a roll of seven lodges on the island, one under the former body, and four under the latter, having surrendered their charters. The English Prov. Grand Lodge died a natural death on the removal of Mr. Ewing to Victoria, but a new one was established under Mr. W.S. Hammond in 1875. The Irish lodges were constituted into a Province in 1884.

New Zealand.

The first lodge in the Colony - Francaise Primitive Antipodienne - was founded at Akaroa bythe Supreme Council of France, August 29, 1843; the second - Ara - at Auckland, by the Grand Lodge of Ireland in 1844; and the third - New Zealand Pacific - by the Grand Lodge of England in 1845. No further charters were issued until 1852, when English lodges were established in Lyttelton, and Christchurch, whilst others sprang up at New Plymouth and Auckland in 1856, at Wanganui in 1857, and at Nelson and Kaiapoi in 1858. In the latter year an Irish lodge (the second in the Colony) was formed at Napier, and in 1860 an English one at Dunedin - where also the first Scottish lodge was erected in 1861. After this the diffusion of Masonry throughout New Zealand became so general, that I must content myself with giving the barest statistics, which, for convenience sake, will be classified so as to harmonize as far as possible with the Provincial systems of the three competing jurisdictions. Between 1860 and 1875 there were warranted in the Colony twenty-five English, eight Irish, and twenty-one

Scottish lodges; while in the ten years ending January 1, 1886, the numbers were respectively forty-seven, seven, and thirty-two.

The lodges in New Zealand are usually classified according to the Masonic Provinces of which they form a part. Of the latter there are five English and three Scottish, of late years dominated Districts, in order to distinguish them from bodies of a like character in Great Britain; and one Irish, to which the more familiar title of Provincial Grand Lodge is still applied. These preliminaries it will be necessary to bear in mind, because the arrangement which seems to me the simplest and best, is to group the lodges according to their positions on the map, which in the present case will correspond very closely with the territorial classification, or division into Districts, by the Grand Lodge of England.

North Island.

Auckland District. - The District (or Provincial) Grand Masters are Mr. G.S. Graham (E.), Sir F. Whitaker (S.), and Mr. G.P. Pierce (I.); whilst the number of lodges under the several jurisdictions is eighteen under the G.L. of England, and six each under those of Scotland and Ireland, that is, if taken according to locality, for all the Scottish lodges on the North Island are comprised within the Auckland District, and the whole of the Irish lodges in both islands within the Auckland Province.

Wellington District. - The only D.G.M. is Mr. C.J. Toxward (E.); and the number of lodges is respectively eighteen (E.), eight (S.), and four (I).

Middle, or South, Island.

Canterbury District. - The D.G.M.'s are Mr. Henry Thomson (E.) and the Rev. James Hill (S.), who rule over nineteen and nine lodges respectively. The seat of government is at Christchurch, where there is also an Irish lodge, the only one in the District.

Otovgo and Southland District. - Mr. T.S. Graham presides over one D.G.L. (E.), and Mr. G.W. Harvey over the other (S.). There are fourteen lodges in each District, i.e., according to the local arrangement, for the Scottish D.G.L. (of which there are only two in the South Island) exercises authority beyond the territorial limits of Otago and Southland. The total number of lodges on its roll is twenty-one, and doubtless Otago has derived much of its importance as a Scottish Masonic center, from the fact of having been originally founded by an association connected with the Free Church of Scotland. At Dunedin and Invercargill there is in each case an Irish lodge.

Westland District. - The only D.G.M. is Mr. John Bevan (E.), who rules over six lodges; and there are three others (S.) which are comprised within the D.G.L. of Otago and Southland at Dunedin.

Marlborough and Nelson District. - These provinces of the Colony are exempt from any local Masonic jurisdiction, under the Grand Lodge of England, which is represented by five lodges. There is also a Scottish lodge (at Blenheim), which is subject to the D.G.L. of Otago and Southland.

Oceania.
Although the various islands and archipelagoes have been treated as far as possible in connection with the continents with which they are ordinarily associated, there are some few of these, lying as it were in mid-ocean, that must be separately dealt with, and their consideration will bring this chapter to a close.

New Caledonia. - This island was taken possession of by France in 1854, and has been used for some years as a penal settlement. At Noumea, the chief town and the seat of government, there are two lodges, L'Union Caledonienne, and No. 1864, Western Polynesia. The former was established by the Grand Orient of France in 1868, and the latter (which is included in the Masonic Province of New South Wales) by the Grand Lodge of England in 1880.

Fiji Islands. - The formation of a lodge - Polynesia - at Levuka, with the assent of the native king, was announced to the Masonic world in a circular dated March 12, 1872.
The Islands were annexed to Britain in 1874, and on February 1, 1875, a Scottish Charter - No. 562 - was granted to a lodge bearing the same name and meeting at the same place as the self-constituted body of 1872. This is comprised in the Masonic Province of Victoria. A second British lodge - No. 1931, Suva na Viti Levu - was established in the archipelago by the Grand Lodge of England in 1881.

Society Islands. - Masonry was introduced into Papeete, the chief town of Tahiti (or Otaheiti), the largest of the Society group, by the Grand

Orient of France in 1834. A Chapter - L'Oceanie Francaise - was established in that year, and a lodge of the same name in 1842.

The labors of these bodies were intermittent, the latter having been galvanized into fresh life in 1850, and the former in 1857. Both lodge and chapter are now extinct.

Marquesas Islands. - A lodge, which has long since ceased to exist - L'Amitie - was established at Nukahiva by the Grand Orient of France in 1850.

Sandwich or Hawaiian Islands. - In 1875 there were three lodges in this group, and more recent statistics show no increase in the number: Le Progres de l'Oceanie, erected by Warrant of the Supreme Council of France in 1850; and the Hawaiian and Wailukee lodges, under the jurisdiction of the Grand Lodge of California. The last named is Maui; the others meet at Honolulu, the capital, where they occupy a hall in common. The earliest of the two American lodges (Hawaiian) was formed in 1852.

These three lodges are composed of natives, Americans, Englishmen, and Germans, between whom the most friendly relations subsist. King Kalakaua was an active member of Le Progres de l'Oceanie, and also his brother, William Pitt Leleihoku, of the Hawaiian Lodge. The former, who has visited many foreign countries, also evinced the same interest in Masonry while on his travels. On January 7, 1874, he was entertained by lodge Columbian of Boston (U.S.A.), and on May 22, 1881, by the National Grand Lodge of Egypt. By the latter body the king was elected an Honorary Grand Master, and afterward delivered a lengthy oration, in which he expressed his belief in Egypt being the cradle both of Operative and Speculative masonry, and thus may be said to have fully reciprocated the compliment which had been paid him by the meeting.

BROTHERLY LOVE, RELIEF AND TRUTH
SUPPLEMENT TO DR. MACKEY'S TEXT
By W. BRO. WILLIAM JAMES HUGHAN

P.S.G.D. of England, P. S. G. W. of Egypt, Iowa, etc.

DR. MACKEY and I had long been regular correspondents and fellow Masonic students, when his lamented decease ended our happy collaboration, which had been mutually helpful and stimulating.

My residence in England obtained for me numerous facilities for the examination of old and original MSS. concerning the Craft. Hence my esteemed friend was often glad to avail himself of my services accordingly, which he always warmly appreciated.

Since Dr. Mackey's regretted death in 1881, several important works have been published and valuable discoveries have been made of ancient records, which, as they concern and in part affect the preceding pages, require to be carefully considered and duly explained. Of these, mention may be made of Bro. R. F. Gould's History of Freemasonry; the Transactions and Reprints of the Quatuor Coronati Lodge (London); Bro. E. Conder's History of the Masons' Company (London); my Old Charges of the British Freemasons, 2d Series, and others.

In loving memory of my dear friend, and in fulfilment of an offer of literary aid made some time ago, I have gone through his comprehensive history, and noted the corrections and additions needful to make it as complete and accurate to date as he would have liked it to be.

His support of what he terms the " Iconoclastic School" can not fail to help us throughout the United States; as we seek to be as constructive as possible, our own desire is that the legends should be kept distinct from authenticated facts, so that the Fraternity may possess a complete history, perfect in all its parts and worthy of 126 the Free and

Accepted Masons throughout the world. His words on the subject at p. 8 are worth reproduction:

"To this school I have for years been strongly attached, and in the composition of this work I shall adopt its principles. I do not fear that the claims of Freemasonry to a time-honoured existence will be injured by any historical criticism, although the era in which it had its birth may not be admitted to be as remote as that assigned to it by Anderson or Oliver."

Book I. - The Old MSS., Etc.

Since the publication of my Old Charges of British Freemasons, in 1872, many copies of these manuscript constitutions have been traced, some of considerable value having been discovered during the last decade. There are now some threescore and ten rolls or books of these "Charges" in existence, the text of certain scrolls being of great importance. The dates of some of the older MSS. have also had to be revised, such as a few noted at p. 15. The date of the "Halliwell" or "Regius MS." has been placed a little later, by a few critics, and that of the "Cooke MS." has been put back to 1450 or earlier.

An unfortunate error was made by the Editor of the "Cooke MS." by reading the final word in the line "And in policronico a cronycle p'uyd," as printed, instead of preuyd or proved, as pointed out by Bro. G. W. Speth in his commentary on that noted little gem of a Book.

The "Harleian No. 2054" (British Museum) is not likely to have been written before 1660 (not 1625, p. 15), and a still older copy of its text was found in 1899, viz., the "John T. Thorp MS." Of A.D. 1629, which is probably the original of both it and the "Sloane" of 1646.

The "Grand Lodge MS. No. 1," erroneously placed by me at 1632 (pp. 15, 69, etc.), is really of 1583, and the numbers of the two York MSS. 2 and 4 should be reversed, the first mentioned being the junior. These points are all detailed in my second volume on the "Old Charges" (of 1895), and in subsequent additions to 1899.

Since Dr. Mackey wrote his history, additional information has been obtained relative to the "Four Crowned Martyrs" referred to in the "Halliwell MS." and elsewhere, which has considerably modified the statements thereon at pp. 16, 27, 34, etc. The legend, so far from being of German origin, is mentioned in England many centuries before there is historic proof of its having acquired currency in Germany. On this subject Bro. Gould's history should be consulted, both in relation to the Steinmetzen and the Masonic MSS. of Great Britain. The fact of the legend having been known in England for so many centuries led the late Bro. the Rev. A. F. A. Woodford to suggest that our Students' Lodge No. 2076, London, should be called the "Quatuor Coronati," and, though rather a singular title for such an organization, we agreed thereto.

The curious name of "Noæchidæ" for Masons, referred to at p. 60, may be traced back to Dr. Anderson's Book of Constitutions, 1738. It was, however, dropped in later editions, but continued by Laurence Dermott in his Ahiman Rezon, which was a pity, the term being so absurd.

The St. Amphibalus legend is not peculiar to the "Cooke" text as the "William Watson" Roll of 1687, first noted in 1890, contains a reference to that ancient celebrity, and I believe that the "Henery Heade" MS. of 1675, in the Library of the Temple, London, also does; but its recent discovery has not allowed time enough for its complete transcription.

There are several MSS. that call Edwin the King's brother, instead of son, as in most MSS. (p. 103), but they are not of much value or antiquity, and belong to the "Spencer" family as respects the text. Dr. Anderson probably had a copy of the "Spencer" or "Cole MS." before him in 1738, as it was printed in 1729.

As to Prince Edwin having been made a Mason at Windsor (p. 98), one or two lately discovered Scrolls contain the same statement as the "Lansdowne" and "Antiquity MSS.," but evidently it was but a local tradition.

Dr. Mackey observes (p. 163) that the reason "why the Temple of Solomon was exclusively selected by the Modern Masons as the incunabulum of their Order can be only conjecturally accounted for." That is so, but on the other hand the extraordinary popularity of works on the Temple of Solomon, and the numerous models made and exhibited, in the latter part of the 17th century, and early in the 18th century, may have led to its incorporation in the Masonic Ritual during the Revival period, 1717 - 23. It can not be said that the "Old Charges" make a prominent feature of that great historic building, and neither are the Biblical worthies familiar to the modern Freemasons conspicuous figures in the ancient MSS. of the Fraternity. The Transactions of the "Quatuor Coronati" Lodge for 1899 are worth a careful study on this point.

Early Records.

Of the most valuable entries concerning Freemasonry in the 17th century may be mentioned those by Elias Ashmole in his famous diary. It is to be regretted, however, that the two editions of the typographical reproduction of that MS. book (1717 and 1774) contain serious errors in the portion relating to his admission into the Craft, and his visitation of a lodge, in 1646 and 1682 respectively. Unfortunately, Dr. Mackey had not facsimiles of these entries, and hence his adoption of the faulty transcripts (pp. 322, 620-21, etc.). The following may be relied on as being an exact copy of the two entries of A.D. 1682.

"March 1682. 10: About 5. p.m. I recd a sumons to appr. at a Lodge to be held the next day, at Masons Hall London.

11. Accordingly I went, & about noone were admitted into the Fellowship of Free Masons, Sr. William Wilson Knight, Capt. Rich: Boothwick, Mr. Will: Woodman, Mr. Wm. Grey, Mr. Samuell Taylour & Mr. William Wise.

I was the Senior Fellow among them (it being 35 yeares since I was admitted) There were prsent beside myselfe the Fellowes after named.

Mr. Tho: Wise Mr. of the Masons Company this prsent yeare. Mr. Thomas Shorthose, Mr. Thomas Shadbolt, . . . Waindsford Esqr. Mr. Rich Young Mr. John Shorthose, Mr. William Hamon, Mr. John Thompson, & Mr. Will: Stanton.

Wee all dyned at the halfe Moone Taverne in Cheapeside, at a Noble Dinner psepaired at the charge of the New-accepted Masons."

On comparing the foregoing excerpt with the one printed at pp. 621-22 of the history, it will at once be seen that Ashmole was not reinitiated, or readmitted into the fellowship, A.D. 1682, by Sir William Wilson and others; but that Wilson and the others named were themselves "accepted," and subsequently paid for the dinner, which was served at the Half Moon Taverrn, in Cheapside, according to custom.

That being so, the elaborate and most ingenious arguments in explanation of the interpolated word "by" are wholly unnecessary, because due to a very faulty transcript. Neither can it be said that the lodge in which Ashmole was initiated in 1646 was of an operative character, because Bro. W. H. Rylands has demonstrated most fully that it was a speculative assembly. See his Freemasonry in the 17th Century ("Mas. Mag.," London, Dec., 1881). So far from the celebrated antiquary having been made an "Honorary Member," it is quite clear that he was admitted to the full privileges enjoyed by the Brethren who elected him.

A very valuable work which was originally published in 1730 (but no copy has been preserved), and a 2d edition was printed as an appendix to the Book of Constitutions, 1738, was not by James Anderson (p. 364) (as generally accepted until recent years), but by Bro.

Martin Clare, F.R.S., who became D. G. M. in 1741. It was entitled A Defence of Masonry, published A.D. 1730, Occasion'd by a Pamphlet call'd Masonry Dissected. In a paper on " The Old Lodge at Lincoln," by Bro. Wm. Dixon (Quatuor Coronatorum, 1891), information is afforded as to this Brother, and copies of minutes given in relation to his authorship of the Defence. So also in another paper of the same year read to the members of the "Quatuor C. Lodge," London, by Bro. R. F. Gould, the Masonic historian, on "Martin Clare, A.M. &. F.RS.," with facsimiles. One minute reads thus: Oct. 2, 1733. " When Brother Clare's Discourse concerning Pritchard, as also some of our Regulations and By Laws were read."

Book II - Masonic History

It was impossible, as Dr. Mackey states at p. 598, "to obtain any continuous narrative of the transactions of the Masons' Company," but happily that condition is now altered by the publication of the Records of the Hole Crafte and Fellowship of Masons, with a Chronicle of the History of the Worshipful Company of Masons in the City of London, by Bro. Edward Conder, Jr., Master of the Company, 1894.

In this important volume the records of the Company are interestingly described, and many are of a very remarkable character. It appears that there were two separate Masonic organizations meeting in the Masons' Hall. The one known as the Masons' Company proper, and the other a Lodge, termed the "Acception." In the first named, the members were "admitted," but in the latter they were "accepted." The Company of Free Masons was so termed, about the middle of the 16th century, the fellowship before being of the Masons only. The prefix was dropped officially after 1653.

There were thus the Free Masons of the Company, and the Accepted Masons of the Lodge, until the former ceased to use the term "Free." Eventually the two prefixes were united as "Free and Accepted Masons," but precisely when we can not say; probably toward the end of the 17th century.

The speculative Lodge of the Acception is noted in the records of the company from about the year 1620, and it was this body that was visited by Elias Ashmole in 1682. The grant of arms was made to the Company of Masons in 1472, and is now preserved in the British Museum, but the copy of the "Old Charges," so often noted in the inventories, has been missing for fifty or more years. This is a great pity, as we are unable to decide for certain what the text was, or how near it agreed with those still preserved.

The "Phillipp's MSS." Nos. 1 and 2 may be copies of the missing Masons' Company MS., of 1650 circa, and so may the "G. W. Bain MS." of the same period, but beyond indicating the probability of such relationship, nothing can be said.

Of the "Harleian No. 1942" text (p. 616, etc.) we have now several copies, so it no longer enjoys the solitary position it once had. Though it and the other similar documents seem to have been written for and used by a company, neither of them can be the missing " Masons' Company MS.," nor can they be copies if the MSS. previously mentioned represent the original Scroll or book which belonged in the Accepted Masons' Hall. They are, however, suggestive of the use of the term accepted, and are thus especially valuable in illustration of the minutes of the "Acception."

I do not consider that the "Sloane MS. No. 3329," British Museum, dates from "between 1640 and 1700," now that the matter has been thoroughly sifted; but more likely to have been written soon after the "Revival of 1717." There is no evidence that it was ever known to Dr. Plot (not "Plott"), the historian of Staffordshire, 1686, and I agree that it is unlikely that separate ceremonies or degrees were worked prior to the 18th century, as Dr. Mackey emphatically states.

My friend declares that the word Free Mason is not to be found in the "Masonic Constitutions," i.e., the "Old Charges," of the operative body, but this is not correct. It does not appear in the very early copies, but the term is met with in several of the rolls of the 17th century.

The mark degree is modern, comparatively speaking, but the selection of marks by the operative and speculative Masons is a very old custom. Even apprentices chose their marks, as evidenced in the "Mark Book" of the Lodge of Aberdeen, of A.D. 1670 onward. As a degree, I had traced it back to 1778 in Dr. Mackey's time, but later on it has been found noted in Lodge Minutes of 1777, London; '1773,' Durham; and 1769, Portsmouth. The last mentioned is in cypher, and has only recently been read. The first entry is as follows:

"At a Royal Arch Chapter held at the George Tavern in Portsmouth on First Septr., Seventeen hundred and sixty nine, Present:

"Thomas Dunckerley, Esq., William Cook Z, Samuel Palmer H, Thomas Scanville J., Henry Dean, Philip Joyes, and Thomas Webb.

"Pro. G. M. Thomas Dunckerley bro't the Warrant of the Chapter, and having lately rec'd the mark he made the bre'n Mark Masons and Mark Masters, and each chuse their mark, via., W. Cook Z,

S. Palmer H, T. Scanville J., Philip Joyes, T. Webb. He also told us of this mann'r of working which is to be used in the degree w'ch we may give to others so they be F. C. for Mark Masons and Master M. for Mark Masters."

Full particulars of this chapter are given in the history of the Phoenix Lodge, No. 257, Portsmouth, by Bro. Alexander Howell, 1894. The Royal Arch was started in that town under the regular or "Modern Masons" in 1769.

Bro. Dunckerly received the Royal Arch Degree in Portsmouth in 1754, but at that time, though worked by the "Moderns," there was no governing body. The ceremony was known in England, Ireland, and Scotland in the 5th decade of the 17th century, and was thus patronized before the advent of the "Ancients" or "Atholl Masons" in 1751. It is well to remember this fact, as Bro. L. Dermott has erroneously been credited, or his Grand Lodge, with having arranged and started the degree. Royal Arch Masonry is referred to in print (A.D. 1743-44) two years before Dermott obtained[149] the degree (1746), and undoubtedly the ceremony was worked in America as soon as it was worked by the "Ancients" in England. Bro. Dermott was initiated in Ireland, 1740 - 41, and in 1752 was a member of Nos. 9 and 10, London (England), when he was elected Grand Secretary. At that time No. 1 was kept vacant.

It was the usage, certainly, for lodges generally to be known by the taverns or hotels in which they assembled, until it happily became the custom to have halls built for Masonic meetings. Lodges, however, had special names long before the year 1767, as recorded at p. 885. In Masonic Records, 1717 - 1894, by my lamented friend and Bro. John Lane, will be found several instances of lodges having adopted distinctive titles, the first to do so according to this excellent authority being the "University Lodge," No. 74, in A.D. 1730, and there was a "French Lodge," also held in London, and so named in 1737, or earlier. It is not a matter of much importance, but it is as well to remember that lodge nomenclature began some one hundred and seventy years ago as respects England, and probably much earlier in Scotland. Neither is it sure that there were only four operative lodges in the city of London in 1716 (p. 879). The immortal quartette of 1717 may have been mainly operative, but even that is not certain, as we are not informed as to their members until the next decade, when assuredly they were severally of a speculative character. We are wholly in ignorance when Dr. Desaguliers and Dr.

---

[149] The degree is noted in the records of St. Thomas's Lodge, London (not "Lancashire," vide p. 822), and is duly referred to on p. 821.

Anderson were initiated, or in what lodges, all particulars as to such being mere guesswork.

Concerning warrants (p. 924), it should be stated that these charters, so well known to the Fraternity since 1750 in England (but much earlier in Ireland), were not issued originally by the premier Grand Lodge of England, but Brethren who wished to be constituted into a lodge petitioned the Grand Master, and on his approval of their prayer a day would be fixed for its constitution, and certified accordingly. In the provinces, a Brother would be deputed to constitute such a lodge by a document signed by the requisite authority; which was a kind of Warrant, but did not nominate the W. M. and Wardens, as since the period mentioned. The fact of constitution made the lodge regular, but there were numerous lodges who did not avail themselves of that favor, and so were irregular, from the Grand Lodge point of view, though as much entitled then to continue their meetings as they were before the Grand Lodge was formed. It is impossible now to decide what lodges joined the new organization between 1717 and 1721; hence my remark, which is referred to in the note at p. 924.

A mass of information had been obtained in 1894 and printed in the volume by Bro. John Lane aforesaid, respecting the old lodges noted by Dr. Mackey at pp. 886-88. The "Lodge of Antiquity" assembled in other places besides those stated, and so as to several of the other lodges; but they need not be recapitulated now. The original No. 2 was erased in 1736. Dr. Mackey (p. 888) assumes that the original No. 3 continued to work from 1723, but as a matter of fact the members gave up their distinctive position, and were constituted into a new lodge, February 27, 1723, taking the No. 11 in 1729. From successive changes it is now 12, and from 1768 was named the "Fortitude," and from 1818 "The Lodge of Fortitude and Old Cumberland." Dr. Anderson puts the matter quite clearly in his Book of Constitutions, 1738, p. 185, when it was No. 1o on the list of London lodges only.

"This was one of the four Lodges mentioned, Page 109, viz., the Apple-Tree Tavern in Charles Street, Covent Garden, whose Constitution is immemorial: But after they removed to the Queen's Head upon some Difference, the members that met there came under a new Constitution, tho' they wanted it not, and it is therefore placed at this number." It is, however, of Time Immemorial continuity.

As to the age of the Master Masons' Degree, no later discovery, subsequent to Dr. Mackey's period, at all serves to make the matter any clearer, save to indicate that the ceremony was not generally worked until fairly on in the 18th century. I published a long account of the minutes of a London lodge from 1725, which mentions the Third Degree in 1727. This is the oldest of the kind known, appertaining to a regular lodge in London, and is of great value. The musical and architectural lodge, quoted pp. 1000 - 1001, was never on the register of the Grand Lodge of England, but its records afford evidence of the ceremony being worked as early as 1725. Minutes published in facsimile by the Q. C. Lo. in 1900.

The lodge opened in Paris as No. 90 (p. 1029) was not constituted until April 3, 1732. The list Dr. Mackey quotes from, though begun in 1730, was continued for two years later. There is no engraved list preserved of 1733; and there was no regular lodge in France until the year I name, i.e., 1732.

The rival Grand Lodge of the "Ancients" was inaugurated in 1751 (not 1753), but Laurence Dermott was not a founder (p. 1105), he having joined in the year 1752, when he became Grand Secretary. Bro. Henry Sadler, in his Masonic Facts and Fictions (1887), objects to these "Ancients" being termed Schismatics, and ably defends them in that well-known work. He considers they were mostly Irish Masons, from whom Grand Secretary Dermott also came, and certainly many of the facts he presents indicate their fondness for that organization. There is no doubt that the date given at p. 1109, viz., July 17, 1751, was the day on which this body was established, but no Grand Master was elected until 1753.

The Royal Arch Degree was not started by these "Ancients" (p. 1108), but only adopted by them as an authorized ceremony. In self-defence the "Moderns," who had worked it before the origin of the "Atholl Masons," but not officially, gradually gave it more prominence. In 1767 they formed a Grand Chapter of Royal Arch Masons and issued warrants for chapters, pushing the degree more even than the "Ancients," though not recognized by their Grand Lodge; so at the union of the two Grand Lodges in December, 1813, the way was prepared for the inauguration of the "United Grand Chapter" in 1817, the ceremony being adopted as the completion of the Master Mason's ceremony, not as a separate and independent degree.

The York Masons who revived their Grand Lodge in 1761 had never any dealings with the "Ancients," and consequently the latter had no right to style themselves "Ancient York Masons." The York Grand Lodge never warranted any lodges out of England, and so the lodges chartered in the United States by the "Atholl Masons" were not "A. Y. M." (Ancient York Masons), but "Ancient" or "Atholl Masons."

I should find it simply impossible to treat of the Introduction of Freemasonry into the North American Colonies in brief, and so shall not attempt it, and must leave Dr. Mackey's interesting Chapter XLVI. untouched. I may, however, just state that, bearing in mind the distinction already noted between regular and irregular lodges; the one duly constituted by authority of a Grand Lodge, and the other not constituted. Let me say that the "St. John's," Boston, A.D. 1733, was the first regular Masonic lodge in North America. There were before then several lodges assembling in Philadelphia, and evidently elsewhere by "time immemorial" usage, and these had as good a right to meet Masonically as any other organization. Everywhere, however, outside the pale of regular Grand Lodge Masonry, and unless such Brethren joined under the new regime, they were accounted irregular. Strange to say, the "Modern" Grand Lodge of England - the premier of the world never had a Pennsylvania lodge on its register. I once thought that a lodge assembling in Philadelphia, Penn. (1730, etc.), had been granted by its constitutional authority, but there is not sufficient evidence to warrant the conclusion. There were regular "Ancient" warrants issued for Philadelphia during the 6th decade of the 18th century and a Provincial Grand Lodge formed. As a matter of fact, singular as it reads, the lodge of 1730, and subsequent lodges of the kind, were never recognized as of English origin, though a Provincial Grand Master was appointed by the "Moderns" for the "Keystone State" in 1730, etc. This was done, though there was not a lodge on its English register from Pennsylvania. An unusual experience assuredly, but not unique as respects some Provincial Grand Masters appointed in England.

I am not aware of any authority for the statement at p. 1252, that the esteemed Bro. E. T. Carson (deceased) had a copy of Dr. Dassigny's celebrated Enquiry of 1744 in his collection, which has lately been acquired by General J. C. Lawrence (P. G. M., Mass.), who is believed to have the largest Masonic library in America, if not in the world. The only copy in the United States is the one I let Bro. R. F. Bower have, who was a distinguished collector and ardent Masonic student. On his regretted decease, his library was purchased by the Grand Lodge of Iowa, which has a great collection of Masonic books, MSS., and curios of immense value. Since my discovery of that volume of 1744, another, and almost perfect, copy has been traced and is now in the important Masonic library of the province of West Yorkshire; and a third has been recognized in the collection of Masonic works in Newcastle on Tyne; so that at the present time, three copies are known, all, however, lacking the frontispiece, and only one of the trio is complete else.

The references in the history of Freemasonry at York, and especially in relation to the additional degrees, i.e., those after the Third, require, occasionally, qualification, in the light of discoveries of late years. It is necessary also to carefully study both portions of my Masonic Sketches and Reprints, as the second part was written after the first was printed, and contains particulars of MS. books discovered whilst the work was in the press. There is an excellent American edition to be had of the same year as the original issue in England.

Chapter XLVIII. is an important one, and deserves particular consideration, for many of the statements are of a very suggestive, not to say startling, character, and advanced by a Brother of great eminence and research. I am not aware of the existence of any evidence in favor of the assertion that Ramsay (not Ramsey) ever sought to introduce any of the additional degrees to the Grand Lodge of England early last century. For that matter, beyond statements of fanciful historians, it has not been proved that he arranged the ceremonies so long connected with his name; and all the declarations concerning the Stuarts and the Craft must be received with caution. Beyond reiterated assertions, the initiation of any of the unfortunate royal family has not at all been clearly established.

Chapter XXX. is of very great interest, but how far it is supported by cold and hard facts it is not for me to say, unless time and space were ample. At all events, it should be read side by side with Chapter XXX. of Bro. Gould's history; so that the reliability or otherwise of some of the sources depended upon should be tested. At p. 280 Dr. Mackey cites the Charter of Arras (Rose Croix), said to have been granted by Charles Edward Stuart. Now, is it likely, is it even possible, that in his father's lifetime he would describe himself as "We, Charles Edward, King of England, France, Scotland, and Ireland?" Surely, in the face of such a declaration, there is no authority to say as to the authenticity of this Warrant "There appears to be no doubt." It could not be authentic if the document contained any such title.

Another subject has also been more thoroughly elucidated of late years, and in consequence thereof some of the authorities quoted in Chapter XVIII. have been found to be unreliable at times, and rather inclined to treat the question as fiction, instead of as history. The Steinmetzen of Germany are not always safe in the hands of such authors as Fallou (not "Fallon") and Winzer. Gould is much safer than either to follow, and the reader may be confident that existing documents will verify all his statements thereon. Considering the paucity of really critical works on the subject, Dr. Mackey has done wonders. Kloss is nearly always to be trusted, either as respects Germany or

France, but in respect to the latter country all mere statements as to the introduction of Freemasonry must be treated with suspicion; for prior to 1732 we have actually as yet no evidence.

Some parts of Dr. Mackey's massive work are indications as much of his valued opinions as of matters of fact, and these, of course, are left alone, and can not well be questioned, now their author is no more. They are, however, of considerable worth, and, whilst the opinions of some other students may not always coincide, so long as they are accepted as inferences, rather than evidences, they are of special interest and importance, and can not fail to throw light on points needing elucidation, because of their suggestiveness.

The foregoing does not aim at being a microscopic examination of Dr. Mackey's history, but simply a fraternal attempt to read it in the light and by the assistance of valuable discoveries made since the year of his lamented decease.

www.ingramcontent.com/pod-product-compliance
Lightning Source LLC
Chambersburg PA
CBHW071156160426
43196CB00011B/2099